Criminal Justice
Recent Scholarship

Edited by
Marilyn McShane and Frank P. Williams III

A Series from LFB Scholarly

Music Piracy and Crime Theory

Sameer Hinduja

LFB Scholarly Publishing LLC
New York 2006

Library of Congress Cataloging-in-Publication Data

Hinduja, Sameer, 1978-
  Music piracy and crime theory / Sameer Hinduja.
      p. cm. -- (Criminal justice recent scholarship)
  Includes bibliographical references and index.
  ISBN 1-59332-124-4 (alk. paper)
  1. Computer crimes. 2. Piracy (Copyright) 3. Sound recordings--
Pirated editions. 4. Intellectual property. 5. MP3 (Audio coding
standard)--Social aspects. 6. Internet--Social aspects. 7. Criminology.
I. Title. II. Series: Criminal justice (LFB Scholarly Publishing LLC).
  HV6773.H56 2006
  364.16'2--dc22

2005028677

ISBN 1-59332-124-4

Printed on acid-free 250-year-life paper.

Manufactured in the United States of America.

To Him.

Contents

List of Tables

Acknowledgments

To begin, God has been, and remains, my everything - and this would not be possible without Him. You have made my paths straight, and You have blessed the work of my mind and my hands. All of this points to Your reality, faithfulness, and provision. Mom and Dad, your unconditional love, support, and prayers have known no bounds, and have kept you close despite the geographic distance. Thank you for cultivating discipline in me and a constant desire to learn, and for teaching me about the unmatched importance of family. Babita, you are my biggest fan, and your love has been a constant source of stability and reassurance in my life.

Justin Patchin, I am honored to have you as my friend. We've gone through this together, and have kept each other inspired and motivated. I am indebted to you in so many ways, and couldn't have hoped for a better companion with whom to run this race. Thank you for your personal and practical support. I hope we have left an impression - not because of what we did, but because of how we are. Amanda Burgess-Proctor, we've shared so many experiences over these years, and my life has been enriched by your fantastic storytelling, your thoughtfulness, and your warmth. I have learned so much from you in terms of both style and substance. Beth Huebner, you have made this journey easier because of your willingness to offer sage advice on graduate school matters, and your insightful comments on scholarly works. I have enjoyed (and now miss greatly) our chats about the highs and lows of our career choice. More than anyone else, you have served as the model of academic success that I have sought to emulate while in graduate school.

Certain professors have also contributed greatly to my development as a scholar: Mahesh Nalla, Christina DeJong, Tim Bynum, Sandeep

Kulkarni, Karen Busch, John McCluskey, and Mark Lanier. I have appreciated your friendship, guidance, energy, and time more than I can express. In addition, each of you have supported my research interests and have challenged me to expand traditional disciplinary boundaries. The following members of Team Bynum deserve acknowledgement for being great friends and colleagues over the years: Joe Schafer, Sean Varano, Ryan Martz, Cheryl Reid, Alison Blair, Catharine White, Jason Ingram, Eric Grommon, and Karen Ream. Other individuals have contributed to both small and large successes in my professional life. These include Kristy Holtfreter, Yan Zhang, Cedrick Heraux, Pete Blair, Brandon Kooi, Jeff Cancino, Meghan Stroshine, Amanda Robinson, Matt Marner, and Michael Alper.

Pastor Mark Evans, you have seen me grow both professionally and personally during this season, and you have believed in me and what I am trying to do with my life. Thank you for seeing my heart and inspiring me towards greatness. Christian Gendreau, I have appreciated your unique and intelligent perspective on things, and your invaluable ability to make me laugh out loud all the time. I am grateful that we have known each other for so long. Tammy Dahl, you have sent so many encouragements this way, and they have always come at the perfect time. Finally, I would like to thank the McPherson's, the Strombeck's, the Lynch's, and the Bryan's.

CHAPTER 1
Introduction

For centuries, scholars and thinkers have sought to explain why individuals engage in criminal behavior. This has resulted in a number of theoretical paradigms that concentrate on singular (e.g., Hirschi, 1969) or multiple factors (e.g., Cohen & Felson, 1979) that influenced our understanding of the onset, incidence, and perpetuation of deviance, delinquency, and crime. Moreover, a few "general" criminological theories have been professed and refined in the last two decades, each ostensibly seeking to predict and explain variation in *all* types of deviant behavior (e.g., academic dishonesty, substance abuse, domestic violence, and embezzlement). These include Robert Agnew's (1992) general strain theory, Michael Gottfredson and Travis Hirschi's (1990) self-control theory, and Ronald Akers' (1985) social learning theory.

Accompanying his seminal examination of white collar crime in the early 20th century, Edwin Sutherland (1947; 1973) maintained that crime theorists should not solely focus on explaining deviance among the lower class, but should expand their paradigmatic scope and seek to explain a wide range of crimes committed by a wide range of offenders. The three general theories mentioned earlier have been posited since Sutherland's assertion, and should by definition have the predictive capacity to explain nontraditional types of wrongdoing such as Internet crime. Indeed, the respective authors of each theory analyzed in this work have specifically stated that their perspective is panoptic and all-inclusive.

The applicability of these theories to traditional forms of wrongdoing has been empirically explored by a host of social science researchers since their initial conceptualization. However, very few studies have attempted to determine their explanatory power on nontraditional types of crime - particularly those fostered through the use of computers and the Internet.

1

With the growing frequency, prevalence, and scope of high-tech illegalities, such phenomena merit immediate and substantive attention by scholars and practitioners, especially those in the domain of criminal justice.

As of yet, however, little research has sought to test the "generality" of general strain theory, self-control theory, and social learning theory by studying a decidedly nontraditional form of deviance that occurs in a decidedly nontraditional environment. Moreover, very few pieces of criminological research have been published on a purely Internet-based illegality[1], and or have attempted to analyze the digital music phenomenon from a social science perspective. In addition, intellectual property will be afforded an increasingly immeasurable value as we rapidly advance into information-based society and economy. Notwithstanding the theoretical implications, the critical role that intellectual property plays in the stability, vitality, and growth of private-sector companies, public-sector organizations, and even individual lives demands that it is secured and precluded from misappropriation, exploitation, and manipulation for illegitimate purposes.

The current work attempts to examine the applicability of these general theories on one specific form of Internet crime: online intellectual property theft, as measured by participation in illegally uploading and downloading unauthorized digital music (MP3)[2] files. Such empirical assessment should determine the extensibility of criminological theory to crimes in cyberspace, and should contribute to the discipline's knowledge base through its testing of the universality of three major theories. Ideally, this study will discern the most salient predictors of music piracy and serve as a foundational inquiry into novel forms of deviance engendered by computers and the Internet. Fruitful policy initiatives may consequently be developed to restrict the propagation of this criminal activity, and may simultaneously work to reduce copyright infringement of other forms of intellectual property in the future.

---

[1] See, e.g., (see Gopal, Sanders, Bhattacharjee, Agrawal, & Wagner, 2004; Hinduja, 2001, 2003).
[2] MP3 is an abbreviation for MPEG Audio Layer 3, an audio compression technology that shrinks the file size of CD-quality audio while maintaining the level of fidelity. It must be stated that the focus throughout this research is on those MP3s that are available online without the legal permission of its owners. This is further explained in Chapter 2.

PRACTICAL BACKDROP OF RESEARCH

MP3 technology has been heralded as the music lover's dream. Its popularity has grown from only being known among small circles of Internet technophiles to competing with "sex" as the most-queried keyword on search engines across the World Wide Web in its pinnacle year of 2000 (Knight Systems, 2000). Since that year, the phenomenon has lost a little momentum, but is still wildly popular. According to the most recent annual statistics available from Google, the most popular search engine as of today, "MP3" was the 10th most popular search term queried among the billions of searches in 2004 (Google, 2004).

One might wonder, what exactly is the basis for such tremendous popularity? To begin, the technology[3] has granted free, unrestricted access to songs of extremely high fidelity by practically every musical artist, past and present. Also, it has allowed individuals to amass enormous collections of digital music files, provide these files to others, make custom audio CDs of favorite tracks, and transfer them onto portable players to satisfy music needs on-the-go. It has spawned massive virtual communities in Internet chat rooms, message boards, newsgroups, and other cybervenues - in existence solely for the purpose of distributing MP3s. Moreover, it has facilitated the growth of hundreds of "dot.com" businesses, allowing millions of dollars to be earned by capitalizing on the profitability and marketability of this method of distributing audio over the Internet. Finally, the pervasive and ubiquitous nature of MP3s has transformed music for the recording industry, the artists, and especially the general consumer.

These are just some of the fruits borne from this revolutionary technological advance. Many would argue it has done a world of good for Internet users and music fans. Others, however, disagree strongly and point towards the inherent illegality of distributing and reproducing copyrighted works without authorization. Despite the outcry from the federal government, the major record labels, and other entities dealing in

---

[3] MP3 audio files are the most popular form of digital music compression technology. Other forms include Ogg Vorbis (.ogg), Advanced Audio Coding (.aac), iTunes (.m4a, .m4p), Windows Media Audio (.wma), and Free Audio Lossless Codec (.flac). For the purposes of simplicity, "MP3" and "digital music" are used synonymously in this paper. "MP3 technology" is inclusive of the compression algorithm and all of the software that facilitates the exchange of unauthorized MP3 files.

intellectual property, MP3s continue to be uploaded and downloaded with relative impunity. According to the Recording Industry Association of America (RIAA), music piracy in the form of bootlegged and counterfeit recordings on *physical media* costs the record industry $5 billion a year, with $1 million lost each day in the United States (RIAA, 2000a). Illegal exchanges of digital music files over the Internet (such as unauthorized MP3s) are exponentially more difficult to track, and one can only estimate through anecdotal evidence the amount of revenue being denied to musicians and record companies through this practice. Admittedly, it is difficult to conceptualize and measure potential sales "lost" by an artist if the unauthorized digital versions of the songs were not available online. Nevertheless, it is unarguable that at least some individuals are losing out on due compensation because their music is being circulated over the Internet without their consent.

Accurate statistics associated with the phenomenon are relatively rare, and are often perceived as biased depending on their protagonist or antagonist source. Some numbers, though, from the International Federation of the Phonographic Industry's 2002 Music Piracy Report paint a compelling picture of the scope and prevalence of participation in online intellectual property theft. Piracy is argued to be the greatest threat to the respective industries of music, movies, and software (IFPI, 2002), and with more instances of plagiarism and misappropriation of textual content, the press and mainstream media may find itself increasingly harmed by piracy of their own produced material in the near future. Copyright industries in 2001 accounted for 5% of the GDP, which equated to $535 billion dollars (IFPI, 2002). The availability of so much copyrighted material worth such a significant amount provides the opportunity and the rewards for potential and actual perpetrators to participate in, and benefit from, piracy.

IFPI (2002) also estimates that at any given time in May 2002, there were approximately three million participants in music piracy providing around 500 million music files for unauthorized downloading by anyone with the inclination to do so. Much of this occurred through point-and-click software that easily facilitates MP3 transfers among users, such as Kazaa[4], the most popular file-exchange software program at that time. IFPI (2002) also estimated that 200,000 file archive sites and web sites

---

[4] As of June 2005, the web site boasts that it has been downloaded over 389 million times, with around 800,000 program downloads each week (Sharman Networks, 2005).

existed online at that time, which hosted or linked to at least 100 million music files without proper permission from, or payment to, the creators and producers of the music works.

Since computer crimes are not easily identifiable (let alone easily measurable), many are currently unaccommodating to empirical research. Crimes such as hacking, child pornography, and Internet fraud can possibly be examined through the use of case studies and through content analysis of message texts and documents transmitted between participants. A quantitative piece would likely have a small number of cases, simply because of the difficulty associated with identifying, soliciting, and tracking participants for inclusion in a sample. Conversely, copyright infringement - the unauthorized duplication or distribution of software, music, movies, and other forms of intellectual property - is a legally-defined crime committed by millions of individuals on a regular basis. As such, this particular act provides a large population from which to obtain study elements (unlike other forms of high-tech wrongdoing), and therefore provides enough cases to conduct rigorous statistical analyses to identify its contributive elements.

THEORETICAL BACKDROP OF RESEARCH

When considering unauthorized MP3 participation and intellectual property theft in general, some criminological and sociological questions inevitably come to mind. What motivates or impels individuals to partake in this illicit activity? Do certain dispositions and inclinations differentiate participants from nonparticipants? What micro- and macro-level factors play predictive roles? In the 20th century, three general criminological theories carved for themselves a substantial niche in the knowledge base of explanations for crime and deviance. Individually and collectively, they appear useful in answering specific inquiries which follow neatly from the aforementioned questions.

First, general strain theory - asserted by Robert Agnew (1992) - may shed light on the impact of maladaptive affective responses on copyright infringement. The primary question to be asked and answered with this theory is: Do feelings of strain or dissonance, when engendered among those consumers who are not able to afford or obtain certain intellectual property but who still desire to appropriate it, induce participation in criminality? Second, Gottfredson and Hirschi's (1990) self-control theory - also known as the "general theory of crime" - appears to also be a valid framework in which to view intellectual property theft. Specifically, if an individual has low self-control, does that make him or her more likely to participate in the behavior when presented with the right opportunity? Third, social learning theory - as proposed by Ronald Akers (1985) - sets the stage for a deep analysis into social elements that facilitate music piracy participation. It may be able to answer the following: How and from who are the techniques and justifications employed to participate in the deviance learned? Is the behavior modeled after the actions of others? How is the behavior reinforced and perpetuated, or punished and ceased?

In addition, these theories might also have interaction effects with each other. Low self-control might increase the likelihood of a person succumbing to the pressures of antinormative peers and pressures, or make a person more inclined to respond in an antisocial manner to stress and cognitive conflict. Moreover, continual exposure to strain might augment the tendency of a person to display characteristics of low self-control, and to be swayed by maladaptive social learning. Testing for statistically significant interactions is beyond the scope of the current work, but merits explanation in future research endeavors.

NECESSITY FOR RESEARCH AND RESPONSE

A host of reasons underscore the importance of studying this phenomenon and developing informed ways of addressing its growth. Theft of digital property over an Internet connection is easier and quicker than doing so from a retail establishment, where the chance of detection, apprehension, and prosecution is exponentially smaller. Nevertheless, both are activities prohibited by the law and induce similar harm. Music piracy, though, is often condoned in some circles as a victimless activity that does not befall tangible or noteworthy harm to any person or organization. Such an argument can be refuted by a host of facts. For instance, the accumulated economic loss incurred is significant to the artist, recording company, and industry, and is said to approximate $4.3 billion worldwide (IFPI, 2002). Through piracy, these associated parties are seemingly preempted from receiving compensation for the creation, production, marketing, and distribution of their intellectual product. The desire to innovate and develop creative works may be stifled if the rewards are less than anticipated, and if persons are able to appropriate the product without paying for the good and service (Harris, 1969; Smith & Parr, 1989). Furthermore, the media- and entertainment-based economy is presumably deprived of investments and profit from their product, and must devote resources to research and develop copy-protection solutions, surveillance and tracking mechanisms, and punitive policies to discourage or thwart attempted theft. It may also reduce jobs in the industry as cutbacks are made to counterbalance the incurred financial losses.

Additionally, if disregard for intellectual property such as music continues unfettered, some conclude that in time, nothing posted on the Internet will be safe from misappropriation. The argument is that a Pandora's box will be ripped open, and articles, thoughts, ideas, graphics, art, sound files, animations, movies, software[5], and more may no longer be the property of their rightful owner(s), but will be free-rein for anyone to copy and use without regard. Indeed, this is already taking place in some respects due to the open and unregulated nature of cyberspace. What seems to be forgotten is this: intellectual property is still property, and is owned by its creator or the company that has purchased its rights. If one does not have the legal authority to reproduce and distribute a copyrighted work, but does so anyway, a crime has been committed[6]. Criminal activity, then, is subject to prosecution, fines, and incarceration. Copyright infringement through unauthorized MP3s must be dealt with and not overlooked or minimized simply because of its nontraditional nature (as compared to crimes which attract more attention and criminal justice resources) or because of the unique "virtual" environment in which the activity occurs.

Moreover, the college-age population who disproportionately participates in the music piracy phenomenon merits attention. Hinduja (2003) argues that a "slippery-slope" effect might be manifested, as digital theft may precipitate more significant forms of computer- and Internet-related deviance. That is, music piracy may possibly serve as a gateway to more severe forms of high-tech crime. Such a correlation has yet to be determined, but its relational viability appears quite real. Finally, the integrity of the educational establishment at which such behavior takes place is undermined, and the ethical and normative standards of individuals who participate are seemingly compromised and weakened, rather than fortified in this scenario.

---

[5] For examples, please see: (Berst, 1997; CyberAtlas, 2001; Dyrness, 2002; Evangelista, 2003; Gentile, 2003; Haney, 2000; Harris, 2003; Jacobs & Allbritton, 2001; Johnston, 2000).

[6] The laws associated with intellectual property are discussed in Chapter 2.

Several research questions are posed:

Do the purported "general" theories of crime have the predictive capacity and flexibility to explain Internet-based criminality?

Are certain elements of each theory more salient than others?

Can the identification of the most relevant contributive factors inform and guide strategies and solutions intended to curb the incidence of certain Internet-based crimes?

To reiterate, the current work attempts to systematically explain one type of Internet crime - copyright infringement in the form of digital music piracy - by conceptualizing three general criminological theories as predictors, operationalizing concepts inherent in these perspectives, and measuring their proposed relationship with involvement in the wrongdoing. Fleshing out the cognitive, behavioral, psychological, and sociological factors that play a role in effectuating copyright infringement will prove valuable as a cogent theoretical foray into the mind and actions of a computer deviant. This undertaking will hopefully help identify some causes of intellectual property theft online, thereby producing new knowledge and insight that will enhance our current understanding of the phenomenon. As such, the application of theory, the empirical examination of contributive factors, and the subsequent construction and implementation of policy solutions to prevent and suppress the illegal activity will ideally result from this research effort.

VALUE AND CONTRIBUTION OF THE RESEARCH

The current study focuses on a controversial and questionable activity involving computers and the Internet. Participation in the MP3 phenomenon may not seem as criminogenic as pirating software, hacking into networked systems, or writing viruses, especially when coupled with its panoptic reach, exponential growth, and unrivaled popularity. However, except under limited circumstances it equates to the contravention of extant copyright law, and therefore is illegal. This illegality has resulted in the crippling of some MP3-based businesses (e.g., the original iterations of Napster, Scour, Audiogalaxy) and the incurring of severe financial penalties on others (e.g., MP3.com), as well as social, civil, and criminal penalties for others[7]. Intellectual property theft via unauthorized MP3s is a computer crime, and its inherently unique qualities render it useful as the subject of this research, particularly when considering its far-reaching social and economic ramifications.

Formal research concerning computer crime has increased over the five years, but still leaves much to be desired in both its scope and theoretical application, as well as with the development of effective policy initiatives. The subject of intellectual property theft in general has been discussed and debated by legal scholars, as the law is constantly shaped and changed by new judicial decisions in this area (see e.g., Lessig, 1997, 1999a, 1999b; Luckenbill & Miller, 1998). A few philosophers (e.g., Tyler, 1996) have also written about the subject to flesh out ideas which may possibly stem the tide of copyright infringement. Software piracy has been specifically studied in the business ethics and management information systems fields, but these inquiries have been primarily descriptive in nature and only a few have developed or tested a theoretical model to shed light on the impetus of the behavior (see e.g., Wagner, 1998). Indeed, most of the current information technology (IT) policies in place have stemmed from anecdotal accounts rather than empirically grounded studies (Rogers, 2001).

Within the social sciences, some scholars (Higgins, 2005; Higgins & Makin, 2004; Sherizen, 1997; Skinner & Fream, 1997) have sought to determine the applicability of sociological and criminological theories on software piracy, but no previous studies in this discipline have examined the MP3 phenomenon. With continual advances in information technology and the increasing presence and distribution of intellectual property online, a rigorous theoretical approach to interpreting and analyzing copyright violators and violations holds much value. Legislators, academicians, and practitioners can benefit from the research, both by garnering a deeper knowledge of the predictors of the behavior, and by obtaining direction in how they might attend to those elements (Denning, 1998). As such, this inquiry is warranted so that the novel occasions for deviance resulting from technological progress do not

---

[7] See e.g., (A & M Records Inc. et al. v. Napster Inc., 2001; CNN.com, 2000b, 2000c; Davis, 2003; Healy, 2003; Jones, 2000; Lipton, 1998; Mendels, 1999; Patrizio, 1999; Philipkoski, 1999a, 1999b; RIAA, 2000b; Rodriguez, 2005; Slashdot.org, 2005; Spring, 2000).

overshadow the promises and profits of our continued progress into an information-centric world.

Most fundamentally, though, this study attempts to assess the generality of three criminological theories which have been professed to explain all types of wrongdoing. It is important to determine if general strain theory, self-control theory, and social learning theory are extensible to Internet crime. The definitional validity of these theories hinge on identifying their relevance in predicting nontraditional forms of wrongdoing rarely explored in empirical criminological research. Such a rigorous theoretical examination is the linchpin of the current research.

ORGANIZATION OF SUCCEEDING TEXT

In this work, an examination of the etiology of MP3s and copyright violation is conducted against a backdrop of correct interpretation of the activity as a civil and often criminal offense in the vast majority of cases[8]. An introduction to Internet audio will first be given to provide fundamental knowledge requisite for a thorough understanding of the issue at hand. Then, a technical breakdown of the MP3 phenomenon will ensue, including an analysis of the specifications of the file format, means of production, and methods of delivery to Internet users. An examination of literature and empirical research on digital music follows, derived from Internet-based news sites and online marketing and research firms, as well as from the academic knowledge base. Next, a review of extant literature on general strain theory, self-control theory, and social learning theory will be provided to demonstrate the pertinence of each framework to traditional forms of crime. Their analogous relevance to the nontraditional crime of music piracy on the Internet will then be posited to depict how the applicability of the theories might be extended.

---

[8] While much social and legal controversy surrounds this issue, copyright infringement is currently defined as an unlawful offense, and the current research is conducted with that perspective in mind. Civil remedies are available for copyright infringement irrespective of the intention or knowledge of the perpetrator or the amount or degree of harm done to the victim. Criminal remedies are available for intentional acts that result in private financial gain or commercial advantage. Financial gain does not only refer to profiting by the perpetrator but also refers to possible financial loss to the victim (RIAA, 2000e). Please see Chapter 2 for more information on digital music laws.

A quantitative analysis on data collected from a sample of university students is subsequently presented to more accurately assess the applicability of each criminological theory on participation in the MP3 phenomenon, and to provide statistical findings which can be used to shape policy to combat online intellectual property theft. These suggested measures will then be discussed in detail, with the intention of framing ideas into feasible practices that can accommodate the benefits of the new digital economy, the music industry, and the perpetually growing wired world.

CHAPTER 2

Digital Audio,
Intellectual Property, and Law

Intellectual property on the Internet and its vulnerability to theft are difficult concepts to grasp. The unique properties of digital music files - for example, their intangible and "virtual" nature, the multitude of parties who endorse or decry their often unregulated availability, and the complicated legal environment that surrounds their creation and distribution - must be explored in detail to provide the reader with a foundational understanding necessary for subsequent analyses and interpretation. Once individuals comprehend how and why this phenomenon has evolved, as well as the reasons behind its controversial proliferation, they can more clearly recognize the factors that undergird it. Furthermore, the knowledge can be extrapolated and used to better appreciate how significantly digital technology has changed the way in which we view innovation and ascribe value to products of one's creative mind.

HISTORICAL BACKGROUND OF DIGITAL AUDIO FILES

The first multimedia personal computers were introduced to the world in 1985 with the Commodore Amiga. These systems not only provided a graphical user interface and a multitasking operating system to individuals, but also integrated relatively advanced sound and graphic capabilities (Patterson, 1998). As Amiga, IBM, IBM-PC Clones (e.g., Compaq), Macintosh, and other personal systems became increasingly advanced in their processing power and functionality, enhanced multimedia capacities were standardized as fundamental features of computers. CD-ROM drives were marketed with new personal computers beginning in the mid 1990s, and complex software applications and games were developed and sold on CDs to utilize the new technology.

Concurrently, audio CDs competed with and ultimately surpassed the popularity of cassette tapes for market share in retail recordings. Music on cassettes were recorded in analog format, but music tracks on CDs were digital in format and could be digitally extracted into waveform format using a computer and software available to the average consumer. Nonetheless, the sheer size of the resultant native audio file precluded ease of distribution and exchange. Waveform files of CD quality consumed approximately 10 megabytes per each minute of audio, and circulation of these high-quality music files just did not happen as most individuals had extremely slow Internet connections. With the explosive growth of the Internet, different audio file formats that allowed for music to be more easily posted and disseminated became popular.

The initial formats included .AU (Sun Microsystems's proprietary audio format), MIDI (Musical Instrument Digital Interface - a format which stores descriptive information on how musical notes should be played in a particular arrangement, rather than the music itself), and WAV (the Microsoft default audio format, and the most popular because of the pervasiveness of Microsoft operating systems on personal computers). Due primarily to issues related to file size, clips posted online were typically created with low-quality bitrates and smaller sample rates better suited for speech and perhaps quotes from television shows or movies.

A monumental event occurred in 1995 when RealNetworks, Inc. released RealAudio 1.0, a streaming audio format to which web surfers could listen within a few seconds of clicking on a hyperlink, rather than waiting until an entire piece of music downloaded onto their computers. While representative of the traditional broadcast model of information dissemination, the quality of RealAudio at that time left much to be desired, and was arguably unpractical for anything other than news bites and speech clips. Thus, listenable popular music of reasonable quality was still not available on the Internet despite the advances in multimedia technology. Another negative was that formats which "streamed" music for playback through the end user's computer speakers could not be saved to enjoy at a later time. MP3 technology, however, was able to overcome these limitations, and ultimately exceeded everyone's expectations through the way in which it facilitated online delivery of high-quality music.

MP3 TECHNICAL BACKGROUND

MP3 (an abbreviation for MPEG-1 Layer Audio 3) is an audio compression format that enables audio files to be compacted into relatively small file sizes while maintaining near perfect fidelity when played back. It is a direct descendant of MPEG-1 (low-bandwidth video compression typically used over the Internet) and MPEG-2 (high-bandwidth audio and video compression that is the standard for DVD technology) (Midgley, 2000). A general idea of the heuristics of the MP3 compression process is useful to note. Compression occurs through the use of perpetual coding techniques, where auditory information from large digital multimedia files that exceeds the perceptual range of human hearing is removed, resulting in smaller file sizes (Crawford, 2000). Its functionality relies on mathematical algorithms developed using knowledge on how the human ear hears sounds. These algorithms are then able to analytically determine which components of the audio data can be heard by the human ear, and those that are inaudible or masked. By discarding those data which do little to contribute to perceivable sound quality, the size of the file is greatly reduced. This process is very similar to how the Internet graphics format JPEG works, essentially eliminating visual data in images that human eyes cannot easily detect (Heid, 1997).

As a general metric, it is said that one megabyte (MB) is typically equivalent to one minute of music in compressed MP3 format. MP3 compression can produce audio files of several different quality levels measured by the amount of data per second required to reproduce that second of sound. A larger amount of data results in higher audio quality, but at the expense of a consequently larger file size. To convert an analog sound recording into a digital format, a process called "sampling" must take place. The more often one samples a waveform per second, the more accurately sound can be reproduced. Audio data on CDs and, as a consequence, practically all MP3 files are sampled at a rate of 44.1khz – where 44,100 16-bit-precision samples are taken each second to accurately reproduce the sound, and separate samples are taken for the right and left speakers in a stereo system.

Exactly 1,411,200 bits (or 176,000 bytes) of data are needed for each second of music on a CD. As a consequence, a three-minute song would occupy 253,440,000 bits (31,680,000 bytes). Compressing it in MP3 format, however, results in a multiplicative decrease of its file size. As such, 1,411,200 bits per second can be reduced to 128,000 bits per second (or 160,000 or 192,000 – common bitrates for MP3 files) by using the compression algorithm. This translates into a file size 11.025, 8.82, or 7.35 times smaller, respectively, than the original. Furthermore, CD audio requires a bandwidth of 1.5 megabits per second in order to play perfectly. The compression technology also significantly reduces the bandwidth requirement for CD quality playback (Karagiannis, 1999). Through this process, audio fidelity is largely preserved while at the same time simplifying and accelerating the transfer and storage of music tracks.

Fidelity refers to the degree to which an electronic system reproduces sound without distortion. For many pieces of music, the MP3 sound quality at 128kbps comes negligibly close to music from a CD (Calpo, 2000). In recent years, the use of 192kbps rates have increased in popularity, but this more accurate high-end reproduction comes with an approximately 33% increase in file size (approximately 13.6% of the original file) when compared to the same file encoded at 128kbps (Calpo, 2000). With the increased availability of gratuitously large hard drives, though, file size no longer seems relevant as individuals tend to seek the highest quality digital audio they can obtain.

In 1987, Fraunhofer Gesellschaft – a prominent technology institute in Germany - began work on the audio file compression algorithm. After perfecting and patenting it in 1989, it was submitted to the International Standards Organization (ISO) to be integrated as an audio subset into the specification for the video compression technology termed MPEG-1[9] (Nijmeh, 2001). MP3 began to gain prominence as an audio-only compression scheme among the Internet diehards at the beginning of 1997 when software to play MP3s was written and released as freeware online. Concurrently, the hardware infrastructure had developed to the point where it could support the software. Intel Corporation finally released a central processing unit (CPU) fast enough to decode MP3 files in real-time, enabling playback as soon as the user clicked on the file, rather than requiring wait time while the song made an uncompressed copy of itself on the hard drive and then began to play (Weekly, 2000). It was not until 1999, however, that MP3 began to take off among the general and less technically inclined online users.

To be sure, MP3 not only "took off," but ushered in a revolution of sorts among a consumer population desiring their music. MP3 players,

---

[9] MPEG is an acronym for Moving Pictures Expert Group, a subcommittee of the International Standards Organization (ISO). That organization sets worldwide standards for business, technology, and society; over 13,700 standards have been published since 1947 (International Standards Organization, 2003).

such as Nullsoft's WinAmp and MusicMatch Jukebox, encoders such as Xing's AudioCatalyst and Telos Systems' Audioactive Production Studio, and organizers such as ShufflePlay and Helium, were rapidly developed and deployed to worldwide users enamored by the promise of this new technology. The hardware and software infrastructure in place was and continues to be vastly sufficient to perpetuate the exponential growth of the phenomenon despite the legal troubles that MP3 has caused certain businesses and individuals (which are discussed below).

With regard to hardware, computer hard drives of multi-gigabyte disk space had been appearing in the retail market at progressively reasonable prices, which afforded many online music aficionados the opportunity to amass large holdings of MP3 files on their systems. Gains in hard drive size also benefited the distributors of the music, as web and file servers that individuals accessed on the Internet could now accommodate larger collections without significant overhead cost. Throughout the 1990s, hard drive capacity increased by 60% each year, and the average size of hard drives sold in 2000 was at least 10 gigabytes (de Fontenay, 1999; Quantum Corporation, 2000). If nothing but MP3 files of an average size of 4 megabytes each were stored on a 10 gigabyte hard drive, an individual would have an easily accessible MP3 jukebox containing around 2,500 songs. Even just a single gigabyte of space could hold approximately 250 high-quality MP3 files.

Moreover, the falling prices of CD burners - drives capable of recording data onto blank CDs – permitted individuals to easily dump an average of 12 hours of MP3 music onto very inexpensive recordable discs (Crawford, 2000). Portable devices which fit hours of compressed music in the resident memory modules also gained a great deal of popularity as prices decreased[10]. Thus, because of the new digital music paradigm fostered by MP3 technology, the distribution of audio over the Internet became less of a broadcasted service. Rather, it took on the qualities of a highly available and valuable property acquired, stored, and circulated as desired.

While the majority of digital music transfers occur to satiate the auditory palates of music lovers, others download and produce MP3s

---

[10] Many new personal and car CD players have the functionality to decode and play files in MP3 format (Consumer Electronics News, 2003; Weekly, 1998) Interestingly, research indicates that the market for audio electronics that play compressed digital music files will grow to almost $44 billion dollars by 2007 (Consumer Electronics News, 2003).

primarily so that they can have a digital backup of their music collection in case a CD is lost, stolen, or scratched. Furthermore, MP3s enable individuals to compile collections of their favorite songs and create a custom playlist on their computer, to play tracks in a sequential manner, and not have to worry about switching CDs in and out of their player. While record companies have felt their grip over the control, production, and distribution of music slowly slipping away, consumers have rejoiced because of the ability to hear the work of musicians before they spend their hard-earned money on an album with perhaps only one or two "decent" songs. In addition, MP3 participants praise the opportunity to be exposed to a wider variety of music genres and to hear the creative productions of thousands of unsigned and yet talented bands and artists. Others argue that the music industry has held an unfair monopoly over the music market and has maintained an inflated price for CDs, compensated artists comparatively little for their efforts, and have reaped sizable profits from these exploitative practices. Conversely, many contend that while it is nice to sample full-length high-quality music for free, they will not be deterred or swayed from purchasing album-length CDs that they can easily take with them to work, to use in their vehicle, and which contain liner notes, lyrics, and cover art (Swiatecki, 2000a).

As mentioned in Chapter 1, other digital music compression formats have been formulated by some of the largest IT companies in the world. Many require certain proprietary hardware or software for playback, and generally include digital protections and limitations to preempt their unauthorized use or dissemination. Most end users, though, had become accustomed to freedom of choice in the ability to control their music experience. The MP3 format therefore became the standard because of its widespread acceptability, comparatively fast download speed, minimal storage requirements, near-CD quality of sound, ease of use, and flexibility (Kibbee, 1999). It did not achieve pervasive popularity among the general populace, however, until the development of a user-friendly freeware software application called "Napster" hit the Internet in 1999.

NAPSTER – A REVOLUTIONARY APPLICATION

Napster - in its original version - was a small peer-to-peer (P2P) file exchange application that transformed users' computers into de facto file servers, enabling them to upload to and download from millions of other MP3 enthusiasts around the world. It was the software – "the killer app" - that revolutionized the worlds of both producers and consumers of music

(Petersen, 2000). As mentioned, no longer were recordings on physical media such as CDs and tapes the only way in which desired songs could be obtained. No longer requisite was the payment of a premium price to possess high-quality music. With Napster, it could be simply and freely be downloaded from the Internet - thereby providing the same aural benefit to the end user, but in the package of a small digital file that could be stored and transferred to others at virtually no cost (apart from the expense associated with owning a computer and an online connection). Millions of individuals were introduced to, and became enamored with, the benefits of MP3 files because of Napster, which served as the catalyst that made a sparsely-known audio compression technology into a global phenomenon.

This is how it worked: interested individuals visited the Napster web site, downloaded the software, and installed it. Upon signing on to the Napster network, the application scanned the end user's hard drive for MP3 files, and catalogued the name of the artist, the song title, and other related variables that designated fidelity of the track and speed of the user's Internet connection. Then, while connected to the network along with thousands of others, the user's catalogue of MP3 files was concatenated into a giant database with the lists of every other individual who was signed on to that particular system. Search queries could then be run for particular artists or tracks, and results were displayed showing the other persons who had available the sought-after MP3 file. Then, with the click of a button, a download could be initiated, transferring the file from the request grantor to the request initiator.

Prior to the invention of this program, MP3s were distributed primarily through Internet Relay Chat (IRC) channels and through downloads from web pages (which often offered unreliable links to MP3 files housed on other servers, and which were usually shut down by the recording industry after a brief period due to their ease of detection) (Harari, 1999). File transferring using specialized but arcane programs were often employed by the Internet-savvy, but the general public was neither aware nor inclined to spend the time and effort to use such a method to obtain music files. Napster's easy-to-use interface and pre-establishment of a network between all of its users greatly conduced to simple, point-and-click accumulation of desired digital music tracks onto the personal and office computers of individuals.

Students at universities and many other music fans with fast Internet connections then began to fill up hard drive space and CDs with MP3s. This was presumably for the purposes of obtaining free music they would otherwise have to purchase, and also simply for the sake of possession to increase the size of their music collection. Unfortunately, this clogged network pipelines and retarded the ability of other individuals from using the shared bandwidth resources for legitimate purposes, such as downloading an open-source operating system for their research work, sending documents and work-related files to other users for the purposes of collaboration, or even merely browsing the World Wide Web (Krochmal, 1998; Stenger, 2000; Swiatecki, 2000b).

As a consequence, academic institutions such as Indiana University[11], San Diego State University, and the University of Chicago were forced to disallow access to the TCP ports used by Napster, which resulted in an outcry of censorship by university students around the nation (Kover, 2000). Other schools attempted to arrive at a common ground, either by regulating the amount of bandwidth an individual could utilize, or by instituting data packet analysis and filtering programs[12] to keep tabs on which users were consuming the largest amounts of data (Stenger, 2000; Swiatecki, 2000b).

Napster allowed for giant repositories of music to be easily accumulated by individuals, providing accessibility to popular songs from virtually any recent decade with incredible ease and functionality, and requiring no extra physical storage space other than that taken up by one's computer. It is true that some MP3s available on Napster were legal files, supported by the artist or band. The vast majority, however, were illegal files of copyrighted works by a sizable number of commercial artists ranging from the latest pop track by Madonna, to the country sounds of the Dixie Chicks, to the hardcore rap songs of Snoop Dogg, to the old-school classic rock of ZZ Top. The crux of the problem was that the owners of the copyright (usually held jointly by the artist and the record company) were denied compensation due to them through unauthorized downloads of their music via the software.

Napster has since evolved into a legal music service (Napster-to-Go) offering over 1,000,000 songs for download for a flat-rate fee of $9.95 per

---

[11] Incidentally, Indiana University and a host of other colleges overturned their decision to ban the program within a few months of their initial decision following the negative publicity that ensued.

[12] Proxy servers and other workarounds can be implemented by the end user to skirt the restrictions in place that deny access to Napster and other file-exchange programs. Therefore, these network management tools seem essential despite their somewhat intrusive nature.

month (Napster.com, 2005). Along with Apple's iTunes, RealNetworks' Rhapsody, Yahoo! Music, MSN Music, EMusic, and Pressplay, legal online services offering digital music have enjoyed success, highlighting the fact that consumers are willing to pay a fair price for digital downloads if a sizable catalog of music is available to them[13]. To note, digital distribution business models for the music industry are discussed further in Chapter 7.

BITTORRENT

BitTorrent is a new peer-to-peer protocol designed by programmer Bram Cohen to facilitate the exchange of files between users (Wikipedia, 2005). There is a central server (called a tracker) which coordinates the actions of all users, and serves as a broker to set up connections between individuals without recording any file content information. The uniqueness and value of the protocol lie in its network design. Files are broken up into multiple fragments and then distributed to requesting users, who then serve those fragments to other requesting machines - often simultaneously downloading (receiving) fragments the software does not have while uploading (sending) fragments it does have to other requesting machines (Dessent, 2005a). Once a user obtains all of the fragments that comprise a file, the file is reassembled in its entirety on the recipient machine. This protocol is particularly useful for large files because it most optimally utilizes bandwidth by spreading the file distribution load to all individuals who each have varying fragments. Furthermore, the problem of "leeching" - where individuals simply download (leech) from others without "sharing the wealth" is reduced because individuals only gain download speed from others when they give upload speed to others. This accordingly provides incentive to all participating individuals to contribute to the efficiency of the file distribution design and its ultimate goal of ensuring that every file request is filled in a timely manner.

A helpful analogy in understanding the process involves visualizing a group of people around a table, each interested in obtaining a complete copy of a book.

---

[13] In 2004, approximately 330 million songs were purchased from legitimate online stores such as iTunes, illustrating that the pay-to-play concept has been embraced by many (Associated Press, 2005).

"Person A announces that he has pages 1-10, 23, 42-50, and 75. Persons C, D, and E are each missing some of those pages that A has, and so they coordinate such that A gives them each copies of the pages he has that they are missing. Person B then announces that she has pages 11-22, 31-37, and 63-70. Persons A, D, and E tell B they would like some of her pages, so she gives them copies of the pages that she has. The process continues around the table until everyone has announced what they have (and hence what they are missing.) The people at the table coordinate to swap parts of this book until everyone has everything. There is also another person at the table, who we'll call 'S.' This person has a complete copy of the book, and so doesn't need anything sent to him. He responds with pages that no one else in the group has. At first, when everyone has just arrived, they all must talk to him to get their first set of pages. However, the people are smart enough to not all get the same pages from him. After a short while they all have most of the book among themselves, even if no one person has the whole thing. In this manner, this one person can share a book that he has with many other people, without having to give a full copy to everyone that's interested. He can instead give out different parts to different people, and they will be able to share it among themselves." (Dessent, 2005b)

BitTorrent is currently the most popular peer-to-peer software being used, and it is estimated that it accounts for approximately 35% of all Internet traffic (Pasick, 2004). Many other programs with file-exchange capabilities have been created since online digital audio became a global phenomenon, and include Gnutella, Wrapster, Napigator, iMesh, Scour, Kazaa, LimeWire, WinMX, Morpheus, Bearshare, and eDonkey. Some of these programs continue to be used by millions of individuals on a daily basis (Black, 2003; Sharman Networks, 2005). As previously mentioned, the primary benefit of MP3s through these and other mediums seems to be the receipt of a valued product and service that otherwise would have to be purchased as a physical recording. Such a concept outraged the producers but delighted the consumers, and other individuals and entities implicated in the phenomenon began to take sides.

PLAYERS IN THE MP3 PHENOMENON

In the controversy, there are seven primary players whose interaction between and among each other fuel the dynamic nature of the issue. On one side, there is the *general public* - who by and large are supporters, endorsers, and participants in uploading, downloading, and otherwise distributing MP3s. *Independent artists* - those not signed to a major music label - often claim allegiance to this side as well because they see MP3s as tools of promotion, and a way to provide their music to anyone and everyone irrespective of whether they have been "discovered" by a recording company (Bowman, 2000). *Internet startups and "dot.com" entrepreneurs* - those who have built businesses around the potential technological, economic, and social benefits offered by MP3s - stand on this side as well. Some have succeeded (or did succeed before the "dot.com bubble" burst), which testifies to the fact that the goods and services they provide are valued and tremendously popular among music aficionados (CNN.com, 2000a).

Hackers[14] are another group who realize a significant value and benefit associated with MP3s. This is likely because their computers are often an extension of themselves for a lengthy period of time each day, and digital music at their fingertips furnishes a constant amount of listening entertainment while they engage in various computing activities. This is also a collective which actively champions the voice of the average Internet user and generally opposes any perceived semblance of capitalistic exploitation (Hafner & Markoff, 1991). Furthermore, hackers commonly organize and assist in the circulation and "sharing" of pirated songs and albums in MP3 format to the masses, and work to "crack" software and digital protections that might hamper or restrict the end user's goals to acquire music for free (see e.g., Thurrott, 2003).

Antagonists to the MP3 phenomenon are less in number but arguably more potent and influential as a whole because of their relative position on the economic ladder. This is partly due to established relationships with the corporate and government sector. Another reason is that the social structure endows them with a disproportionate amount of power to define

---

[14] The term "hacker" is chosen for use here for the purposes of simplicity. In cyberspace social circles, "hacker" is properly used only for those who explore systems for the purposes of well-intentioned knowledge discovery, while "cracker" is the term used to signify those who break into systems – and who break copy-protection mechanisms – for illicit gain.

and enforce their constructed definitions of legal, and thereby acceptable, behavior. That is, what comes to be known as propriety seems shaped not so much by legal, institutional, or societal factors but is rather an extension of economic self-aggrandizement by those in a privileged and influential position. The federal government and the courts have largely defended the interests of private corporations and businesses, and have imposed restrictions and harsh penalties on entrepreneurial MP3-based enterprises (e.g., MP3.com, Napster, Inc.) and individuals because of their alleged copyright-infringing practices (A & M Records Inc. et al. v. Napster Inc., 2001; CNN.com, 2000b, 2000c; Davis, 2003; Healy, 2003; Jones, 2000; Lipton, 1998; Mendels, 1999; Patrizio, 1999; Philipkoski, 1999a, 1999b; RIAA, 2000g; Spring, 2000).

The most powerful player is the *recording industry*, a $40 billion dollar behemoth of authority and clout (King, 2001; RIAA, 2003). Its chief voice is the Recording Industry Association of America (RIAA), a trade consortium comprised of record companies that distribute approximately 90% of legitimate sound recordings in the United States, and seek to foster a "business and legal climate that promotes [their] members' creative and financial vitality" (RIAA, 2000i). Through the introduction and distribution of MP3s online, the traditional medium (and "cash cow") of distribution through packaging, marketing, and selling recordings on compact discs and tapes has been forcibly weakened. *Commercial musical artists* signed to the major record labels are generally hostile towards the unauthorized availability and distribution of their creative works, as they believe revenue is being denied to them since their label can no longer control how their music is obtained (Breen, 2000)[15]. Indicative of the consensual attitude towards the phenomenon and its attendant software facilitators, one popular artist publicly denounced Napster as "bulls---t hippie capitalism," and others have expressed similar sentiments (Bowman, 2000; RIAA, 2000f). The final group consists of *attorneys* who trumpet the cause of either position, both eager to litigiously prove that the intents and practices of one side are not damaging to the other.

---

[15] Some major artists who are in support of the technology include Limp Bizkit, The Offspring, Chuck D, Deftones, and AFI.

REVIEW OF MP3-RELATED RESEARCH

Intellectual property is legally defined as:

1. A category of intangible rights protecting commercially valuable products of the human intellect. The category comprises primarily trademark, copyright, and patent rights, but also includes trade-secret rights, publicity rights, moral rights, and rights against unfair competition.
2. A commercially valuable product of the human intellect, in a concrete or abstract form, such as a copyrightable work, a protectable trademark, a patentable invention, or a trade secret. (Garner, 1999:336)

Digital intellectual property can be characterized as a "public good," in that its utility is not decreased or removed if given to other individuals. Such a characteristic encourages the distribution and "sharing" of such property, often with the implicit assumption that others will distribute and "share" similar property to collectively meet the desires of all who participate. In addition, digital intellectual property is an "information good" as the marginal cost of production is virtually zero. Software and digital music are two types of digital intellectual property, and Bhattacharjee, Agrawal, & Wagner (2003) have stated that they differ from each other in five primary respects:

1) Fidelity. The fidelity of digital music is not as high as the quality of the same music from an original CD, because digital music is compressed. Fidelity is not an issue with software

2) Size. Songs in digital format generally have much smaller file sizes than software applications, enabling their transfer at quicker speeds

3) Price. Songs in digital format are generally much less expensive than software applications

4) Volume. The variety and availability of digital music is vastly greater than that of software applications

5) Support. No product support or service from the author or manufacturer is needed for digital music, unlike software applications.

These differences endow digital music with unique qualities which augment its attractiveness as a valued commodity to be acquired, and which point to reasons why the music industry refused for years to embrace the changes this new format has introduced to their business model.

To determine the extent to which unauthorized digital music distribution over the Internet has proliferated and how it might affect the music industry's revenue stream, a handful of empirical studies have been conducted. These, however, have been primarily sponsored by music business stakeholders in an attempt to validate or refute claims that the availability of digital audio files adversely affects CD sales, the recording industry, and the artists themselves. Most of these examinations occurred in 1999 and 2000, the years in which Napster served as the catalyst that propelled MP3 technology into the limelight. Subject matter included: participation with MP3s (Angus Reid Worldwide, 2000b; DMA, 2000; Jay, 2000; Kibbee, 1999; Pew Internet & American Life Project, 2000); determining the acceptability and extent of music piracy among certain populations; assessing the influence of piracy on CD purchasing behavior (Angus Reid Worldwide, 2000a; Jay, 2000; Kibbee, 1999; King, 2000a, 2000b; Latonero, 2000; Learmonth, 2000; Reciprocal Inc., 2000a, 2000b; Stenneken, 1999); identifying whether individuals would be willing to pay for digital downloads (Kibbee, 1999; King, 2000a; Pew Internet & American Life Project, 2000; Stenneken, 1999; Webnoize, 2000); determining how the behavior was learned (Latonero, 2000); determining the contributive role of high-speed Internet access (Cravotta, 2000; Davis, 2003; Healy, 2003; Latonero, 2000; Petreley, 2000); and generally examining ideas and opinions related to the technology and its consequences for all parties involved (Jay, 2000; Latonero, 2000; Stone, 2000).

None of these studies analyzed behavioral influences or motivations that conduce to the criminal activity, and no theoretical perspective was used to create the hypotheses or to shape inferred conclusions. Moreover, the methodology and research design of most was questionable, and the underlying motive for commencing the study was typically manifested in the suggested policy solutions. It is predictable, then, that no dominant theme consistently emerged concerning the relationship between unauthorized MP3s and the economic health of attendant players in the industry. Nonetheless, a rough sketch of the prevalence of participation in music piracy was obtained through the research.

Recently, a few exploratory academic studies utilizing small sample sizes have been published concerning the MP3 phenomenon. For instance, in a sample of over 200 college students from 2000-2001 (Bhattacharjee et al., 2003) found that price of music and available bandwidth are positively related to participation in digital music transfers, and that the issues of digital music fidelity and level of income were not significantly related to downloading "known," "favorite," or "popular" music tracks. In another study (Gopal et al., 2004) developed a structural equation model of behavioral determinants related to music piracy, and included: ethical inclinations; conceptions of justice and belief in laws; "club size," where individuals partner with others to increase the availability of desired music among the group; income; gender; age, and amount of money saved. The model provided a good fit to the data retrieved from surveying 133 undergraduate students primarily majoring in business and in their third year of school.

As anticipated, ethical individuals and those with strong conceptions of justice were less likely to commit intellectual property theft for the purposes of providing music to others. Older individuals participated less in the activity, as would be expected. The amount of money saved was a strong predictor of club size, as a greater perception of reward (i.e., not having to pay for music on a physical CD) increased the likelihood that the individual would exchange music with others. Income was not found to significantly predict club size. The researchers also identified that receiving an article delineating the prosecution and penalties of a college student who distributed unauthorized MP3 files did not have a significant effect on club size. This research is the first to conceptualize music piracy from a behavioral perspective, and therefore merits accolade despite its incompleteness.

With regard to theoretical applications, Banerjee et al. (1998) stated that piracy is a result of decisions that individuals consciously make. Other scholars (Gopal & Sanders, 1997, 1998; Gopal et al., 2004; Im & Van Epps, 1991; Kievit, 1991; Thong & Yap, 1998; Wong, 1995) have asserted that the decision to pirate is influenced by individual ethical conduct. While such statements stimulate inquiry into the cognitive impetus for behavior, a host of additional factors (e.g., cognitive, behavioral, psychological, and sociological) seemingly play a contributory role. Scholars have recently begun to explore these elements, with a recent study of 318 undergraduate students revealing that low self-control significantly influenced software piracy participation, and that rudimentary social learning theory variables also had some predictive effect (Higgins, 2005; Higgins & Makin, 2004). Further inquiry is required, though, that explicitly specifies more of the elements that might explain some proportion of the variance in the behavior. This is essential to obtain a thorough understanding of the etiology of the piracy phenomenon.

THEFT, LAW, AND AMBIGUITY – HISTORY AND RELEVANCE

Theft, law, and ambiguity all intersect to provide some insight into the etiology of the dishonest acquisition of property. The common law definition of larceny serves as the historical starting point for theft and dishonest acquisition of property. Traditionally, a trespassory taking was necessary in order for larceny to occur, and larceny was only applicable when considering certain forms of property. Over time, this law has evolved to encompass more forms of the act and more forms of the property that can be dishonestly acquired. The maintenance of the social order has also been paramount to the development of theft laws, as legal mandates tend to define and uphold the boundaries of behavioral propriety to preserve the social, political, and economic system in place. Jerome Hall, in his seminal work Theft, Law, and Society (1935), points to an appropriate example which arose in England in the late 1400s when the country was transitioning from a feudal and agricultural economy into one based on trade and mercantilism.

In this setting, merchants who sold goods to customers would hire individuals - or carriers - to transport and deliver the goods on a horse-drawn cart. Some carriers, however, decided to keep the goods for themselves. At the time there was no law which defined such an action as illegal because social norms dictated that goods belonged to the individual who had possession of them (Hall, 1935). That is, while the goods were with the carriers, they belonged to them, and no theft had occurred if the carriers chose to appropriate what was in their possession. Any harm that befell merchants was their own fault, because they had chosen to hire someone untrustworthy to deliver their goods. The English merchant class vociferously demanded that this activity be deemed illegal, though their number was much smaller than the population of poor English men who were the ones fulfilling the role of carrier and delivering the goods.

In 1493, judges who came from well-to-do backgrounds and who did not represent the interests of the majority population of the lower class ruled in favor of the merchants and created a new crime and definition of theft that outlawed the retention of deliverable goods by carriers (Hall,

1935). This decision – which reflected a paradigmatic shift in social and business practices – safeguarded the economic interests of the privileged merchant class at the expense of the poor, and curtailed behaviors that potentially threatened the status quo. Over the centuries, the criminalization of dishonest acquisition has significantly expanded, and the contributive force of economic and political interests cannot be overlooked.

Ambiguity in the actual content and application of the law during the Mercantilian Revolution appears to have contributed to the crime. For example, common sense in the 21st century would indicate that keeping something owned by another but entrusted to one's care is unethical and illegal. In the 15th century, though, it was a socially acceptable behavior and no alarm or question was raised when it occurred. If carriers were well-versed in definitions of property and made conspicuously aware of the wrongful nature of misappropriating propriety that belonged to someone else, perhaps no problem would have arisen. Some five hundred plus years later, ambiguity in the Information Revolution appears to once again be relevant in contributing to illegal activity - this time concerning intellectual property theft over the Internet.

Arguably few carriers were aware that their actions might be criminal since the inception of their occupational duty, but were made aware of the unacceptability of their behavior through the visible processes and outcomes of the legal system. Similarly, it can be posited that a significant number of MP3 enthusiasts do not completely understand the illicit extent of their point-and-click actions online. Even if news and media outlets have introduced that notion to them, it is highly unlikely that they thoroughly comprehend why their behavior is inappropriate and the reasoning behind policy intended to restrict and penalize such activity. Nonetheless, uploading and downloading music files would not be a crime if the content being exchanged had no commercial or personal worth. Any creative work, however, is fundamentally imbued with value and the usurping of that value without proper authorization is the issue at hand.

THE VALUE OF INFORMATION AND INTELLECTUAL PROPERTY

"Although intellectual property has become a salient topic in economic and political circles, it has generally escaped the attention of criminologists. Such negligence is unwarranted. It is time to grant that intellectual property is as valuable as customary forms of property, that its infringement is as significant as burglary and robbery, and that its violation and protection merit careful investigation." (Luckenbill & Miller, 1998:116).

Seminal in part to the current research was an interesting article in Justice Quarterly by David F. Luckenbill and Susan L. Miller (1998), who assessed the relevance of two competing theories related to intellectual property. The first was termed the "intellectual property protection" argument, and speculated an increase in laws protecting the creative works of authors and punishing violators of copyright. The second was termed the "intellectual property access" argument, and projected a decrease in protective laws and prohibitive actions concomitant with a rise in the amount of legislation that increased access to creative works.

The authors described how the development of exploitative information technologies foreboded and facilitated the misuse and misappropriation of works without proper remuneration and rights that should be duly afforded to the originators and owners (Dordick, 1986). Home satellite dishes, audio-to-digital converters, decoding boxes, videocassette recorders, and audiocassette recorders were articulated by the researchers as technologies that have greatly enabled individuals to acquire, copy, alter, and distribute intellectual property to which they have no legal right (Luckenbill & Miller, 1998). It was predicted that as these and similar technologies became more prevalent, intellectual property crime (and the difficulty in addressing it) would rise (Office of Technology Assessment, 1986). Luckenbill and Miller's paper was published in 1998, a year in which the MP3 phenomenon was still relatively incipient. It can be argued that digital music has had much greater ramifications than the aforementioned devices for the distribution of creative works due to its global scope and availability on the Internet.

Historically, government agencies paid attention to traditional types of property crimes but ignored those of the intellectual variety (Luckenbill & Miller, 1998). By the turn of the 20th century, though, supporters of rights restricting the copying and dissemination of creative works had successfully compelled the state to propose and enact legislation in line with their position after developing strong political and economic ties (Bettig, 1996). As time went on and more effort was expended by owners of intellectual property to seek the assistance of the government to protect their interests, lawmakers mobilized to quell copyright concerns that the entertainment industry voiced following technological advances such as the player piano (in 1908), broadcast radio (1931), photocopies (1968), the VCR (1976), the DAT recorder (1990), and portable MP3 players (1998) (Schoen, 2002).

Luckenbill and Miller (1998) assert that a primary reason for the historical apathy of the state towards protecting intellectual property may have hinged on the fact that most individuals lacked the capacity to violate these laws. For example, many recording and duplicating devices were prohibitively expensive for many years, but the cost of these pieces of hardware eventually became quite affordable for the average person. Furthermore, in recent years the advent of the Information Age has facilitated the opportunity and means to covertly distribute copyrighted data without a significant threat of detection, apprehension, and punishment, and at a comparatively small cost[16]. Thus, the combination of lower participation costs and the greater number of deviant possibilities to exploit has jointly provoked legislators to action.

Researchers also have largely ignored the importance of studying intellectual property, disproportionately focusing attention on conventional conceptions of property (Gilbert & Lyman, 1989; Reiman, 1995). Legal scholars, however, have studied it to a great extent and continue to do so. Their interest resides primarily - though not exclusively - in the semantics of laws as crafted and delineated in the books and in their consequent application[17]. Analyses of the prevalence, role, and efficacy of intellectual property laws have been extremely limited - a deficiency which Luckenbill and Miller attempt to address through their work. They examined federal legislative action involving copyright on both civil and criminal levels from 1949 through 1992, and uncovered a host of interesting findings. First, significant growth in the amount of legislation over this time period took place, and 91.5% of the 423 bills that were introduced favored the owners of copyright rather than the consumers (Luckenbill & Miller, 1998). Simply put, as the private-sector became increasingly vociferous in petitioning the state to support their interests, a greater number of legislation was proposed and passed.

The scholars also analyzed civil copyright cases compiled by Administrative Office of the United States Courts from 1955 to 1993, and criminal copyright cases compiled by the Executive Office of the United States Attorneys from 1997 to 1993. Civil complaints increased from

---

[16] All that is needed is a computer, an Internet connection, and some freely available software.

[17] See e.g., Lessig (1997; 1999a)

approximately 300 per year in the 1950s, to about 2,000 per year in the 1990s, as a greater number of civil violations were deemed worthy of pursuing formally, while the amount of criminal complaints generally decreased from 93 in 1977 to 12 in 1989 (Luckenbill & Miller, 1998). With regard to the actions of the courts, they acted on a larger proportion of civil cases but a smaller proportion of criminal cases over the years in which the data were available. Finally, of those that were handled by the courts, the researchers found that many ended in guilty convictions and relatively few in dismissals (Luckenbill & Miller, 1998).

Also examined were statistics compiled by the Motion Picture Association of America to obtain an understanding of investigations into, and legal resolutions of, film piracy. An increase (32.6% in 1986 to 47.5% in 1994) in the amount of criminal action and a significant decrease (67.4% in 1986 to 30.6% in 1994) in civil action was identified (Luckenbill & Miller, 1998). Over that same time period, the rates of sentencing and conviction of intellectual property offenses remained relatively stable, while the severity of sentences declined.

Overall, the findings suggested that legislators supported the private-sector and the courts were more diligent in attending to intellectual property cases, but law enforcement remained largely apathetic in fervently seeking to identify and apprehend copyright criminals (Luckenbill & Miller, 1998). Two reasons are suggested. The first is that the copyright laws were implemented to promote a symbolic purpose and to proclaim a certain value system, rather than as specific delimiters of behaviors that would be punitively addressed. The second revolves around the issue of limited resources and expertise to identify and combat intellectual property violations, coupled with the politically- and socially-mandated focus on traditional personal and private property crimes (to the exclusion of nontraditional forms of illegality). It may be that civil cases are the only viable option because of the restrictions that are placed on the activities of law enforcement entities (Luckenbill & Miller, 1998).

COPYRIGHT LAW

Those who publish the creative products of musicians on the Internet in MP3 format without authorization tend to rationalize the questionable nature of their activities. This can take the form of disclaimers on a web site offering unauthorized free music, such as those that qualify the presence of unauthorized MP3s on their page as "promotional" or "educational." Others caveats used as justification include, but are not limited to, the following: "Any files downloaded must be deleted from your computer within 24 hours," "The author is to be held blameless in all respects for the data available on this site," "The author of this site is not responsible for the illegal transfer and possession of copyrighted material by its visitors," or "This site is non-profit, and is only providing an evaluation service to visitors before purchase of the respective music CDs" (RIAA, 2000h). Rationalizations are also manifested in participants' outcries that MP3s are not *absolutely* CD quality, that "clips" of songs are legally acceptable, that the music being downloaded is for personal use only, that there is no profit being made, or that a site only containing hyperlinks to MP3s on someone else's file server is legal because it does not actually store the copyrighted material.

These justifications are all invalid in light of the fundamental principle of copyright – only the owner has the lawful ability to distribute or reproduce that creative work, and anyone or anything that directly or indirectly contributes to unauthorized dissemination or duplication of another's intellectual property is committing a crime. Disregard for the copyrights of intellectual property, manifested through the purposeful dissemination of unauthorized digital music files, is a federal offense (RIAA, 2000e). The illicit activity falls under the auspices of "Internet crime," which can be defined as any illegal act fostered or facilitated by the Internet and a computer, whether the computer is an object of a crime, an instrument used to commit a crime, or a repository of evidence related to a crime (Royal Canadian Mounted Police, 2000).

As quoted from the United States Copyright Office, the owner of a copyright has the exclusive right to do (or authorize another to do) the following:

To reproduce the work in copies or phonorecords;

To prepare derivative works based upon the work;

To distribute copies or phonorecords of the work to the public by sale or other transfer of ownership, or by rental, lease, or lending;

To perform the work publicly, in the case of literary, musical, dramatic, and choreographic works, pantomimes, and motion pictures and other audiovisual works;

> To display the copyrighted work publicly, in the case of literary, musical, dramatic, and choreographic works, pantomimes, and pictorial, graphic, or sculptural works, including the individual images of a motion picture or other audiovisual work; and

> In the case of sound recordings, to perform the work publicly by means of a digital audio transmission. (Copyright Office of the United States, 2000a)

The term "copyright" is defined as the legal right granted to an author, composer, playwright, publisher, or distributor, to exclusive publication, production, sale, or distribution of a literary, musical, dramatic, or artistic work (de Fontenay, 1999). Copyrights cover both published and unpublished works, and are secured immediately upon the expression of an original work in fixed, tangible form (Copyright Office of the United States, 2000a).

Sound recordings have two copyrights, one on the underlying musical work (notes and lyrics), and one on the actual recording itself (the arrangement and layering of the performance by the artist, the backup singers and musicians, the producers, and the sound engineers, as written to a physical medium (e.g., cassette tape or CD) (Harari, 1999). Each copyright grants the owner explicit and sole permission to modify, distribute, reproduce, perform, or display the work. With the uploading and downloading of digital music over the Internet, however, these copyrights are violated. For instance, uploading an unlicensed MP3 to a web or file server that can be accessed by others through their web browser or through a file transfer program is a form of distribution. If the copyrighted work is not owned or authored by the uploader, that person is breaking the law. When an individual requests MP3s from a web or file server, or uses a file exchange program to download MP3s onto his or her hard drive, an exact copy of that sound recording is made on the recipient's computer system. This violates the reproduction tenet of the copyright law, as non-owners must have explicit permission to duplicate protected works, whether for profit or merely for personal listening pleasure, and regardless if it is for a transitory or permanent period of time.

The RIAA stresses two legal concepts that come into play with Internet music piracy – copyright infringement and vicarious liability. When a person knowingly facilitates violation of copyright, infringement has taken place (RIAA, 2000e). This can occur online as web sites link to other servers that host unauthorized MP3s, even if the files are not housed directly on the initial web site. Another instance might be when a person sets up an automated system to advertise MP3 files for download in a chat channel. While that person is not specifically initiating the transfer of files, he or she is making available MP3s for distribution without the consent of the copyright holders. Vicarious liability occurs when a person is able to control the activities of a copyright violator and fails, and also receives some pecuniary benefit from his or her role in facilitating infringement (RIAA, 2000e).

There are a few pieces of important legislation that necessitate mention to provide a richer understanding of the attendant legal issues. Each is explicated below, as is its relevance to the current controversy surrounding digital music distributed over the Internet.

U.S. Copyright Law {Title 17 U.S.C. Section 101 et seq., Title 18 U.S.C. Section 2319}

This federal law gives the exclusive rights of reproduction, adaptation, distribution, public performance, and public display of copyrighted works to its owners. Individuals who exercise those rights without a license from the copyright holder are committing infringement, and thereby subject to penalties unless shielded by the Fair Use Doctrine (discussed below). An individual can be held civilly liable if he or she infringes on a copyright unknowingly, or without forethought or specific intention. Criminal liability can occur if an individual duplicates copyrighted intellectual property for the purposes of obtaining profit or "gain" from it. This is not limited to financial returns, and can include the possibility of denied revenue to the artist. When the illegally-reproduced works are used for commercial advantage, resultant penalties include incarceration for up to five years and fines up to $250,000 (Copyright Office of the United States, 2000b). Additional civil liabilities may include payment for damages incurred by the copyright holder, or statutory damages of up to $150,000 per infringed work.

Fair Use Doctrine

The doctrine of "fair use" from the 1976 Copyright Act, Section 107, allows a user to duplicate a copyrighted work for educational or research purposes such as criticism, news reporting, teaching, or scholarship, as long as the work is not used for profit and its potential value is not negatively affected (Copyright Office of the United States, 2000b; RIAA, 2000e). The value of a song, however, can be impacted even if only a small clip of it is expropriated, regardless of how high the fidelity is, and irrespective of the fact that no monetary gain is derived. "Profit" can constitute any form of received benefit outside the exceptions in this clause. To be clear, distribution of the work over the Internet for the purposes of exchanging commercially-produced music without remunerating the artists does *not* fall under the exemptions of the "fair use" doctrine.

The Audio Home Recording Act (AHRA) of 1992

Arising from the development of physical digital playback products such as MiniDisc (MD) and Digital Audio Tape (DAT) players, the AHRA required manufacturers to pay a royalty from the sale of each device and device media sold to musicians, songwriters, and record companies as compensation for lost revenue, and to implement mechanisms to prevent serial copying or multi-generation duplication. The Diamond Rio PMP300 player was claimed by the RIAA to be in violation of this law. However, the U.S. 9th District Court of Appeals ruled against the RIAA's charge by holding that the Rio was not an audio recording device, but rather a playback device incapable of intrinsically facilitating music piracy (CNN.com, 2000c; MP3.com, 1998). Consumers were given permission to make private, non-commercial copies of copyrighted music with these devices and exempted from litigation for infringement. Incidentally, a computer is not covered under the auspices of the AHRA, as it is not solely designed for digital audio playback and recording, and has multiple noninfringing purposes as well.

The Digital Performance Right in Sound Recordings Act (DPRA) of 1995

The DPRA afforded copyright owners of sound recordings (distinguished from "musical works") control over the public performance of their work, such as granting or denying permission for digital dissemination and broadcasting (RIAA, 2000c). It also allowed for artist compensation when their works were transmitted digitally, excluding the mediums of radio and television. Previously, copyright owners of sound recordings were not allowed to authorize public performances of their work; this law enabled them to do so.

The No Electronic Theft Act (NET) of 1997

The NET Act, signed into law by President Clinton in 1997, specifies that copyright violations are now criminally prosecutable and punishable with up to $250,000 in fines and three years in prison, even when there is no profit motive to the activity (RIAA, 2000g). Those who derive financial gain from the behavior can be imprisoned for up to five years and/or be liable for up to $250,000. Additionally, offenders may also be found civilly liable for damages of up to $150,000 per copyright infringement. "Financial gain," according to the law, is not necessarily restricted to monetary benefit, and also includes the receipt (or expectation of receipt) of a valued item, which can include MP3 files and other digital intellectual property (Congress, 1997).

The Digital Millennium Copyright Act (DMCA) of 1998

The DMCA essentially criminalizes any act of circumventing copy protection. As such, an individual may legally make MP3s from a music CD, unless that CD is copy-protected. An increasing number of CDs are created with technological restrictions to prevent digital audio extraction and subsequent conversion to MP3 files. According to the DMCA, then, any action that attempts to bypass the protection in place - even for ostensibly legitimate purposes - is unlawful and subject to sanctions. The action may be to make a backup of a CD for personal use – either to one's hard drive or to a CDR – and is actually legal. If circumvention of a protective control is necessary to accomplish that goal, however, the action becomes illegal, rendering the DMCA a law that "extends rights to consumers even as it effectively prevents them from exercising those rights" (Harmon, 2001).

Secondly, the DMCA amended the DPRA to cover transmission over the Internet, as well as through cable and satellite services (Copyright Office of the United States, 1998). Finally, the liability of Internet Service Providers (ISPs) was clarified with the creation of the DMCA. It was determined that ISPs are not responsible for keeping tabs on what their customers transmit online or post to web pages and file servers for others. However, if an ISP is aware, or is made aware, of copyright-infringing practices, that business has a legal obligation to act accordingly and remove the material, or risk facing liability (RIAA, 2000c).

MGM v. Grokster (2005)

In this case, a lawsuit was brought against the creators of the peer-to-peer file exchange software products Grokster, Morpheus, and Kazaa by 28 of the world's largest entertainment companies in an attempt to place liability on the innovators of the software for copyright-infringing practices (i.e., music piracy) committed by the software's end users (Duke Law School, 2005; Electronic Frontier Foundation, 2005). Similar to the decision in Sony Corporation of America v. Universal City Studios, Inc. (Sony Corp., 1984), the lower courts deemed the software products capable of "substantial noninfringing uses." This meant that the software innovators could not be held liable for the actions of users. Specifically, the US. Court of Appeals for the 9th circuit declared that Grokster et al. did not "materially contribute" to copyright infringement, and could not have had reasonable knowledge of specific infringement because they did not maintain a searchable index of shared files on a centralized server. However, in June 2005 the Supreme Court struck down the ruling of the lower courts, and unanimously declared that Grokster et al. can be held liable for copyright infringement that occurs through their technology. In the words of Justice David Souter, "We hold that one who distributes a device with the object of promoting its use to infringe copyright, as shown by clear expression or other affirmative steps taken to foster infringement, is liable for the resulting acts of infringement by third parties" (Crawford, 2005). While the specifics are as yet unknown, it is expected that this ruling will have broad implications for the manufacture and use of software related to the distribution of music, video, and other forms of intellectual property over the Internet.

CIVIL AND CRIMINAL SANCTIONS RESULTING FROM COPYRIGHT VIOLATION

Law enforcement acknowledges that while the chances are very slim that a person will get arrested for intellectual property theft, it is still a possibility (Spring, 2000). Other detrimental outcomes are more likely, however. For instance, upon joining a file exchange network like Kazaa or Morpheus, a computer system is rendered more vulnerable to viruses and spyware. In addition, by opening up a file directory on a computer system so that others can download your files, that computer has become a veritable conduit of music piracy and subject to apprehension and prosecution (Spring, 2000).

To illustrate, the U.S. Attorney's office obtained the country's first conviction under the NET Act in August 1997 against a 22-year old University of Oregon student who distributed thousands of songs, software, and movies after setting up his computer as an accessible file server (Patrizio, 1999; Roth, 1999). In 1998, a suit was filed against a 20-year old junior at Arizona State University for posting approximately 50 copyrighted works by popular artists on his web site (Lipton, 1998). Another suit was filed in Washington against an individual who made over 1,100 copyrighted songs available on a server (Lipton, 1998). In October 1999, Carnegie Mellon University used specialized software to detect potentially copyright-infringing materials on the dorm room network of a random selection of 250 students. They subsequently disconnected Internet service from the 71 individuals who were found to be hosting illegal music archives, and stated that Internet access could be regained following attendance at a discussion forum on the topic of copyrights (Mendels, 1999; Philipkoski, 1999a). Penn State, in the spring of 2003, revoked broadband Internet access from 220 students in residential halls after it was discovered that they were committing intellectual property theft (Davis, 2003).

Finally, in a lawsuit that made headlines largely because of the incredible amount of possible financial penalties, four students at Princeton, Michigan Technological University, and Rensselaer Polytechnic Institute were charged in 2003 with creating and administrating local area file-sharing networks that made available over one million songs to other students (Healy, 2003). With possible damages up to $150,000 per song, fines might have totaled $150 billion dollars. However, a settlement was reached and the students were each required to pay between $12,000 and $16,000 in restitution for their criminal activities. This was the first time that monetary penalties have been exacted from individuals for music piracy in the United States, and perceivably sought to demonstrate that the illegal activity is seriously regarded and will not be tolerated. Finally, 11,700 lawsuits have been filed against MP3 pirates by the RIAA between September 2003 and June 2005 (Associated Press, 2005; CNN.com, 2004; Slashdot.org, 2005). While the minimum penalty is $750 *per violation,* cases have generally been resolved out of court for between $3,500 and $4,500 (Rodriguez, 2005).

Online businesses, too, are coming under increased scrutiny for their potentially-infringing practices. For instance, Napster defended its original-version services by reasoning that its software allowed users the same privileges that the Diamond Rio portable MP3 player accorded; that is, the ability to duplicate copyrighted works for private, non-commercial purposes (CNN.com, 2000c). The RIAA argued that the service was a haven for online piracy and violated the AHRA. Napster countered that it was only providing a technology which serves as a conduit for users to exchange music, and that it was not responsible for, nor could it possibly control, the unethical and illegal behavior of its user population of millions (CNN.com, 2000c). The plaintiffs won the case in 2001 when the court ruled that Napster must block all copyright-infringing files, which effectively led to its demise[18].

MP3.com was sued by the RIAA in January 2000 and later found guilty of copyright infringement resulting from their practice of allowing users to create digital "lockers" (Breen, 2000; CNN.com, 2000b; RIAA, 2000b; Swiatecki, 2000b). Music CDs could be placed in one's CDROM drive at the home or office, and information would be sent to the web site detailing the artist and album of the particular disc. Then, upon noticing that the end user did in fact possess the physical CD (indicating actual or purported ownership), previously created MP3s of each track were placed in the individual's personal locker. This consequently allowed the user to access his or her CD collection, in the form of streaming digital MP3 tracks, from any computer at any location simply by connecting to the MP3.com web site. Thus, individuals could access their music collections remotely without having to constantly carry around the physical discs themselves. Apart from placing a CD into one's CDROM drive and connecting to the MP3.com web site — a service named "Beam-It" allowed members to have a digital copy of an album placed immediately into their locker after purchasing that album from an online CD retailing partner. This was known as MP3.com's Instant Listening Service (RIAA, 2000b).

To do this, and allow for millions of individuals to have digital copies of their CD collections online, MP3.com "ripped" (the term used for extracting digital audio from a CD into a waveform audio file) and "encoded" (a term referring to the compression of a waveform file into an MP3) approximately 45,000 albums, an activity for which they did not have permission from the artist or record company to do (Swiatecki, 2000b). The RIAA made the case that the service offered cannot determine ownership of a CD, and only relies on possession of a CD to

---

[18] Napster's technology and business model has since been reformulated into a pay-to-play service called Napster-to-Go.

give users the ability to listen to that music in digital format on demand from MP3.com. Further, the industry claimed that MP3.com does not have the legal right to broadcast, stream, or otherwise disseminate creative content and property that belongs to other musicians as well as the respective recording companies without a license or approval (Jones, 2000; Rosen, 2000). MP3.com countered that the music industry should not be able to control how a purchaser of a CD listens to that music. Additionally, MP3.com stated that it was benefiting artists to a much greater degree than the RIAA is by providing a direct link to their target audience, and well as the tools to promote their music in a new, profitable, and prolific distribution model (Robertson, 2000).

A settlement occurred a short time later, as the U.S. District Court ruled in May 2000 that MP3.com was guilty of copyright infringement due to its unauthorized appropriation of the property of the recording industry, its music companies, and its artists. Further, the "Beam-It" and "Instant Listening" services were found to facilitate a blatant disregard for the rights of the music industry to control and license the creative content it owns to others (Menta, 2000; MP3 Newswire, 2000). This ruling has served as precedent and shaped the future of online music business ventures by reinforcing the requirement that all delivery of music to the end user requires licensing and permission from the copyright holders.

It is perhaps difficult to appreciate the value of intellectual property if an individual is not in an intellectual property-related field. Further, it seems difficult simply due to the fact that society is somewhat accustomed to receiving various forms of information at no direct cost, especially when using the Internet. Finally, the confluence of the vast availability of software, movies, and music (if an individual knows where to look online), and an atmosphere of ignorance, confusion, and irregularly applied punitive policies, appears to contribute to a mentality that undermines an intrinsic respect for commercially valuable products of the human intellect.

Copyright laws are in place to give incentive to individuals - such as music artists - to innovate and produce creative works. It can be argued that if the virtual community of today is not able to respect the intellectual property of musicians and record companies, and continues to download and distribute digital audio files without authorization, the Internet users of tomorrow may be even less likely to ascribe to ethical behavior. A downward spiral might consequently ensue, possibly resulting in a complete and utter disregard for creative "fruits" of labor.

Unquestionably, many persons around the world create and freely distribute their intellectual property for others to use and enjoy[19]. However, some individuals and companies desire to reap the financial benefits of creating commercially valuable product in order to make up for their investment of time, money, and effort. Similar to Jesus' parable in Matthew 13 of the thorns which choke out the crops that attempt to flourish, a weed of disregard for intellectual property - left to germinate and grow on a society-wide level - could ultimately "choke out" the originative and inventive dogmas of our culture. As more and more aspects of our lives are affected (and more of our needs are met) through the capacities afforded by the Internet, this will drastically affect the structure and function of our networked economy and society. The elements that precipitate a person's decision to pirate music, and the theories that explore them, are detailed in Chapter 3.

---

[19] See e.g., the Free Software Foundation, the Open Source Foundation, and the thousands of independent artists not signed to a record label.

General Strain, Self-Control, and Social Learning Theories

The current research attempts to clarify the cognitive, behavioral, psychological, and sociological influences of online intellectual property theft in the form of digital music piracy. Towards that end, three general criminological theories appear applicable in inducing the phenomenon. These include general strain theory, self-control theory, and social learning theory, and prior to empirically analyzing their relevance as explanatory frameworks, it is important to provide a detailed description of their precepts. In the subsequent sections, each theory is introduced, and a number of studies which have respectively tested the salience of their approach are reviewed and discussed. Additionally, a breakdown of how certain elements of the theories might impel an individual to engage in music piracy is posited for the purposes of explaining to the reader why the behavior might occur.

GENERAL STRAIN THEORY

Strain, in essence, is the maladaptive response experienced by some individuals who seek to attain culturally or socially promulgated goals, but are thwarted by a variety of hindrances. This consequently leads them towards goal achievement via unethical or illegal means, or towards harmful responses at the perceived sources of their strain (Agnew, 1985). Since its initial promulgation by Robert Merton (1938; 1968), the concept of strain has been refined by a host of prominent sociological and criminological scholars including Cohen (1955), Cloward and Ohlin (1963), Agnew (1985; 1989; 1992); and Messner and Rosenfeld (1994). Agnew's conceptualization has received the most attention and empirical examination in recent years, and has been proffered as a general theory capable of explaining all types of deviance and criminality. It attempts to understand the detrimental effect that immediate social and environmental pressures can have on a person, as manifested through the affective vehicles of anger and frustration.

In his general strain theory, Agnew (1992:50) vocalized three primary types of strain that may affect an individual: the threatened or actual failure to achieve positively valued goals; the threatened or actual removal of positively valued stimuli; and the threatened or actual presence of negatively valued stimuli. The first type is exemplified by the notions of classic strain theory through its focus on the disjunction between aspirations and expectations/achievements – or, the ideal and the real. Also implicated are idealized conceptions of fair, equitable outcomes with those that actually occur. That is, certain emotive responses often result from an individual's failure to live up to certain expectations or from experiences of perceivably unjust outcomes, which lead to deviant methods of coping or compensating. The second type of strain regards the removal of certain positives in a person's life, such as healthy friendships, relationships, or environments (e.g., involving home, school, or work). For instance, stressful life events have the tendency to incite feelings of pain, anger, and frustration (and arguably subsequent criminality) as the strained individual attempts to prevent or come to terms with circumstance.

The third type of strain is the presence of irritating, frustrating, angering, painful, or otherwise noxious factors in a person's life. These may stem from social, environmental, or relational influences, and delinquency might ensue as the individual attempts to manage, curtail, or eradicate its effect. To reiterate, Agnew expands the concept of strain to include not only the thwarting of goal attainment, but also the removal of conducive entities and the introduction and persistence of detrimental entities in one's life. Also asserted by Agnew (1992) is the magnitude, recency, duration, and clustering (i.e., occurring closely together in time) of strainful events, and the positive relationship between those factors and the adverse impact of strain.

To note, certain elements moderate the link between strain and delinquent outcomes, such as the availability of coping resources and positive environmental and social support, as well as differences in personality, temperament, and aspirations (Agnew, 1992:71). For example, those individuals with an internal locus of control, with normative levels of self-confidence and self-efficacy, and who associate primarily with law-abiding peers will be less likely to engage in deviance to cope with strain (Agnew, 1992). Accordingly, Hoffman and Miller (1998) have argued that strain is not an "isolated cause of delinquency, but a facilitative mechanism that interacts with coping strategies to increase the probability of delinquent behavior." These conditioning factors, then, must be acknowledged and accommodated when attempting to test the viability of the relationship between strain and any deviant or criminal outcome.

Empirical Support for General Strain Theory

Empirical research since the theory's "general" reformulation in 1992 was initiated by Agnew himself, and followed by an assortment of other rigorous studies. In the first theoretical test, Agnew and White (1992) studied data collected from the Rutgers Health and Human Development Project, a longitudinal study which interviewed New Jersey youths about their experiences with delinquency and drug use. They first created multiple scales of strain, including those representing negative life events, life hassles, negative relations with adults, parental fighting, neighborhood problems, unpopularity with the opposite sex, occupational strain, and clothing strain. When contemporaneously measuring strain's influence on delinquency and drug use among 1,076 kids, the researchers identified a significant link between stress around the home and the two outcomes. They also discovered that the relationship between strain and these antinormative behaviors was conditioned by delinquent peer associations, social control elements, and self-efficacy, which was defined as "perceived personal control over the environment" (Agnew & White, 1992:488). In terms of the amount of variation explained, R^2 values of .402 for delinquency and .489 for drug use were derived, inclusive of all of the aforementioned predictors. Next, the relationship between a summary measure of strain at Time 1 and delinquency and drug use at Time 2 (three years later) was explored among 798 youths. Strain was found to significantly predict delinquency at Time 2, and had a larger effect than any of the differential association, social control, or self-efficacy elements (Agnew & White, 1992). It was not, however, related to drug use in the longitudinal analysis.

Paternoster and Mazerolle (1994) performed a more extensive test of the theory through longitudinal analysis of adolescents from the first two waves of the National Youth Survey. They employed a shorter lag period (one year) than the three-year gap between re-interviews in Agnew and White's (1992) study. In addition, they replicated most sources of strain constructed in that previous work, and extended the analysis by examining the interaction effects of strain with delinquent peer groups, self-control, self-efficacy, conventional social support, and moral inhibitions (Paternoster & Mazerolle, 1994:240).

Despite the fact that none of the interactions were found to be significantly related to delinquency, some general support was discovered for the theory. Specifically, negative relationships with adults and friends, negative experiences with school, various stressful life events, and living in a noxious neighborhood environment were significant predictors of delinquency (Paternoster & Mazerolle, 1994). Also identified was the facility of strain to weaken conventional social bonds and strengthen unconventional bonds. Temporal ordering of this relationship, however, was not clear because measurement of the concepts occurred at the same time. In another longitudinal work, (Hoffman & Miller, 1998) found that strain (operationalized as negative life events) was significantly related to changes in delinquency when controlling for other exogenous factors. Contrary to one of Agnew's hypotheses, however, self-esteem and self-efficacy appeared unrelated to the relationship between strain and delinquency.

In a study that offered strong support for the theory's tenets, four scales - negative relations with adults, school/peer hassles, neighborhood problems, and negative life events - were employed by Mazerolle and Maahs (2000) as strain measures, along with one composite additive scale of all the variables that comprised the aforementioned facets. Utilizing data from the National Youth Survey, the researchers found a linear and systematic relationship between delinquency and strain. Further, they found that conditioning variables such as negative peer influence, low moral inhibitions, and a behavioral inclination towards delinquency increased the likelihood of wrongdoing on both a cross-sectional and longitudinal basis.

Broidy (2001) examined the relationship among strain, crime, and two mediating variables - negative affective states such as anger and the availability of legitimate coping avenues - among 896 undergraduate students. A significant positive link was identified between strain and anger, unfair outcomes and anger, and strain and negative emotions. Interestingly, blocked goals reduced the likelihood that individuals responded to anger with strain, while negative emotions were positively related to legitimate coping mechanisms. Finally, negative emotions such as anger increased the likelihood of crime commission. Anger has been identified as an intervening variable between strain and criminal outcomes in a host of studies (e.g., Agnew, 1985; Agnew & Brezina, 1997; Agnew, Cullen, & Burton, 1996; Brezina, 1998; Mazerolle & Piquero, 1998; Piquero & Sealock, 2000), which have highlighted its importance as the medium through which violence is manifested following exposure to strain.

Strain, anger, and delinquent behavior in the forms of violence, drug use, and school-related deviance were further explored by Mazerolle et al. (2000). The researchers found that strain exhibited a direct effect on violence when controlling for the precepts of differential association and social bond theory, and some demographic measures. It was also found that strain mediated the relationship between anger and violence. Strain, when it occurred to those who were angry, tended to produce violent outcomes, while anger did not necessarily lead to violence unless strain was present (Mazerolle et al., 2000). Such findings contrast expectations associated with general strain theory but emphasize the fact that strain can exert a criminogenic influence through anger. Additionally, it was determined that strain and anger do not directly affect drug use or school-related deviance at the bivariate level, and that anger did not serve a mediating role between strain and such nonviolent outcomes (Mazerolle et al., 2000).

More support for the notion that variations in affective states resulting from strain predict different types of criminality was found among a population of 150 youthful offenders (Piquero & Sealock, 2000). In particular, anger was identified as a significant predictor of personal but not property crimes, while depression was unrelated to either type. Supporting the contentions of previous research (Broidy & Agnew, 1997; Mazerolle & Piquero, 1998), the scholars also found that the strength of relationship between strain and consequent emotional responses varies based on the types of crime under analysis, and that a link between anger and interpersonal violence and between depression and self-destructive behavior merits additional exploration. A similar conclusion was reached by Aseltine, Gore, and Gordon (2000) when they examined the effect of life stressors on delinquency through the inclusion of school, work, family, and financial strain variables among high school youths in Boston. Their analysis revealed general support for general strain theory, but identified a link only between anger and more serious and violent forms of criminality. Specifically, feelings of anger and hostility stemming from stressful life events appeared to predict aggressive responses more so than nonaggressive responses or drug use (Aseltine et al., 2000).

The effect of strain on the sexes has also been analyzed by a few researchers in this area. Hoffmann and Su (1997) found similarities across gender for the applicability of general strain theory to delinquency and drug use. Another study published the same year demonstrated that men were more likely than women to partake in delinquency following exposure to strainful stimuli (Agnew & Brezina, 1997). In a conceptual piece, Broidy and Agnew (1997) asserted that gender influenced the types of strain and the negative affective states experienced, as well as the resultant methods that individuals employed to cope. Specifically, they hypothesized that males are often subjected to financial strain - which frequently results in property crime, and to interpersonal strain - which frequently results in violent crime (Broidy & Agnew, 1997:297). They further stated that strain experienced by women typically includes disproportionate subjection to social control, and a restriction of opportunities to partake in criminal behavior - which largely seem to result in self-destructive outcomes like eating disorders and drug use (Broidy & Agnew, 1997:297). These self-harming behaviors appear to stem in part from certain emotions that accompany strain among women, such as depression, shame, and guilt.

Mixed support for general strain theory was generated by Mazerolle (1998), however, who did not find any difference between the effects of strain predictors on delinquency across gender categories. Nonetheless, he did find that gender differentiated the effect of negative life experiences on violent crimes, with men more likely to externalize anger and women more inclined to internalize such an emotion. These studies jointly highlight the fact that qualitatively different responses appear to result depending on the emotional outcome immediately resulting from the strainful experience, and point to the importance of revised conceptualizations of strain when attempting to understand differences in delinquency among males and females.

Finally, two constructs were found to be significantly associated with the possibility that individuals reacted to strain with delinquency: negative emotionality and constraint (Agnew, Brezina, Wright, & Cullen, 2002). The former refers to the proclivity to interpret events as aversive or malicious, and to respond to them in a hostile or antisocial manner; the latter concerns self-control, discipline, and delayed gratification. Overall, delinquency was found to be higher for juveniles who experienced strain in familial, neighborhood, and school contexts. As might be expected, juveniles high in negative emotionality and low in constraint had an increased predisposition towards delinquent responses from strain. A wide variety of scales were constructed and utilized in this analysis, including those measuring: family strain; the presence of conflict with parents: whether the parents sometimes lose control and feel they might hurt their child; feelings of hatred towards school; if the juvenile is picked on by other kids; and the presence of neighborhood strain. To be sure, any or all of these factors may contribute in some manner towards deviant manifestations.

Certain conclusions based on this literature review can be made. The main tenet of general strain theory - that a positive relationship exists between strain and delinquency - has been supported through both cross-sectional and longitudinal research. Variables in the form of personality, temperament, self-control, self-efficacy, self-esteem, deviant peer associations, conventional bonds, moral beliefs, and social support systems have conditioned the effect of the primary predictor on the delinquent outcome, but not to a conclusive degree. Additionally, the types of offenses directly or indirectly produced by strainful circumstances appear to vary, depending on both the content of the strain and the affective way in which the individual responds (which is often related to gender differences) (Broidy & Agnew, 1997; Mazerolle, 1998). Further analysis is required to more accurately tease out the intervening role of emotions, and the way in which the aforementioned mediators affect the strain/delinquency relationship. It also should be noted that conceptualizations of strain theory have been integrated with other theoretical perspectives, such as those in the biological (Walsh, 2000), structural (Agnew, 1999; Brezina, Piquero, & Mazerolle, 2001), and developmental (Agnew, 1997; 2002) spheres.

General Strain Theory Applied To The MP3 Phenomenon

As mentioned earlier, anger and frustration are the two primary emotional outcomes resulting from strain, and the literature has largely explored the path from anger to crime and delinquency. When considering the subject matter at hand, frustration seems to be much more relevant as a causal element. Accordingly, its applicability to music piracy is hereby explained. Individuals who are strained in certain ways may attempt to cope with the resultant emotion(s) by participating in online intellectual property theft. On its surface, the relationship between stress-inducing stimuli and this specific type of deviant behavior appears to be a stretch. However, Agnew's first type of strain - the threatened or actual failure to achieve positively valued goals – may be relevant. Specifically, strain in the form of financial, age, mobility, and parental restrictions on music, and in the form of a perceived necessity to achieve a certain status level among peers or family members, may cause some to unlawfully obtain and transfer copyrighted music from online sources. Further elaboration of these points is necessary before proceeding.

Most individuals are not able to purchase the desirable commodity of music CDs without limit, simply because of their price. This point is more pronounced among children, teenagers, and college students, whose fiscal resources are often minimal to none due to the fact that they have not yet acquired a well-paying job (and perhaps due to unwise budgeting). The desire to possess and listen to certain songs and artists, and the inability to purchase them either because they are not affordable or because they cannot take precedent over bills, payments, and other more pressing destinations for one's dollar, results in a conflict that must be resolved. To note, though, even those who do make a comparatively large amount of money are still inclined to participate in the wrongdoing, as if the fact that they *could* easily afford purchasing the CD is irrelevant[20]. Seemingly, the appeal of obtaining something for nothing is too strong to resist for many, regardless of their socioeconomic status.

The strained individual has the choice to commit larceny by pilfering a coveted music album from a retail establishment, but runs the risk of detection, apprehension, and punishment. The advent of MP3 technology, though, provides the conflicted person with another option that is more socially acceptable and more difficult to monitor, curtail, or thwart. As a result, the dissonance stemming from the inclination to possess and the incapacity or disinclination to pay can be overcome through the discovery and download of the desired music from P2P file exchange networks, chat rooms devoted to the dissemination and exchange of unauthorized MP3s, bulletin boards and newsgroups created for the same purpose, web sites, file servers, and even from others via instant messaging programs.

Age, mobility, and parental restrictions also may contribute to the strainful circumstance. Some music albums have explicit content or lyrics and are marked with a sticker or logo that indicates to sales clerks that purchases must be made by an adult or with an adult present. The desire among those underage to obtain and listen to this type of questionable music may induce some amount of strain. Also, children and teenagers

---

[20] Please see some white-collar crime research examples (e.g., Benson, 1985; Benson & Moore, 1992b; Coleman, 1989; Rosoff, Pontell, & Tillman, 2002) for evidence towards this end.

who are not yet able to drive, or who do not have access to a vehicle, may not be able to venture to stores to purchase certain coveted music, and thus the lack of mobility inherent in such a scenario may hasten strain. Limitations set by parents on the types of music that their child may possess can also lead to strain, particularly if that type of music is popular and culturally embraced by their child's peer group. Aspirations for peer acceptance, social status, and even the simple desire to possess (or at least be familiar with) the music of certain genres, artists, or bands - coupled with the inability to do so because of parental restrictions - may activate strainful feelings[21].

The significance and acuteness, then, of such uncomfortable stimuli may be attenuated through the maladaptive response of music piracy. What is essential, however, is the presence of negative affect stemming from the strain. In these cases, it would be frustration and aggravation resulting from thwarted ambitions for a desired product that consequently lead to music piracy.

An analogy might assist in understand this point. Some individuals in office environments congregate around the water cooler to discuss a variety of topics, such as popular television sitcoms from the previous night. Those who did not watch the shows being discussed might feel as if they do not fit in because their unfamiliarity with the subject matter precludes their participation in the dialogue. Indeed, their status level might be reduced in some capacity in that social group if they continually are present for the discussions but never actually watch the sitcoms, and strainful feelings might result. To resolve the dissonance stemming from this predicament and to be able to relate to coworkers around the water cooler, individuals can choose to familiarize themselves with the television shows by watching them – an activity that can generally be done at no cost to them.

College students aspire for peer acceptance in a similar way, and may need to demonstrate familiarity with, and appreciation of, certain music to fit in and relate to their social group. To counter the strain and negative affective state of frustration that might result, one solution requires them

---

[21] As mentioned in the literature review, Agnew & White (1992) employed a one-item measure of "clothing strain," where individuals indicated whether their parents were able to purchase for them the types of clothing they desired. It was not, however, significantly related to delinquency or drug use in their study. Nevertheless, this parallels the same type of strain that an inability to purchase socially desirable music might effectuate.

to purchase CDs and thereby acquaint themselves with the music that their peers embrace. Unfortunately, the cost of CDs is somewhat prohibitive, particularly for those in school. Another solution would be to download that same music quickly and easily from free but illegitimate sources on the Internet. *Ceteris paribus,* it is obvious which choice is more appealing in offsetting potential or actual strain.

Agnew's initial presentation of his theory was relatively nascent in its development, and scholars over the past decade have attempted to augment and refine its explanatory capacity. The current work takes another step in that direction by applying it to an Internet-based crime in the form of music piracy for the purposes of testing its generality. Additionally, most empirical examinations of strain have utilized middle- or high-schoolers, or nationally representative samples of youths; the current study employs a population of university students. While detailed hypotheses are presented below, general strain theory appears relevant to predicting Internet crime by focusing on the inability to achieve a positively valued goal - the possession of a socially, culturally, and individually esteemed commodity: commercial music. Individuals may desire to purchase the creative works of certain artists or bands, but might be unable to do so. Furthermore, certain social pressures may be present - such as the fact that one's peer group is participating in the MP3 phenomenon, and it may consequently be important for an individual to partake in music piracy to "fit in." The desirability of being perceived as "cool" among one's friends and acquaintances stemming from having a large collection of MP3s, or being well-versed with popular artists and bands, is another positively valued goal which arguably may incite the behavior.

SELF-CONTROL THEORY

Self-control theory was articulated in its most developed form by Michael Gottfredson and Travis Hirschi in their 1990 work The General Theory of Crime. The scholars defined crimes as "acts of force or fraud undertaken in the pursuit of self-interest" (1990:15). In their view, criminal acts generally provide only immediate and short-term rewards, are easy and simple to enact, are exciting, require little skill or planning, impose pain on others, and can relieve frustration temporarily (Gottfredson & Hirschi, 1990). By extension, the argument made is that all types of wrongdoing can be explained by low self-control and the opportunity structure surrounding the act.

With self-control theory, the line of criminogenic explanation continues to proceed in the opposite direction of Aquinas' quixotic belief that man is essentially good and by committing crime actually harms his own humaneness and natural tendency to abide by the law (Vold, Bernard, & Snipes, 1998). Since the 13th century then, the firmly ensconced assumption about human nature is that individuals will take advantage of others without qualms or misgivings if left to their own devices. Self-control theory embraces that paradigm as a foundation for its interpretation. The underlying premise is as follows: all people are intrinsically motivated to break the rules of society, but differences exist in people's innate ability to suppress or restrain urges and drives, and in their needs for excitement, risk taking, and immediate gratification (Lanier & Henry, 1998).

Because of deficiencies and weaknesses in their intrinsic personality and character, individuals with low self-control are more likely to engage in crime to accomplish a goal or to resolve a conflict in the most expeditious and effortless manner. Gottfredson and Hirschi (1990) also assert that those persons who demonstrate difficulty in (or apathy toward) accomplishing long-term goals or maintaining long-term relationships, and those who engage in extreme and decadent activities (such as smoking, drinking, and promiscuity) are predisposed towards illegal behavior. Nonetheless, most people do not break the rules because they have been effectively socialized by various institutions. Some, however, have either been inadequately socialized or not socialized at all, and this lack of constraining values frees them to commit crime (Lanier & Henry, 1998). Gottfredson and Hirschi (1990) state that inadequate parenting during childhood is a primary reason why some individuals are improperly trained to exhibit self-control.

The theory also incorporates the concepts of stability and versatility (Gottfredson & Hirschi, 1990:117-9). Stability refers to the fact that because of the relatively permanent trait of self-control, the role of other influencing factors later in life is rendered largely impotent in impelling criminality. By extension, differences in individual offending should remain generally invariant; those individuals who possess high self-control will be "substantially less likely at all periods of life to engage in criminal acts" (Gottfredson & Hirschi, 1990:89). To note, it seems that assessing self-control among college students in the current study will presumably measure a characteristic that has, and will continue to, affect their life decisions in a certain way. According to Gottfredson and Hirschi (1990), if self-control is significantly related to the music pirating habits of respondents, this factor is not dependent on time and its influence will not vary in the person's past or future.

Versatility regards the explanatory power of low self-control predicting all varieties of criminality, deviance, and even unfortunate occurrences like accidents, debunking the argument that certain causal factors produce different criminal specialties. Taken to its logical conclusion, both traditional and nontraditional, blue-collar and white-collar, and real-world and "virtual" crimes are possible by those who lack a sufficient amount of self-control. These are two of the primary underpinnings of Gottfredson and Hirschi's framework, and are largely what render it a "general" theory.

While low self-control is a necessary condition to increase the likelihood of committing a crime, Gottfredson and Hirschi affirm that it is not a sufficient condition. Opportunity plays a crucial role, and the scholars draw on routine activities theory (RAT) to speak to its relevance. Proposed by Alfred Cohen and Marcus Felson (1979), RAT attests that the conditions necessary for a crime to occur include a suitable target, the absence of a capable guardian for the target, and the presence of a motivated offender. Gottfredson and Hirschi's chief concern involves the role of guardians and targets; the motivation of offenders is regarded as nonproblematic (Sellers, 1999). In its very simplest terms, then, it is the degree of availability to a target that produces the opportunity to engage in deviance. Pratt and Cullen (2000:933) echo similar sentiments by stating that "although people vary in levels of self-control, the world is filled with criminal opportunities; after all, crime is easy to commit and requires little planning." Due to the tremendous (and almost ubiquitous) availability of digital music files online and the presence of a population potentially disposed towards exhibiting low self-control in a college environment, this theoretical perspective appears highly salient to the subject matter at hand.

Self-control is considered a nucleus of sorts around which every other known factor associated with the crime can be configured, and is perhaps best understood as an underlying construct which integrates a variety of conceptions about crime (Akers, 1991; Pratt & Cullen, 2000). Gottfredson and Hirschi do not operationally define "self-control," and it is therefore difficult to measure its causal influence on crime. As such, and as identified by other scholars (e.g., Akers, 1991), the identification of the former can be made by identifying participation in the latter. Research subsequent to the theory's initial assertion has therefore sought to indirectly assess low self-control to determine its underlying predictive influence on deviant and criminal behavior. Furthermore, as long as self-control and crime are measured using independent items, any arguments of tautology are preempted (Pratt & Cullen, 2000). Gottfredson and Hirschi (1990) also recommended testing the theory through the proxy of participation in "analogous" behaviors which demonstrate low self-control; this has been done in much of the relevant research. To note, the current study measures self-control through separate attitudinal and behavioral operationalizations; this is discussed in detail later in the text.

Empirical Support for Self-Control Theory

There have been a multitude of tests examining the linkage between low self-control and criminal acts, operationalizing its six delimited facets: impulsivity, simple tasks, risk seeking, physical activities, self-centeredness, and temper (Gottfredson & Hirschi, 1990:89). Many of these inquiries have found support for the general theory. Moreover, it has been applied to a variety of crimes, ranging from imprudent behaviors (e.g., Arneklev, Grasmick, Tittle, & Bursik, 1993) to general law violations (e.g., Piquero & Tibbetts, 1996). The relationship between self-control and white-collar crime has also been examined, but little to no support was found (e.g., Benson & Moore, 1992a; Steffensmeier, 1989). To note, most research has not empirically examined how poor parenting is a causal predictor of low self-control. Instead, studies have disproportionately concentrated on the relationship between self-control and deviant and illegal behaviors; the current work is no exception.

In one study, Gibbs and Giever (1995) analyzed the independent effect of self-control on criminal-equivalent behaviors among a sample of 236 undergraduate students, and characterized such individuals as a group marked by high self-control because college enrollment requires some amount of academic success. Indeed, they state that they "would expect to find very few wholly unrestrained individuals in a group of university students" (1995:243). According to the researchers, higher levels of self-control also lent itself to greater levels of participation in the study and in more valid measurements based on the responses retrieved. Dependent variables included class cutting and levels of drinking alcohol - both technically noncriminal but appropriate for testing Gottfredson and Hirschi's theory since they demonstrate low self-control and share characteristics with actual crime (1995:250). Via both Ordinary Least Squares (OLS) and logistic regression, self-control was significantly related to the outcome measures. However, the R^2 findings were relatively low (.139 for class cutting and .230 for alcohol consumption) and suggested the existence of other explanatory elements not included in the models.

Grasmick et al. (1993) were the first to test an unidimensional operationalization of the six components of self-control, and their work resulted in the creation of a single factor 24-item scale with four items for each component[22]. That is, the items comprising the six dimensions articulated by Gottfredson and Hirschi demonstrated enough variance in common to be used as a singular scale assessing self-control. In their analyses, three predictions were tested. First, the interaction between self-control and opportunity should be positively and significantly related to force and fraud; this was supported with standardized coefficients of .156 for force and .235 for fraud. Second, since Gottfredson and Hirschi assert the necessity of opportunity in inducing those with low self-control to commit crime, the interaction term should be larger than the singular predictive effect of self-control. This was corroborated in part, as the interaction term was significant and the main effect of low self-control was not when measured against acts of force. Both were, however, when measured against acts of fraud. The third prediction was that opportunity should not be singularly related to either force or fraud beyond its interactive effect with low self-control. Contrary to that hypothesis, the relationship between opportunity and the two general types of crime was significant, introducing some ambiguity into the causal chain[23].

A large number of studies have used the Grasmick et al. (1993) scale both partially and fully to assess the relevance of self-control on a variety of deviant and criminal behaviors (Arneklev et al., 1993; Longshore & Turner, 1998; Longshore, Turner, & Stein, 1996; Piquero & Rosay, 1998;

---

[22] In their original analysis, Grasmick et al.'s final scale had 23 items due to the removal of a Physical Activity measure (which increased the resultant alpha from .805 to .812) that most aptly and reliably measured the nature of the characteristic as presented by Gottfredson and Hirschi (1990). When factor analyzing the variables, however, a five-factor solution was identified; nonetheless, the resultant scree plots revealed a significant drop-off between the first and second factors, and so a one-factor model was forced . (1993:16).

[23] Incidentally, Grasmick et al. (1993:25) also suggest incorporating variables that affect individual motivation, such as those related to strain, to explain more variance and live up to the billing it was given by its originators. This highlights the possibility in future research to incorporate key individual components of each general theory to best predict online intellectual property theft such as music piracy.

Piquero & Tibbetts, 1996; Wood, Pfefferbaum, & Arneklev, 1993). Arneklev et al. (1993) found a link between low self-control and "imprudent" behaviors such as excessive drinking or a gambling predilection, and Wood et al. (1993) identified a strong relationship between self-control and theft, vandalism, certain forms of violence, and drug use. It is interesting to note that of the six elements conceptualized by Gottfredson and Hirschi and operationalized by Grasmick et al. (1993), physicality has been consistently identified as a very weak predictor (Arneklev et al., 1993; Cochran, Wood, Sellers, & Chamlin, 1998; Grasmick et al., 1993; Wood et al., 1993). On the contrary, the risk-taking and impulsiveness elements of the theory have been consistently identified as strong predictors (see e.g., Brownfield & Sorenson, 1993; Keane, 1993; Wood et al., 1993).

The Grasmick et al. (1993) scale was also utilized by Piquero and Tibbetts (1996) to test the applicability of self-control on deviance by 642 university students between the ages of 17 and 35. They found that four and five percent in drunk driving and shoplifting respectively could be explained by the direct influence of self-control, as well as its indirect influence through situational factors such as perceptions of pleasure and shame. When employing 19 out of the original 24 items in the scale, Piquero and Rosay (1998) found that self-control explained 7% and 13% of the variance in fraud and force measures when controlling for general demographic characteristics. Indeed, when considering the utility of the scale, they asserted that it is acceptable for "tapping into the components alluded to by Gottfredson and Hirschi" (1998:170). Additional works have differentiated between property and personal crimes to more accurately assess the predictive capacity of the theory. Longshore, Turner, and Stein (1996) specifically tested the scale on a sample of offenders with a history of drug use, and found a weak but theoretically expected relationship between self-control and acts of both force and fraud. In a study on drug users' proclivity towards property and personal crimes, Longshore (1998) determined that low self-control and high opportunity - as well as the interaction of the two - was significantly related to the outcome variables. The amount of explained variation was quite modest (4%), but did lend credence to the theory's main precepts.

Additional strong corroboration for Gottfredson and Hirschi's theory was found by: Evans et al. (1997), who assessed its predictive capacity on 17 personal and property crimes and 18 other forms of deviance; Gibbs et al. (1998), who demonstrated that low self-control among college students is significantly related to cheating, drinking, suspension or expulsion, and skipping class; and Burton et al. (1998), who keyed out the theory's relevance to a variety of wrongdoing including the filing of false insurance claims, workplace theft, interpersonal violence, drug use, and automobile accidents.

One project related to interpersonal aggression relates tangentially to the current work. Christine Sellers (1999) retrieved some interesting results when studying self-control and domestic violence data from a subset of 985 students at a college in Florida who were then involved in a dating relationship. Although the statistically significant results were relatively weak when isolating the element of self-control, it could be concluded that low self-control played at least some role in predicting the probability of using violence against a dating partner (Sellers, 1999). Coupled with other factors such as opportunity and the perception of reward, the explanation gained slightly more strength (Sellers, 1999). From a broad perspective, the use of physical aggression appeared to offer short-term gratification to the offender, both in terms of the receipt of pleasure - perhaps through enhanced arousal and a feeling of excitement or thrill, and the reduction of pain - perhaps through relieving frustration or ending an argument (Sellers, 1999). The researcher also maintained that the most common form of courtship aggression involved physical actions that require little effort and no planning which can take place at any time, such as slapping or shoving (Sellers, 1999). Consonant with findings from previously mentioned studies, this underscores the salience of spontaneity and speedy gratification in effectuating wrongdoing – which conceptually seems relevant when considering the behavior of music piracy.

Finally, Pratt and Cullen's (2000) meta-analysis of 21 studies identified impressive support for self-control theory, consistently finding an effect-size estimate - the standard correlation coefficient (r) - over .20 for the construct of self-control. These results remained even when including variables measuring opportunity and the elements of other criminological theories, and despite different operationalizations of the construct by various scholars. It is also worthy of mention that the researchers found that social learning theory variables, when included in studies of self-control, increased the explained variation of deviant or criminal behavior - highlighting their validity and importance as predictors of criminality.

Interestingly, Pratt and Cullen's (2000) meta-analysis identified 82 attitudinal measures and 12 behavioral measures of self-control. Attitudinal measures include those in the Grasmick et al. (1993) scale, while behavioral measures consist of instances of analogous behaviors. behavioral measures, in fact, were recommended by Hirschi and Gottfredson (1993) over attitudinal items, and this assertion has attracted criticism for the tautology inherent in utilizing measures of deviance as a predictor of deviance. Pratt and Cullen (2000) found that while behavioral measures had a slightly larger effect size, they were similar in magnitude as their attitudinal counterparts - demonstrating that employing one measure over the other will not significantly affect the predictive capacity of self-control, and testifying to the robustness in operationalizing the theoretical construct in multiple ways. With this in mind, the choice was made in the current study to include both attitudinal and behavioral measures of self-control to provide a more nuanced perspective as to the role of that dispositional trait on music piracy. This is explained in detail in Chapter 4.

The present research is cross-sectional, and does not purport to offer inconclusive evidence concerning the causal relationship between the theories and the crime. Nonetheless, Gottfredson and Hirschi (1990) argue that cross-sectional research of self-control is not inherently subordinate in quality, utility, or rigor to longitudinal research, and may in fact be more beneficial in some instances. To note, the meta-analysis by Pratt and Cullen (2000) found that the explanatory strength of low self-control is weaker in longitudinal research conducted to test the applicability of the theory.

To summarize, Gottfredson and Hirschi's general theory consists of two primary components: self-control and criminal opportunity. Individuals, then, are more apt to engage in wrongdoing if they have low self-control - a stable dispositional trait on an individual level. Furthermore, they can be characterized as impulsive, insensitive, short-sighted, and risk-taking (Gottfredson & Hirschi, 1990:90). These persons are also inclined to partake in "analogous" behaviors such as smoking, alcohol and illegal substance use and abuse, speeding, truancy, and even an increased proclivity towards accidents and illness (Gottfredson & Hirschi, 1990; Junger & Tremblay, 1999; Paternoster & Brame, 1998, 2000). Its relevance as a predictor of music piracy is explicated in the following text.

Self-Control Theory Applied To The MP3 Phenomenon

Individuals with low self-control, when presented with the opportunity to obtain high-quality, commercially-produced songs over the Internet through a few "point-and-click" maneuvers of their mouse, may not be able to bridle their inclinations, and may consequently engage in the activity of music piracy. College students are a population of individuals who have the opportunity to access the Internet either through a personally-owned computer or a university-owned machine, install P2P file sharing programs, and participate in unregulated data transfers (often over high-speed connections) with either no cost on campus or at an affordable cost at an off-campus location (such as their home). Indeed, with the continued decrease in computer and connectivity prices, the development and propagation of advanced physical media (such as fiber-optic lines) for data transfers, new technology involving file compression, smaller packet sizes, and quicker routing, the opportunity for those interested to have access to, and use, the Internet continues to grow. Suffice it to say that the opportunity is there, and will be in increasing fashion.

The differentiating variable, then, may be self-control. Reflexive responses to immediate stimuli (such as the availability of MP3 files), rather than careful reasoning as to the acceptability, wisdom, and ramifications of certain actions, might occur among those with underdeveloped amounts of self-control. Indeed, typical college students are already arguably at an age where self-control is not foremost on their mind, particularly if they have recently left the "nest" and are living outside of the regular supervision of parental authorities for the first time. Persons at this age also tend to experiment a great deal (see e.g., Apter, 2001; Plant & Plant, 1992). Internal pressure to participate in a host of questionable activities which previously would have been impossible or unacceptable are now more plausible, appealing, and even desirable. Accordingly, low self-control is a characteristic which might be more frequently found among this population than among children or full-fledged adults.

It is also important to discuss if music piracy is characterized by the distinguishing features that Gottfredson and Hirschi (1990) contend as related to crime, such as the precursor to short-term gratifications of excitement, monetary gain, and relief from situations that induce aggravation. Seemingly, participants may experience *excitement* when locating and obtaining an unauthorized MP3 file of a song they have wanted to hear. This excitement may be augmented when they realize that no cost is incurred when downloading the music file to their computer system for unlimited playback. More excitement may result from dissemination of that file to friends or family, as the meaning, importance, or relevance of the song is shared through its collective experience. Excitement again comes into play when the individual realizes that vast amounts of high-quality and easily accessible music by practically any musician or band from practically any time period is available.

Monetary gain is relevant primarily through the realization that no expenditure of funds is necessary to receive and enjoy this commodity, or to pass it along to others. In fact, nothing physical or tangible is required in the acquisition and distribution of these files apart from a computer system and an Internet connection. Most - if not all - of the software necessary for involvement in the MP3 phenomenon is freely available online. These factors widen the net of potential pirates because no purchases must be made beforehand to facilitate the activity. With golf, for example, golf clubs, balls, and a bag need to be purchased prior to participation. The skills and knowledge essential to competence on the golf course also often necessitate the purchase of lessons as well. These requisite expenses serve as a funnel to reduce the amount of golfers in the general populace. With music piracy, if an assumption is made that individuals have a computer and an Internet connection as an arguable "necessity" for personal and professional reasons (particularly among college students), no other equipment is needed. Lessons to participate are also absolutely superfluous because of the simplicity of software applications that assist interested users.

Finally, downloading (and transferring) MP3s may provide *relief from aggravating situations* if one considers that individuals may have a desire to enjoy certain songs or albums but lack the funds to legitimately purchase them from a retail outlet. Perhaps a specific music file is (to the initiating downloader) useful in some way for admiration or esteem among friends, or for use in a school project, or to send to a loved one. Perhaps that person has also sought to purchase the music file on CD from legal sources, but has been unsuccessful in all attempts to locate it. These examples provide support for the possibility that copyright infringement through the acquisition of unauthorized MP3s may relieve aggravation stemming from situational factors. To note, this aggravation as mentioned by Gottfredson and Hirschi points to the role of strain in effectuating criminality or deviance, and alludes to some overlap between the theoretical paradigms. This overlap is further discussed following the presentation of social learning theory.

SOCIAL LEARNING THEORY

Refined and developed during the course of subsequent years, social learning theory was initially proffered as a guiding theory in 1977 by Ronald Akers, and was based in part upon his research with Robert Burgess (1966) and the earlier works of such scholars as Edwin Sutherland (1947; 1949a; 1949b), Albert Bandura (1969; 1973; 1977; 1963), Gabriel Tarde ([1890] 1903), and B.F. Skinner (1953; 1971). As a general theory of crime, it seems intuitively applicable to new forms of criminal behavior stemming from technological advances, and in fact has been suggested and utilized for the study of nontraditional crimes (Akers, Krohn, Lanza-Kaduce, & Radosevich, 1979; Rogers, 2001; Skinner & Fream, 1997). Seemingly, unethical or unlawful behavior involving a computer and the Internet requires the presence of at least some of the principles of social learning theory to occur; it is not an action that just anyone can do without learning certain techniques and mentalities.

Social learning theory is an amalgamation of four singular theoretical tenets into a cohesive whole. An explanation of each is required before proffering its application to MP3 participation. They include: differential association; imitation and modeling; definitions; and differential reinforcement. *Differential association* occurs as social interaction with family, friends, and acquaintances provide and strengthen normative definitions of acceptable and unacceptable conduct. In this environment, motives, drives, rationalizations, and methods for behaving in certain ways are learned and internalized. This first facet of social learning is based on Sutherland's (1947; 1949a; 1949b) differential association theory, which holds that an individual who associates more with supporters of criminal patterns of behavior (irrespective of whether they are actual offenders) than those with anti-criminal patterns of behavior will be more likely to violate the law. Second, behavior is also learned through *imitation and modeling* of the actions of others during the socialization process. Individuals already immersed in the deviant activity provide a palpable exemplar to emulate, thereby transmitting knowledge, attitudes, beliefs, and techniques that significantly influence a potential criminal's participation in the wrongdoing.

The third component of social learning theory refers to *definitions,* which are evaluative criteria designating certain behaviors as good or bad, and thus qualifying them as appropriate, desired, or justified (Akers et al., 1979). These also are learned from social interaction, and are instrumental in determining commencement of, or abstention from, a certain activity.

Definitions roughly parallel the neutralization techniques proposed by Sykes and Matza (1957). However, rather than being created and utilized by a singular individual to free himself or herself from the constraints of law and normative standards, they stem instead from social interaction and are shared by a group. They are meanings that define an action as wrong or right – "discriminative stimuli" (Akers, 1985) - which serve as cues to participate in or refrain from the behavior. This is analogous to what people have called the most important principle of Sutherland's (1947; 1949a; 1949b) theory - that crime will result from an excess of "definitions" favorable to crime.   Accordingly, the fourth and final principle comes into play after deciding to partake in or refrain from a particular path of action. Behavior is now shaped by the consequences that result from it – also known as operant conditioning (Skinner, 1953) – and this notion is subsumed under the construct of *differential reinforcement*. Positive reinforcement results when a beneficial outcome is produced by the action, thus strengthening the behavior. Negative reinforcement occurs when behavior is strengthened or continued through the avoidance of pain. Conversely, positive punishment ensues when negative stimuli following a behavior serve to weaken it, and negative punishment takes place when a beneficial outcome is denied after an action, also weakening the behavior (Akers et al., 1979:638; Skinner, 1957); . The continuance or cessation of behavior, whether lawful or illicit, stems from such a conditioning process due to social and nonsocial influencers. Akers writes:

> "Progression into more frequent or sustained use and into abuse is also determined by the extent to which a given pattern is sustained by the combination of the reinforcing effects of the substance with social reinforcement, exposure to models, definitions through association with using [or participating] peers, and by the degree to which it is not deterred through bad effects of the substance [or behavior] and/or the negative sanctions from peers, parents, and the law." (Akers et al., 1979:638).

Thus, it is important to understand that social forces expose the individual to prescriptive and communally esteemed conduct, and provide or teach cognitive restructuring techniques to assuage or render irrelevant any pressing misgivings. They also provide palpable models to emulate, and train the person or persons in the identification of positive and negative outcomes that may result (Akers, 1996).

Akers has also proposed a sequence by which criminal behavior is learned and then manifested. Differential association with others who hold definitions favorable to the crime first occur. This social group then models criminal behavior, which is consequently imitated as activity-supporting definitions are shared and adopted. The continuance or desistance of these imitated behaviors is based on reinforcements – both social and nonsocial (Akers et al., 1979). To note, since individuals are exposed to culturally transmitted definitions, and also are provided with models to imitate and reinforcement to stimulate either prosocial or antisocial behavior, they can behave in a conforming or conflicting manner to a culture, subculture, or even their own personal value system (Akers, 1994). In sum, once a social environment is created consisting of associations with persons inclined to criminality, patterns of imitation and the internalization of definitions can then follow, with reinforcing stimuli later playing a large role in determining perpetuation. Akers further states that the theory links individual and social processes, as structural conditions influence a person's differential associations, models of behavior, definitions conducive or aversive to crime commission, and differential reinforcements (Akers, 1992, 1998).

Empirical Support for Social Learning Theory

Akers has emphasized that the social learning paradigm is empirically testable through the operationalization of the four particular constructs (Akers et al., 1979). To corroborate this statement, he reviewed a large body of research in 1994 and asserted that:

> "...almost all research on social learning theory has found strong relationships in the theoretically expected direction....When social learning theory is tested against other theories using the same data collected from the same samples, it is usually found to account for more variance in the dependent variables than the theories with which it is being compared." (Akers, 1994)

Many studies in criminology and sociology have been conducted to assess the relevance of the theory. It is useful, therefore, to familiarize oneself with the most important pieces and findings prior to applying its precepts to a heretofore unanalyzed phenomenon.

In one examination in 1979 in which Akers was a primary investigator, the applicability of social learning theory to adolescent drug and alcohol use was tested via a self-report questionnaire given to 3,065 Midwestern students in grades 7 through 12. It was found that the combined components of the social learning framework accounted for 68% of the variance in marijuana use and 55% of the variance in alcohol use (Akers et al., 1979). Cigarette smoking and substance abuse among adolescents has also been longitudinally analyzed using the principles of social learning, generally showing support in predicting usage over time (Akers & Cochran, 1985; Akers & Lee, 1996; Catalano, Kosterman, & Hawkins, 1996; Krohn, Skiller, Massey, & Akers, 1985). Additionally, the application of a sensation-seeking component to social learning has been explored recently on substance use (Wood, Cochran, Pfefferbaum, & Arneklev, 1995). It was found that positive reinforcement is fostered through intrinsic rewards (such as obtaining a rush and immediate gratification) associated with participating in a marginal activity. An initial speculation would be that similar intangible benefits also result from unlawful computer behavior, such as unauthorized MP3 participation.

Outcome variables utilized in the testing of this theory have also included perceptions of the appropriateness of deviant behaviors ranging from cheating to suicide. Lersch (1999), for instance, surveyed over 500 undergraduate students to empirically validate the influencing power of social learning on academic dishonesty. Of the four tenets of the theory, the most significant predictors of deviant behavior were acceptance of favorable definitions toward cheating and level of immersion in a peer group which endorsed the activity. Agnew (1998) discovered that the theory was applicable in the approval of suicide, as those who had been exposed to ideas or thought processes conducive to suicide were more likely to perceive it as an acceptable (or at least justifiable way) to deal with one's problems. Relevant to the instigating role of an individual's peer group, Adams (1996) focused on the role of labeling in effectuating delinquency through social interaction with others engaged in (or in support of) the deviance. His findings affirmed the viability of social learning as a general theory, and also corroborated the significance of differential association on participation in criminal activity. Similarly, Brownfield and Thompson (1991) found that delinquency was dependent on associating with friends who were delinquent, a finding consistent with prior research (Akers et al., 1979; Orcutt, 1987; Winfree, Backstrom, & Mays, 1994). The theoretical perspective has also been used to examine participation in gangs. For instance, gang affiliation was strongest among those 9th grade youths in a self-report study who were differentially associated with gangs and had learned or assumed gang-related attitudes (Winfree et al., 1994). In another study involving incarcerated delinquents, the tenets of differential association and definitions were proven significant in determining gang membership. That is, gang members differed from others in the amount of gang-related attitudes they had acquired and in their proclivity toward gang activities (Winfree et al., 1994).

Sutherland's primary tenet of differential association – disproportionate exposure to law-violating peers - has been successfully operationalized in previous studies (e.g., Matsueda, 1982). Indeed, there is no paucity of research emphasizing the significant relationship between one's association with a delinquent subgroup and one's participation in delinquent and criminal activities (see e.g., Adams, 1996; Hawkins et al., 1998; Orcutt, 1987; Warr, 2002). This occurs through training the individual in proficiencies to commit the act, providing extrinsic and developing intrinsic rewards such as gratification and respect among the peer group, and by decreasing the constraining or inhibiting power of cultural norms, societal dictates, and personal bonds toward normative, lawful conduct (Kaplan, Johnson, & Bailey, 1987). These aspects of differential association appear highly relevant to music piracy, and their possible applicability is described below.

Social learning theory appears to hold much value for the explanation of computer crimes, and has been applied to them in a few studies. One research piece published in 1997 utilized a self-report questionnaire to assess the influence of differential association, imitation and modeling, definitions, and differential reinforcement on the incidence of computer criminality among 581 undergraduate students at a major southern university. Five types of high-tech deviance were measured: whether the respondent "(1) knowingly used, made, or gave to another person a "pirated" copy of commercially sold computer software; (2) tried to guess another's password to get into his or her computer account or files; (3) accessed another's computer account or files without his or her knowledge or permission just to look at the information or files; (4) added, deleted, changed, or printed any information in another's computer files without the owner's knowledge or permission; and (5) wrote or used a program that would destroy someone's computerized data (e.g., a virus, logic bomb, or trojan horse)" (Skinner & Fream, 1997).

With the inclusion of all relevant variables in a regression model, 37% of the variance was explained by software piracy while password guessing accounted for an additional 20%. Furthermore, 16% of the variance was explained by unauthorized access to browse another's files, and 40% was explained by a computer crime index composed of the sum of respondents' frequencies in engaging in the five aforementioned types of deviance (Skinner & Fream, 1997). Gaining access to change files and writing a destructive program were not included in the regression analysis because of extremely small case numbers. Differential association and definitions were found to be strongly and consistently influential on the outcome variables, imitation varied somewhat in its strength depending on the computer crime variable utilized, and differential reinforcement in the form of perceived certainty of apprehension was not related to wrongdoing. Generally, though, the predictive value of three of four social learning theory variables was demonstrated by the findings, supporting its use as a guiding framework.

Rogers (2001) further explored the relationship between social learning theory and computer crime in his doctoral dissertation. In accordance with his hypothesis, computer criminals were significantly differentiated from non-criminals on the basis of their associations, but the strength of relationship was quite moderate ($\eta^2 = .11$). Also, the individual theoretical tenet of differential reinforcement was found to be a significant predictor of computer criminals, but with an even smaller level of variation explained ($\eta^2 = .04$). In this particular analysis, the sample size totaled 132 respondents.

Social learning theory holds much merit because it expands on differential association and incorporates other chief propositions concerning the acquisition of criminogenic tendencies. In this context of interpersonal interaction, motives, drives, rationalizations, and methods for behaving in certain ways are learned, internalized, and sustained. It is this author's contention that the theory can be logically extended to online intellectual property theft. It is hypothesized that the primary method in which individuals are introduced to, and become involved in, digital music piracy is through social learning, whether online in cyberspace via asynchronous (message board, discussion group, web page, email) or synchronous (chat channels, instant messaging programs) communication, or in real space via face-to-face interpersonal interaction. In the next section, each of the four components of social learning theory is specifically applied to music piracy.

Social Learning Theory Applied To The MP3 Phenomenon

Differential Association

MP3 propagation and exchange on the Internet is a wildly social event. A great number of music aficionados congregate in cyberspace for the distinct purpose of obtaining and exchanging digital music. The particular behavior of uploading and downloading digital music is validated and reinforced by the sheer number of participants and the casual way in which requests for songs (and advertisements of the availability of other users' collections) are asserted. Via a simple illustration, an understanding can be obtained of how unauthorized MP3 participation is effectuated by the first component of social learning theory – differential association. If an individual visits a chat channel and someone mentions that he is looking for an MP3 of Britney Spears' latest hit single, those not knowledgeable of what an MP3 is are likely to inquire, and will conceivably be inundated with words of accolade referencing this new technology that allows for the distribution of near-CD quality music files over the Internet, preempting the need to purchase CDs to listen to favorite artists and bands. Techniques to obtain this type of digital audio files might then be taught to the "newbie," or person unfamiliar with the technology, as well as motives (free, high fidelity music in replace of CD purchasing has a tendency to impel many to participate), drives (one heard with increasing frequency is the necessity to "get back" at the monopolistic recording industry that has exploited music consumers), and rationalizations (such as how "everyone is doing it," or how music should be "free," or how the chances for getting caught for distributing copyrighted works are very small).

When MP3 became a "buzzword" among the technologically-inclined and the general public, the phenomenon took on a life of its own. The media and popular culture quickly noticed its sensationalistic quality and introduced it into the public eye. Thousands of articles have been written about it, hundreds of news sources have covered it, and individuals of various demographic groups have actively embraced it. Not only has this attention served to augment the notoriety of MP3 and allow a greater number of individuals to take advantage of its characteristics, it also has expanded the scope of evaluative criteria rendering it favorable. Even if the press makes reference to copyright law or the recording industry's hostility towards software that facilitates piracy, the amount of coverage given to the phenomenon and the statistics proffered to depict its overwhelming popularity (such as the number of users of P2P file exchange programs, or the estimated amount of CD album sales lost by the music industry) testify to its panoptic reach. In fact, such attention may even subtly imply that those who are not yet riding, or who have not yet caught on to, the wave of digital music are seriously missing out on something special.

The media is specifically mentioned as a role player in the social learning process (Akers, 1998). Individuals might interpret from the veritable onslaught of information they receive about MP3s that the positives it generates substantially outweigh any perceived or real negatives resulting from participation. It may be that persons partake in a cost-benefit analysis and come to the conclusion that the questionable behavior is desirable and even essential for fear of "missing out." Subsequently, obtaining and exchanging MP3s with other individuals may engender positive reinforcement (both tangible and intangible) which - coupled with the lack of any substantive threat of repercussion for downloading or distributing such files[24] - might more profoundly ensconce the individual in the practice. This immersion then can establish the person as an experienced digital audiophile who is able to pass on techniques, rationalizations, definitions, models of behavior to imitate, and reinforcing stimuli to introduce and inculcate others into the scene. Upon internalization of this learning process by the next generation, the cycle can continue. Thus, a powerful social system to support the existence and perpetuation of MP3s can come into existence, facilitating their propagation across the Internet and the growth of the population who participates.

It should be noted that Akers explicitly differentiates between the differential association construct and the idea of "peer pressure." The former is subtle and has a tendency to shape an individual's behavior without his or her awareness, while the latter is couched in overt practices by others to induce the commission of a desired behavior by a person (Akers, 1998). In cyberspace, differential association might not be as salient because an individual could simply leave a particular chat channel or environment in which MP3s are being exchanged if the perceived or actual actions of others do not align with certain personal standards or mores of conduct. While it is true that a person can experience ostracism

---

[24] The likelihood of being on the receiving end of a civil lawsuit filed by the recording industry is very small, simply because of the vast number of possible defendants online.

online, the consequences are transitory, and can be countered through the use of a new screen name or user ID, which effectively provides a brand-new identity and persona to its claimant. At the same time, it might be argued that differential association is more pronounced online than in real space because a great number of physical, social, and contextual cues are obviated. Accordingly, this increases the influence of the textual communication one witnesses and takes part in, because there is nothing else to distract, interfere, or add as an ingredient to the contemplation, processing, or interpretation of an action.

To note, Chantler (1996) has argued that computer-related crime may be more dependent on differential association than traditional crime because of the fact that those who want to engage in the former must acquire the technical skillsets necessary to do so - skills not learned through common, everyday experiences. In addition, it has been documented that those who participate in computer-related deviance are more apt to associate with others of like mind than would normally be the case for conventional forms of deviance (Chantler, 1996). This association occurs in a variety of venues, both offline (e.g., local area network (LAN) computer gaming parties, technology-related conferences, grassroots computing organizations that sprout in small localities) and online (e.g., chat channels, newsgroups, message boards, mailing lists). For instance, persons interested in digital music congregate in various settings for the purposes of discussing and learning more about the utilization of the file format technology, hardware and software associated with MP3s, news updates concerned with copyright infringement or P2P applications, as well as to partake in general conversation on artists, musicians, genres, albums, and songs (Mindenhall, 2000; Weisbard, 2000). To note, research has identified a similar example of differential association among computer hackers, as online peer groups are formed to share network intrusion knowledge and provide practical, emotional, and psychological support for hacking activities (Rogers, 2001).

Due to its inception decades ago, social learning theory in its original form does not explicitly mention the role of the community generated via computer-mediated communication. It has been established that the pressures exerted by a collective unit in the physical world are just as strong and influential in a faceless, nameless, virtual milieu (Etzioni, 1999; Miller & Gergen, 1998). Another interesting point is that the majority of traditional deviant behavior, particularly as analyzed by Akers, is communally-oriented in nature - performed and validated in a group setting. Downloading and uploading MP3s are inherently individualistic and private behaviors - generally executed by one person at his or her computer in the solitude of a home or office. It is typically required, however, that persons interact with others *online* (to varying degrees, depending on the software interface used) to obtain digital music. The communal aspect thus undoubtedly comes into play in cyberspace. Still, associations with other people *offline* may also affect participation, even if only through casual conversation about the technology or about particular music or artists. This double dose of societal pressure seemingly exerts a substantial amount of influence on individuals, which guides and shapes their level of participation in the phenomenon.

Imitation

Once individuals are immersed in an atmosphere conducive to the learning of techniques, motives, and rationalizations, the patterning of their activity based on the words and actions of others can follow. This is the easiest way for the commission of the act to occur, and due to the rampant popularity of MP3s, there is no lack of suitable models to emulate or mimic in behavior. For example, in a chat channel specifically related to digital music, a person need only spend a few minutes watching the unfolding dialogue before certain recurrent themes are detected. One might be the way in which music files are requested or offered. Another might be the way in which users gain access to private file servers consisting of hundreds or thousands of songs for download.

Because there are no other distinguishing characteristics evident in a virtual setting apart from the traits evidenced by one's own way of communicating via a keyboard, a newbie can blend in with a population of experienced users simply by acting in a similar manner as them. As mentioned earlier, the anonymous, detached, and wide-open features of the Internet necessarily remove certain nonverbal cues which generally factor into the way individuals typically would respond to one another. These include gesture, posture, facial animation, variations in voice, social role, status, affiliation, and a host of demographic characteristics (Flaherty, Pearce, & Rubin, 1998; Walther, 1992; Walther, Anderson, & Park, 1994). Their absence makes it difficult to quickly categorize people and reflexively act towards them based on previous experience or preconceptions. Therefore, in an online setting with only textual messaging as the vehicle of communication, simply following the lead of others and acting likewise removes any perceived marginality and results in quick assimilation into the culture. Saint Ambrose's advice to Saint

Augustine, "When in Rome, do as the Romans do," seems perfectly applicable in an online setting. Imitation of the behavior of other MP3 participants that one meets in cyberspace can then take place, further facilitating the commission of the act. Specifically, the actions of more experienced users are copied by those new to the scene through specific prescribed instruction or through emulation of methods to acquire or exchange unauthorized MP3s.

Definitions

Definitions are also used to further the social learning process and to inculcate a favorable attitude toward participation in the phenomenon. These generally reflect the opinion that the MP3 phenomenon is not wrong and is in fact to be heralded for increasing the availability of music to the average consumer and for allowing more artists to be heard. For the ordinary individual, it is relatively difficult to come up with definitions unfavorable to partaking in the activity because the recording industry and musical artists seem so removed from the simple, largely anonymous process of downloading 3-6 megabyte files[25] from a computer across the Internet. It is perhaps not easily comprehended how this practice, multiplied by hundreds of thousands of individuals, could actually be harmful.

Chat room environments are disproportionately favorable to MP3 participation, and this influences those in attendance as the statements and actions of each user significantly reinforce the perceived legitimacy of the activity. Definitions which characterize the activity as positive, beneficial, and commonly accepted are very present in the textual interaction among members in MP3-related chat rooms. These definitions not only champion the benefits of participating in the phenomenon, but also subtly convict or denigrate those who are not yet well-versed in the exchange of MP3s, and who have not yet realized its benefits. Television and the print media have mentioned the issues associated with copyright and the grey areas associated with the technology, but dialogue in MP3-related chat channels hardly ever breaches the subject of intellectual property rights and infringement. In fact, these channels would not be in existence if their originators and frequenters were not wholly supportive of the file format and the free exchange of high-quality music it precipitates. Therefore, the

---

[25] Most, but not all, songs are approximately this file size.

impression given to those new to the setting is extremely skewed and particularly myopic. Without any mention of "the other side of the story" in these venues, individuals cannot make an enlightened, informed decision as to whether or not they should personally support participation with MP3s. As such, most "newbies" succumb to the inundation of positive definitions and become acclimatized to the pro-MP3 atmosphere quickly and easily.

Both Sutherland (1947) and Akers (1998) posit that factors such as frequency, duration, and intensity of the differential associations and definitions also influence the social learning process. When considered in the context of the MP3 phenomenon, *frequency* concerns how often a person is blanketed with statements endorsing music piracy, or how often a person interacts with those who pirate music. *Duration* depends on the amount of time spent in an environment supportive of piracy, whether participating in a P2P network, interacting with a discussion thread on a MP3-related newsgroup or web site, or communicating with MP3 aficionados via a personal messaging program or chat room. *Intensity* refers to how pointed, enthusiastic, cogent, and passionate both the providers of definitions and the definitions themselves are, and how influential they are in guiding, shaping, or bringing about certain behaviors. To note, definitions can also be general or specific, with the former geared primarily to influencing either conforming or deviating behavior, and the latter more suited towards affecting specific actions (Akers, 1998).

A further delineation is made between "positive" and "neutralizing" definitions favoring criminality. Positive definitions are much rarer, and openly champion the deviant or criminogenic behavior as beneficial. Neutralizing definitions are much more common, and - in line with Sykes and Matza's (1957) techniques of neutralization - attempt to rationalize or justify the undesirable behavior as acceptable or appropriate even though an awareness of its undesirability or erroneous nature is present. Both of these seem prevalent in cyberspace, as a blatant disregard of intellectual property is evident among so many persons[26]. The relative anonymity and distributed nature of the Internet allows many individuals to incautiously endorse participation in an illegal practice without care for potential consequence or backlash from such statements (or the actions they seek to

---

[26] A piece by Moore and McMullan (2004) identified some tendency to neutralize unauthorized MP3 participation among 171 university students.

foster). Such positive definitions are presumed to be more prevalent among those substantially ensconced in the MP3 scene, and who participate in it to a disproportionately high degree.

Neutralizing definitions are likely more frequent among new and casual users - those not yet deeply rooted in the activity and not yet able to completely disregard any qualms stemming from engaging in the act. This is arguably because their appropriateness is still a question mark in the mind of new participants, and some mental gymnastics must take place to reconcile incompatible feelings through a process of rationalization. Over time, as the individual becomes more accustomed to the behavior (and benefits in significant ways), there may come a time where no justifications are necessary in order to proceed; the action now becomes almost reflexive, undertaken without contemplation or deliberation. Neutralizations also prevent the imputation of a deviant identity onto the actor, and preclude the development of resultant guilt stemming from the wrongful behavior. The theoretical relevance of Sykes and Matza's (1957) techniques of neutralization to music piracy is not analyzed in the current work, but has been briefly discussed elsewhere (Moore & McMullan, 2004) and deserves greater attention in future research.

Differential Reinforcement

After deciding to engage in or refrain from a behavior, social and nonsocial reinforcers aid in the persistence and escalation of the activity. Social reinforcement online can occur if an individual needs a particular song in MP3 format that someone else possesses, and attempts to trade with that person for another requested song file. Thus, the acquisition of something desirable by both parties at no cost to either will foster a pleasant acquaintanceship, and will perpetuate the activity of exchanging MP3s. Additionally, those knowledgeable about MP3s, the latest music released, file servers and web servers where the best and most popular music files are stored, and those with extensive and varied collections of MP3 files are considered "elite," and are respected and admired in the MP3 community. As affinity-seeking is a natural function of human behavior, continued immersion in the MP3 scene may aid in providing these social benefits. Nonsocial reinforcement might result after discovering the excellent quality sound recordings available in MP3 format, and realizing how simple it is to amass a great amount of music without any monetary cost, sans the price paid for a computer and an Internet connection (which many individuals already possess). Other benefits of the technology itself, such as the ease of distribution to family, friends, and associates, and the ability to make audio CDs or to burn them in their original file format onto recordable discs for portability and use at different locations, seemingly reinforce involvement in the MP3 scene.

A person may have a proclivity to participate in certain deviant behavior, due to learned attitudes, beliefs, and definitions favorable to commission. However, he or she will likely refrain from participation if under the impression that punishment is imminent. Conversely, he or she will likely engage in the behavior if a perception is held that rewards or benefits will result from the act. These preconceptions and perceptions are shaped by previous actions - either one's own, or learned through the experience of another - that resulted in reward or punishment (Akers, 1996). Social learning theory proposes that individuals adhere to dominant prescriptive behavior online, but that positive reinforcement (e.g., the procurement of free music, social status among friends, ease and convenience of access) or negative reinforcement (not having to pay approximately $15 for a CD for only one or two appealing songs) might make the individual more likely to change direction and participate in the activity. Social and nonsocial rewards, then, are potent enough to overrule subscription to an ethical set of values, rendering them discardable so that commission of the crime and reaping of the perceived rewards may occur.

One lesser-known form of positive reinforcement regards affective outcomes from participation. Downloading an MP3 is an inherently emotional action. It provides immediate gratification when one desires to listen to a particular song. It also presents the rewards of convenience and self-satisfaction as high-quality music of relatively small file sizes can be shared with friends and colleagues without the need for their provision as a physical recording on tape or CD. By extension, it gives individuals somewhat of a guilty pleasure by providing a valued commodity for free, something for which they normally would have to pay. Irrespective of whether the download of an MP3 later effectuates the purchase of an album, that incipient pleasure is present and accordingly increases the incidence and frequency of the behavior.

An example of how social learning theory is applicable offline also deserves comment. A college student might be introduced to the MP3 phenomenon by her roommate, who seems to always have an exceptional variety of music blaring from her computer speakers – including oldies from the 1960s, disco tracks from the 1970s, love songs from the 1980s, alternative grunge rock from the 1990s, boy-band pop from the 2000s, and even albums and singles that have not even been officially released to the public. Knowing that it is highly unlikely that someone can afford such a vast CD collection and also pay for college and living expenses at the same time, the curious student might ask the source of all the great tunes. The roommate can then acquaint the student with the technology, and show her how many other people in the residence halls are exchanging files with each other through the local area network. Moreover, the unfamiliar student can be taught how millions of individuals globally use P2P applications or visit certain chat channels to obtain practically any song, from any time period, by any artist, all within a few minutes through effortless use of their keyboard and mouse to search for and download MP3s.

The socialization process can continue through informal discussions with friends and classmates on the topic of music. The knowledgeable roommate might initiate the newbie into the scene by showing her how to download her first MP3, and then the process of imitation can take place as one individual learns and models the behavior of the other. This event has undoubtedly unfolded itself numerous times in college dorm rooms across the United States. Definitions favorable to MP3 use are likely to proliferate in this context, win the allegiance of the student, and become internalized with little (if any) dissension or dispute. The college student thus becomes enamored with MP3s and proceeds to accumulate large quantities of files. She then emails love songs to her boyfriend back home, sets up a server on her computer to distribute copies of her MP3s to others, leaves her computer on for weeks at a time to continue transferring files, and develops a web page to promote the distribution of digital music on the Internet. Reinforcement occurs as she sees all of her peers downloading MP3s and through the realization that she no longer must buy music CDs to meet her needs for tunes. Moreover, the behavior is further legitimated and ingrained as the sheer number of participants in the phenomenon (for all intents and purposes) any possibility of detection and discipline for her individual actions.

Social learning theory points to the methods and manners in which an individual might be introduced to a criminal activity. As illustrated above, its four theoretical components of differential association, imitation and modeling, definitions, and differential reinforcement can conceivably be applied to music piracy in the same manner that they have been applied to more traditional forms of crime. The ways in which a social group contributes to the commencement and persistence of a behavior is important for analyses, particularly because the behavior under study appears to flourish via its communal nature and the amicable context in which it occurs.

Interrelationships Between the Theories

Scholars have not ignored the possibility of interrelationships between general strain, self-control, and social learning theory. It is interesting to note, for example, that when comparing social learning theory and self-control theory, the former asserts that crime results from learning something (e.g., techniques, rationalizations, motives) while the latter contends that crime results from not learning something (e.g., how to defer short-term pleasures for long-term gains). However, Gottfredson and Hirschi (1990:168) have argued that low self-control and social circumstances do not interact to induce criminality because those with low self-control participate unequally in social institutions and relationships and actually avoid attachment to others due to the underlying dispositional trait. As such, low self-control - their sole predictor of participation in crime - is not and cannot be learned in a social setting (Gottfredson & Hirschi, 1990:95).

Nonetheless, Evans et al. (1997) suggested Gottfredson and Hirschi overstated their case when asserting that social learning does not play a contributive role in criminality. These researchers studied 555 individuals[27] through self-report surveys and included two social learning measures related to differential association and definitions favorable to law violation. The former was operationalized by a question concerning the respondent's number of criminal friends, and the latter by "statements concerning the degree of tolerance for criminal behavior, moral validity of breaking the law, and level of agreement with committing criminal acts" (Evans et al., 1997:487). They reached the conclusion that criminal associations and criminal values may augment the influence of low self-control on deviant outcomes, either through introduction to the activity, pressure to partake in it, modeling of the behavior, or redefining it in an acceptable light and as a pleasurable endeavor worth the risks of apprehension and punishment (Evans et al., 1997)[28].

---

[27] The analysis was limited to Whites because their response rate was disproportionately higher than other demographic groups.

[28] Other important research involving delinquent peer associations and delinquent value systems support this finding (e.g., Heimer, 1997; Matsueda & Anderson, 1998; Warr & Stafford, 1991). Thus, a relationship between low self-control,

The incorporation of strain and social learning variables with self-control in an explanatory model has also been suggested (e.g., Evans et al., 1997; Grasmick et al., 1993; Mazerolle & Maahs, 2000; Pratt & Cullen, 2000; Wright, Caspi, Moffitt, & Silva, 2001). For instance, Wright et al. (2001) sought to determine how certain variables measuring self-control, social control, and differential association were related to crime. They discovered that low self-control is positively related to delinquent peer association, and that self-control and social control were both independently and interactively related to crime. Mazerolle and Maahs (2000) identified that variables measuring social learning theory and self-control theory, when included with general strain theory variables, affect delinquency independently in both a cross-sectional and longitudinal model. This appears to cry out for an integrationist approach to collectively account for each theory's relevant precepts.

More variation in music piracy, then, may be explained through the juxtaposition and integration of theoretical concepts from each of these paradigms. The primary purpose of the current research is not to integrate theoretical propositions into a cohesive or unifying whole in an attempt to explain intellectual property theft online. However, future analyses should venture in that direction.

---

social learning, opportunity, and crime has been substantiated. In another piece, (Agnew et al., 2002), evidence was discovered linking the personality trait of "low constraint" to criminality as a mediating variable between strain and delinquency. This speaks to a demonstrable association between strain, low self-control, and crime. A juxtaposition of the three general theories, then, is almost demanded - and an integrative approach subsequent to the current research endeavor may hold much promise in predicting the most variance in the dependent variable under study.

CHAPTER 4

Instrument, Sampling, and Variables Under Study

The present study seeks to determine whether general strain theory, self-control theory, and social learning theory are all valid explanatory frameworks in which to study and understand criminality that is conceptually different from traditional types in two ways. First, the phenomenon at hand - music piracy - is facilitated by a computer, and computer-related criminality has rarely been the subject of academic empirical examination or policy development by criminal justice personnel. Second, the phenomenon occurs online - over the Internet in an intangible, nonphysical, virtual realm. It is hoped that through this research endeavor, a comprehensive picture of predictive elements associated with online intellectual property theft will be obtained.

POPULATION

The subject population of the current study is undergraduate students at a large public university in the Midwest region of the United States. The empirical validity of many criminological theories has been tested through the use of data collected from samples of college and university students; indeed, this is a widely prevalent and accepted method in the criminology and criminal justice disciplines (Mazerolle & Piquero, 1998; Nagin & Paternoster, 1993). Most students have high-speed access to the Internet in their residence hall rooms, or through cable modem or DSL connectivity in their off-campus homes. Others may primarily use a dialup modem to connect to the university's network, and while speeds are significantly slower in this context, online access is still attained. Students in the 21st century are required to use the Internet for a variety of academic reasons, including research, correspondence, and various types of scholarly projects. Moreover, tasks as essential as registration for courses are only possible online, demonstrating the tremendous necessity of connectivity for those currently enrolled in the university. Notwithstanding school-related responsibilities, the Internet has become valuable for meeting social and personal needs, and thereby plays a large, functional role in the lives of most students.

An increased frequency of online activity by students enhances the likelihood of being introduced to, and participating in misbehavior on the Internet. While this author will leave some of the more seedier and outrageous examples to the reader's imagination, online intellectual property theft in the form of music piracy is one such activity in which students may participate. Augmenting the likelihood of the behavior's occurrence are a host of factors, including a lack of enforcement of rules governing acceptable use of computer and network resources, a deficiency in delineating ethical and unethical standards of behavior by instructors and other authority figures, and a higher level of curiosity, experimentation, and general deviant inclinations among the college-aged population[29].

INSTRUMENT

An extensive survey instrument was constructed and refined in order to gather data to examine the veracity of the aforementioned hypotheses. It has been included in Appendix A. The questionnaire commenced with a short general introduction of the study, stated the protections afforded to the subject, provided a summary of how data was being collected, and gave contact information both of the primary investigator and chair of the relevant institutional review board. Questions representing the three general criminological theories were then presented to the respondent. First, six questions intended to measure strainful life experiences were given, and stem from Broidy's (2001) empirical test of Agnew's (1992) general strain theory. These items asked the respondent to reflect on the last six months and indicate whether they received a bad grade in a class, broke up with an intimate partner, experienced weight gain or loss, been fired or laid off from a job, had money problems (i.e., had difficulty

---

[29] Research on the subject of cheating, plagiarism, and software piracy has sufficiently illustrated this point (Agnew & Peters, 1986; Buckley, Wiese, & Harvey, 1998; Eining & Christensen, 1991; Im & Van Epps, 1991; Wong, Kong, & Ngai, 1990).

paying tuition, rent, bills), or been a victim of a crime. Possible responses were true or false. Next were six items from the 24-item scale created by Grasmick et al. (1993) operationalizing the six constituent elements of self-control, in order to assess the relationship of this intrinsic characteristic to music piracy among the sample. This decision stemmed from its extensive empirical utilization and agreed-upon appropriateness in the previously reviewed studies. The variables included: "I often do what brings me pleasure here and now" (to measure impulsivity); "When things get complicated, I tend to quit or withdraw" (simple tasks); "I find no excitement in doing things I might get in trouble for" (risk seeking); "I try to look out for others first, even if it means making things difficult for myself" (self centered); "I don't lose my temper very easily" (temper); and "I feel better when I am on the move rather than sitting and thinking" (physical activities). As is evident, one question was selected for each of the six theoretical components of Gottfredson and Hirschi's (1990) conceptualization of self-control. In the current research, these were considered "attitudinal" measures of self-control.

Five questions measuring various types of antinormative conduct that range in severity were next presented. Their purpose is to provide a rough sketch of whether "analogous" behaviors are related to participation in nontraditional criminality in the same way that they are related to conventional forms of crime (Cochran, Wood, Sellers, Wilkerson, & Chamlin, 1996; Paternoster & Brame, 1998, 2000; Tremblay, Boulerice, Arseneault, & Niscale, 1995). They included whether the respondent had: skipped more than 10 class periods in the past year; lied to a professor/instructor either via email, telephone, or in person at least once in the past year; plagiarized on a school assignment at least once in the past year; drank alcohol before he or she turned 21; or driven a vehicle while under the influence of alcohol at least once in the past year. These variables were considered "behavioral" measures of self-control.

The subsequent section of the survey presented thirty-seven questions largely measuring social learning theory. The large number of items was deemed essential to most accurately grasp the four elements of the theory – differential association, imitation, definitions, and differential reinforcement. Finally, twenty-two questions intended to elicit the frequency and scope of their actual participation in the activity were subsequently given, and the instrument terminates with an assortment of items seeking demographic information from the respondent. A conscious effort was made to create and present questions in as neutral a manner as possible, so as not to offend individuals or prejudice their answers. This was imperative not only to conduct good research, but also because self-reported criminality is the dependent variable. Candid and forthright responses must be encouraged so that internal validity is not threatened, and so that consistency in interpretation is fostered - as best as possible - to most accurately evaluate key concepts in the work.

Due to the fact that the survey was closed-ended, its structure constrained the responses and therefore prevented individuals from providing comments, feedback, or more richer answers to the questions. This was necessary, however, due to resource limitations associated with the project. The vast majority of items were provided with a Likert-scale answer set; the remainder were either true or false, or had answer choices specific to the inquiry posed. Also, the direction of answer choices was varied to prevent automatic and lackadaisical responses by participants.

SAMPLING PROCEDURES

While creating a sampling frame of classes to survey, much care was taken to ensure that the resultant group of individuals were representative of the entire student population at this university. Three primary stages of data selection took place. First, a list of the fifteen colleges was obtained, as well as a list of departments and schools inside each college. Second, two or three majors inside each college were selected so that specific classes that might be surveyed could be identified. Some majors were somewhat conventional in nature, and offered classes which all undergraduates would have the opportunity to take - such as introductory courses in Computer Science and Psychology. Other majors were highly specific and offered classes that only those in that department would take - such as Biochemistry, Zoology, and Finance. These courses ranged from the 100-200 level (generally populated by freshmen and sophomores) to the 300-400 level (largely consisting of juniors and seniors).

Once a few majors in each college were randomly chosen, the third stage of data selection occurred. A concerted effort was made to randomly select 1 or 2 lower-level and 1 or 2 upper-level classes through the use of the university's online course catalog. A comprehensive list of these potential classes to survey was then created, and emails were sent to each respective professor or instructor. In these emails, a description of the project was given, along with a link to a web page where the survey instrument might be viewed. A request was then made for approximately 20 minutes at the beginning or end of the class period so that the surveys could be administered. Overall, 169 professors representing 185 classes were emailed, and 15 professors representing 16 classes agreed to the request.

The aforementioned method is known as purposive sampling for heterogeneity. This technique seeks to obtain a certain number of people in specified groups (such as college majors), and is not inordinately concerned with proportionality but rather to obtain a sufficiently diverse sample on one or more characteristics. Determining the prevalence of music piracy among university students across the gamut of possible majors was a goal of this study, rather than restricting it to those in specific disciplines, such as computer science or criminal justice. "The general strategy is to identify important sources of variation in the population and then to select a sample that represents this variation" (Singleton & Straits, 1999:158). Individual area of study was one notable variable in which students would differ - and which may accordingly affect their ideologies toward music piracy. Therefore, a minimum of two classes (one lower-level and one upper-level) from a minimum of two majors in each of the colleges in the school where this research was conducted was deemed necessary to facilitate cross-disciplinary comparison of individuals. The classes and majors selected were chosen based on this author's judgment after consideration of the population at hand and the goals of the study. For the purposes of this analyses, stratified random sampling would not have added much value in terms of precision or generalizability, as the primary objective was not to perfectly mirror the demographic proportions of the student population but to garner a sample generally representative of that larger group. Despite the fact that permission was given in only 16 of 185 classes, a broad amount of majors were expected to be represented in those 16 courses due to their interdisciplinary content.

During the data collection phase, the researcher and the subject matter were introduced, and the fact that there would be no cost associated with participating except for the time spent in composing a response. Students were verbally informed of the anonymous nature of the survey, that participation was completely voluntary, and that it would take approximately 20 minutes to complete. They were also instructed to refrain from revealing their name, student number, or any other identifying information when filling out the questionnaire. In addition, potential respondents were made cognizant that only group totals would be consolidated and released at the culmination of the project. This was essential to protect the rights of the respondents, to encourage a greater number of truthful responses, and to garner a reliable cross-section for measuring the relevant constructs. It was hoped that the written and oral introduction to the survey would assuage any inhibitions the respondent might have.

The study was restricted to undergraduate students because they are more representative of traditional conceptions of the "college population," and because one might argue that they are categorically different in many ways than those in graduate school. Nonetheless, the demographic question related to the respondent's year of study did include a "graduate school" answer choice in case a graduate student was enrolled in a higher-level undergraduate class to earn elective credits. Those who identified themselves as graduate students were removed from the analysis.

PRETEST

Prior to its administration in classrooms, the instrument was pretested among a select group of colleagues in this author's department, as well as in two upper-level undergraduate criminal justice classes (N=52). The retrieved data showed that a sizable number of participants downloaded MP3s, and indicated that there would be sufficient variation in the dependent variable to facilitate statistical analyses. Furthermore, more informed decisions were made possible as to which variables should be kept and which should be removed (further explained below), and identified that a greater variety of items measuring pirating behavior were necessary. For example, the instrument employed in the pretest only asked about current participation in the phenomenon; the revised survey inquired about participation in years past. Through the pretest, feedback on clarity, consistency, and content of the survey items was also retrieved and considered. Many of these comments were subsequently incorporated to preclude conceptual and operational problems from compromising the validity of the retrieved data. This fine-tuning of the instrument greatly assisted in the objective of posing properly constructed questions and obtaining responses which most accurately represented the primary concepts in the study.

As mentioned, the pretest was useful in refining and paring down the number of items on the questionnaire. Indeed, the primary sentiment revealed by students who took the pretest was that the instrument was too lengthy. It initially consisted of 124 questions; however, upon reflection of the results stemming from the pretest, it was determined that many items were superfluous for measurement purposes. As a consequence, a concerted attempt was made to only include those that were most statistically and theoretically relevant.

SPECIFICATION OF VARIABLES OF INTEREST

Strain

Following data collection, confirmatory factor analyses (CFA) was conducted on the six initial strain items to determine which items loaded together best for inclusion in the statistical analysis[30]. A cut point of .5 was selected, which left three variables from which a factor score would be created to measure strain in the statistical models; see Table 1 for their factor loadings and reliability alpha.

Table 1. Strain Factor Score	Factor Loadings
Broke up with an intimate partner	0.546
Experienced weight gain or loss	0.734
Had money problems (e.g., not being able to pay tuition, rent, bills)	0.635
(Cronbach's α = 0.287; Eigenvalue = 1.240)	

Self-Control

CFA was also conducted on the initial six attitudinal self-control questions. Respondents could select among "Strongly Disagree," "Disagree," "Neutral," "Agree," and "Strongly Agree" as possible responses. Three items loaded above the selected cut point of .5 (see Table 2), and were consequently used to create a factor score measuring attitudinal self-control.

---

[30] It should be noted here that the reliability of factors is dependent on the number of indicators per factor and largely independent by the number of cases (or the interaction of N with the number of factors). Also, there is general agreement that more indicators per factor is better than fewer. At least three indicators are desirable, and a large number per factor is not desirable unless N is sizable (Marsh & Hau, 1999).

Table 2. Attitudinal Self-Control Factor Score	Factor Loadings
When things get complicated, I tend to quit or withdraw	-0.634
I try to look out for others first, even if it means making things difficult for myself	0.582
I feel better when I am on the move rather than sitting and thinking	0.588

(Cronbach's α = -0.051; Eigenvalue = 1.087)

Then, a list of five "analogous" behavioral measures of self-control were compiled; possible responses were true or false. CFA revealed only four statements with factor loadings greater than .5. See Table 3 for the loadings and reliability alpha statistic.

Table 3. Behavioral Self-Control Factor Score	Factor Loadings
I have skipped more than 10 class periods in the past year	0.619
I have lied to a professor/instructor either via email, telephone, or in person at least once in the past year	0.680
I have plagiarized on a school assignment at least once in the past year	0.598
I have driven a vehicle while under the influence of alcohol at least once in the past year	0.595

(Cronbach's α = 0.472; Eigenvalue = 1.557)

Social Learning

Thirty-seven social learning theory variables were initially created, and CFA was utilized to determine the appropriateness of the item groupings for each of the four elements of differential association, imitation and modeling, definitions, and differential reinforcement. To note, the imitation construct of social learning theory was particularly difficult to operationalize, due to its apparent theoretical overlap with differential association. As mentioned earlier, imitation follows immersion in an environment where socialization takes place, but such a concept was difficult to capture in the construction of survey items. CFA and reliability analyses were performed on variables *conceivably* measuring imitation. They revealed multiple factors, weak loadings, and extremely poor alphas - posing a sizable problem. This author sought to find a way to include imitation as a separate concept because of its importance as a distinct theoretical element, and was hesitant to only measure differential association, definitions, and differential reinforcement like other studies had done (e.g., Lersch, 1999). In Akers et al.'s (1979) test of the theory, imitation was weakly related to the frequency of alcohol and marijuana use. The researchers qualified the low levels of variance explained by stating that imitation is the most narrow of the four empirical phenomena and that "the interrelationships specified in the theory would indicate that removing imitation has less effect because its impact is still reflected to some extent in the remaining broader measures" (Akers et al., 1979:647).

From a practical perspective, though, MP3 participation truly seemed to be influenced by individuals modeling the behavior of other music pirates, and thus its individual inclusion seemed imperative. It appeared that imitation and differential association could be highly interrelated, and so a determination was made to include all variables of both of those groups in an exploratory factor analyses model. The two primary factors seemed to differentiate the variables in a theoretically expected manner; and measures concerning influences in real life (offline) clustered separately from those measures related to online influences.

It may be that differential association takes place largely in an offline context – where interaction is presumably more frequent, profound, and subtly persuasive in its effect on the actions of a person. Imitation, then, is perhaps more of a direct, perceptible, and conspicuous process, as well-ensconced participants are concurrently online with those who are new to the phenomenon, and the behavior of the former is immediately observable for emulation by the latter. In sum, differential association was operationalized by four variables specific to offline interaction: "My friends support my MP3 usage"; "I associate with others in real life (offline) who are supportive of MP3 usage"; "I was introduced by another person in real life to MP3s"; and "I have learned the techniques of using

MP3s from my friends" (see Table 4). Imitation[31] was represented by three variables endemic to the environment of cyberspace: "I have learned the techniques of using MP3s from television or print media"; "I have learned the techniques of using MP3s from online sources (web pages, chat rooms, etc)"; and "I associate with others online who exchange MP3s with me" (see Table 5).

Table 4. Differential Association Factor Score	Factor Loadings
My friends support my MP3 usage	0.825
I associate with others in real life (offline) who are supportive of MP3 usage	0.821
I was introduced by another person in real life to MP3s	0.761
I have learned the techniques of using MP3s from my friends	0.698

(Cronbach's α = 0.774; Eigenvalue = 2.421)

Table 5. Imitation/Modeling Factor Score	Factor Loadings
I have learned the techniques of using MP3s from television or print media	0.817
I have learned the techniques of using MP3s from online sources (web pages, chat rooms)	0.829
I associate with others online who exchange MP3s with me	0.576

(Cronbach's α = 0.595; Eigenvalue = 1.686)

The final set of items measuring definitions were as follows: "One of the reasons I download MP3s is because I will not purchase the music"; "One of the reasons I download MP3s is because I feel the recording industry has been overcharging the general public for music tapes and

---

[31] Skinner and Fream (1997) measured imitation by asking respondents about the sources from where they might have learned computer crime techniques, such as from family, teachers, books or magazines, television and movies, or computer bulletin boards. Their rationale was that even though such items do not measure modeling exactly as it was proposed by Akers, they could shed light on imitated sources that provide a means for behavioral learning.

CDs"; "One of the reasons I download MP3s is because many musicians and the recording industry make millions of dollars anyway, and downloading MP3s of their songs does not really cut into their income"; and "One of the reasons I download MP3s is because I think music should be free" (see Table 6). The final set of differential reinforcement items included: "It is a great benefit to sample new music through MP3s"; "It is a great benefit to be able to transfer assorted MP3s onto an audio/data CD or a portable MP3 player so that I can have music on-the-go"; "It makes me feel good to download a song that I have wanted"; and "It is a great benefit to me to be able to access music freely" (see Table 7).

Table 6. Definitions Factor Score	Factor Loadings
One of the reasons I download MP3s is because I *will not* purchase the music	0.656
One of the reasons I download MP3s is because I feel the recording industry has been overcharging the general public for music tapes and CDs	0.724
One of the reasons I download MP3s is because many musicians and the recording industry make millions of dollars anyway, and downloading MP3s of their songs does not really cut into their income	0.775
One of the reasons I download MP3s is because I think music should be free	0.656

(Cronbach's α = 0.658; Eigenvalue = 1.986)

Table 7. Differential Reinforcement Factor Score	Factor Loadings
It is a great benefit to sample new music through MP3s	0.889
It is a great benefit to be able to transfer assorted MP3s onto an audio/data CD or a portable MP3 player so that I can have music on-the-go	0.881
It makes me feel good to download a song that I have wanted	0.791
It is a great benefit to me to be able to access music freely	0.803

(Cronbach's α = 0.862; Eigenvalue = 2.836)

This final set of fifteen variables measuring the four tenets of social learning theory did appear to warrant further examination. Could it be determined whether the constructs can be distinctly operationalized and measured? Or, is overlap in their measurement inevitable due to the tight interrelationships among the concepts? It was useful to discover whether the data might lend additional understanding to this theoretical complexity.

Empirically Disentangling the Tenets of Social Learning Theory

To begin, an exploratory factor analyses with varimax rotation was conducted on these fifteen variables presumed to accurately and separately measure the four tenets of social learning theory. Four Eigenvalues over 1 were identified, but the scree plot indicated that there were only two primary factors, the first explaining 26.29% of the variance, and the second explaining 13.23% of the variance. The rest of the explained variation appeared to be statistical noise. Looking at the factor loadings across the four dimensions and choosing a cut point of .45 or higher (as this threshold seemed to separate those variables which loaded decently on a factor from those that did not), all four differential association and all four differential reinforcement variables loaded on the first factor (see Appendix B, Table A). Furthermore, all three imitation variables and all four definitions variables loaded on the second factor. Admittedly, this researcher's conceptualization of the tenets may be susceptible to error and consequently may have confounded their distinct nature when creating the variables.

Notwithstanding that possibility, it may simply be difficult to perfectly disentangle differential association from differential reinforcement and measure them as two separate constructs. What are some reasons for this finding? It might be an artifact of a cross-sectional research approach to the dynamic concept of social learning. However, it might point to a conceptually valid interrelationship. The presence of peers who support, inculcate, encourage, endorse, and share certain motives, rationalizations, and drives related to an activity is intrinsically a positive and rewarding element that is perpetuated through continued participation. Similarly, the presence of these peer associations (and the attendant social and nonsocial benefits) will perceivably diminish if the behavior is reduced in frequency, and individuals may wish to preserve that peer group and consequently continue an activity in order to avoid pain associated with their possible loss. This, of course, is equivalent to negative reinforcement.

It is more difficult to posit why the variables ostensibly measuring imitation and definitions loaded on the same factor. Imitation refers to the modeling of actions of others, and the transmission of knowledge, attitudes, beliefs, and techniques associated with those actions. It appears to connote more of a physical replication of a person's behavior. If individuals download MP3s after watching a friend or family member in real life, this would seem highly applicable. In cyberspace, however, such physical replication is not possible simply due to the lack of material cues and the fact that all interaction takes place through computer-mediated communication. As such, imitation online would appear to result from observing and internalizing typed words and commands that represent knowledge, attitudes, beliefs, and techniques of MP3 participation.

Once a person who wants to participate in the phenomenon meets and interacts with an individual already well-versed with MP3s, the latter person can serve as a palpable model to emulate solely through that which is recognizable and evident in their textual content. Any demarcating line between content that induces imitation and content that induces definitions is blurred, because the same actions might affect one, the other, or both tenets of social learning theory. Definitions, as mentioned earlier, are evaluative criteria designating a behavior as good or bad and thereby qualifying them as appropriate, desired, or justified (Akers et al., 1979). Their learning and internalization may not occur in a disparate moment from when imitation takes place. That is, the social setting on the Internet which provides sources of imitation and definitions in support of the activity may promulgate both through the same elements and individuals, thereby obscuring any attempt to disconnect the two and measure each on an individual basis.

The next step was to run factor analyses with promax rotation, under the assumption that the variables were correlated with each other. The first run included the variables measuring differential association and differential reinforcement. All of the factors loaded relatively highly on the one factor that was identified (supported by the resultant scree plot), further reinforcing the fact that these items may not measure distinctly different concepts (see Appendix B, Table B). A reliability analysis revealed an alpha of .878, indicating collective measurement of the same construct. When separated into their two groupings, the reliability alphas for differential association and differential reinforcement were .774 and .862, respectively. A decision was made, then, to maintain the operationalized separateness between the two constructs by utilizing each distinct set of variables rather than combining them.

The second run included the imitation and definitions variables. Contrary to what happened in the first run, two factors were identified with each set of variables loading separately from the other. The reliability alpha value for these items together was .659; their alpha values when separated into the two tenets was .595 for imitation and .658 for definitions (see Appendix B, Table C). These analyses highlight some of the complexities inherent in attempting to empirically distinguish between the four theoretically defined elements of social learning theory, especially when considering an Internet-based activity.

Dependent Variables

Thirteen dependent variables in the current research sought to measure the frequency of an individual's participation in music piracy. Respondents were asked to indicate how many MP3 files they personally downloaded last week and in an average week (0, 1-5, 6-10, 11-20, More than 20), and last month and in an average month (0, 1-25, 26-50, 51-100, More than 100) this year, last year, and two years ago. Furthermore, they were asked to indicate how many they downloaded in totality during each of the past three years (0, 1-10, 11-100, 101-1000, More than 1000), how many they had downloaded over the course of their life thus far (0, 1-100, 101-500, 501-2000, 2001 or more), and how many total complete music albums in MP3 format they had obtained online (0, 1-5, 6-10, 11-20, More than 20).

These variables were factor analyzed using promax rotation, and the resultant scree plot depicted a tremendous drop between the first and second (and subsequent) Eigenvalues. The first explained 55.39% of the variance across the model, while the second explained 14.03%. As such, a one-factor solution was forced; see Table 8 for the detailed loadings. Additionally, the alpha value for these thirteen dependent items was .930, indicating that if a respondent answered a certain way for one of these questions, it was extremely likely that he or she answered the same way for the other questions.

Table 8. Music Piracy Dependent Variable Factor Score	Factor Loadings
How many MP3 files downloaded in the last week?	0.590
How many MP3 files downloaded in the last month?	0.646
How many MP3 files downloaded since the beginning of 2003?	0.751
How many MP3s do you, on average, download per month?	0.744
How many did you download in an average week exactly one year ago?	0.810
How many did you download in an average month exactly one year ago?	0.814
How many did you download in an average week exactly two years ago?	0.772
How many did you download in an average month exactly two years ago?	0.776
How many MP3 files did you personally download in 2002?	0.819
How many MP3 files did you personally download in 2001?	0.783
How many MP3 files did you personally download in 2000?	0.673
How many total complete music albums in MP3 format have you obtained online?	0.604
How many total MP3s have you downloaded over the course of your life thus far?	0.836

(Cronbach's α = 0.930; Eigenvalue = 7.201)
Note: one factor solution forced

Similar questions have been utilized in the descriptive studies on MP3s conducted by various research firms (Angus Reid Worldwide, 2000a, 2000b; Jay, 2000; King, 2000a; Latonero, 2000; Learmonth, 2000; Pew Internet & American Life Project, 2000; Reciprocal Inc., 2000a, 2000b; Webnoize, 2000). In addition, determining immersion in intellectual property theft through items inquiring about the frequency of participation in the activity has been supported by research on software piracy (Rahim, Seyal, & Rahman, 1999; Sims, Cheng, & Teegen, 1996; Solomon & O'Brien, 1990; Wood & Glass, 1995). Inquiring about the number of illegal songs acquired by the individual has been supported in MP3 research based on a behavioral perspective (Gopal et al., 2004).

Other questions in the survey asked the number of hours each week the respondent spends looking for MP3s and what activities are done with MP3s (e.g., creating an audio CD from MP3 files, made an MP3 from an audio CD or another sound source, listening to them on a computer, listening to them on a portable MP3 player, burning them to CD, sharing them with friends, selling them). The individual is also asked to assess the ratio of his or her download/upload time spent transferring MP3 files online (I do not participate with MP3s, 0% of the time downloading and 100% uploading, 25% and 75%, 75% and 25%, 100% and 0%) and the percent of MP3s possessed that are not personally created from CDs the individual owned, or are not of songs that the individual owns on CD. Three questions then followed that sought to capture perceptions of the legality of downloading and uploading MP3s. These include: "Do you believe that receiving or providing MP3s should be illegal?"; "As far as you know, is receiving or providing MP3s illegal?"; and "Do you refrain from obtaining MP3s because you believe it is illegal?."

Finally demographic information was solicited through inquiries as to the respondent's race, gender, age, year of studies, major, parents' annual household income, employment status, living situation, type of Internet connectivity, variety of Internet use, and proficiency of Internet use. A copy of the questionnaire is provided in Appendix A; it can be consulted for additional details on the items utilized in this study.

HYPOTHESES

There are three primary hypotheses in this study, and can each be empirically tested utilizing the variables created for statistical analyses. While their content might be intuitive to the reader, they must be clearly expressed prior to statistical modeling, so that the tests are most optimally constructed and so that there is no conceptual confusion with the purpose of the research. The resultant findings should provide substantive insight into which elements most strongly influence the music piracy phenomenon, and should point in the direction of the most appropriate policy solutions. These three hypotheses are detailed below.

Hypothesis 1

Participation in music piracy varies based on the extent to which an individual is proficient in using the Internet, and on the range of online activities in which the respondent has participated. Specifically, those who are highly skilled in performing various Internet-based activities, and those who take broader advantage of the possibilities available online, will be more likely to engage in music piracy.

Hypothesis 2

The elements of general strain, self-control, and social learning theory are all significantly related to Internet music piracy. That is, each "general" theory is appropriately named and has the capacity to explain variation in a crime that is highly nontraditional both in content and in context.

Hypothesis 3

The general theory that explains the most variation in online music piracy is social learning theory, because above all this particular crime is learned from, and supported by, the influence of individuals and institutions in society. self-control theory and general strain theory will be second and third respectively in explanatory power when considering the three general theories.

LIMITATIONS

Limitations are inherent in any social science research endeavor, particularly because of the capricious nature of human behavior, and also because of the virtually unlimited number of influences that may play predictive or determinative roles. General strain, self-control, and social learning theory will not perfectly explain criminal activity, and scholars have pointed out some vulnerabilities in their constitution that deserve comment before delving into the analyses. Furthermore, methodological choices related to survey instrument design and data collection sometimes lead to over- or underspecification of the significant findings. These do not invalidate the results, but provide a caveat for cautious interpretation and generalization. As such, they are also presented here for consideration.

Theoretical Limitations

Concerning general strain, Broidy (2001) reported that the specific negative emotion experienced largely determines the legitimacy of the coping mechanism employed. That is, anger led to illegitimate outcomes, while other negative emotions (e.g., frustration, disappointment, sadness, loneliness)[32] were associated with legitimate coping. In addition, even though individuals may be similar in their strainful experiences, many do not engage in deviance. Social science scholars have attempted to point to the factors that condition the relationship between negative affect and wrongdoing. Morality, self-efficacy, personality, coping resources, social support, social control, and peer associations all moderate the proclivity towards delinquent behavior following strain (Agnew, 1997; Agnew et al., 2002; Agnew & White, 1992).

Gottfredson and Hirschi's (1990) general theory of crime has been faulted for many reasons. Critics have pointed to the inherent tautological nature of its explanation, its underdeveloped conceptualization of the role of opportunity and reward in the etiology of crime, and its superficial portrayal of the nature of the behavior that the theory is designed to explain (e.g., Sellers, 1999). In addition, even if social institutions effectively develop a bond to convention among individuals and a consequent ability to repress drives to fulfill immediate self-interest, it is plausible that they may still participate in wrongdoing. Finally, the definition of crime employed by Gottfredson and Hirschi (1990) arose from classical thinking in which individuals were believed to act in ways that maximized pleasure and minimized pain. In the theory, there is a panoptic assumption that human beings perceive pleasure and pain in exactly the same way. That is, no allowance is made for varying degrees of each of these constructs among persons, which might result from different biological, psychological or socio-cultural factors. These all shape the way an individual perceives what is pleasurable and what is painful – and while it can be argued that there are extant overall generalities among all humans, it is important that individual and cultural nuances be taken into account when considering any wrongful activity, including one as unique as music piracy.

With regard to social learning,, one limitation is that Akers does not factor in the element of spontaneity and quick, spur-of-the-moment

---

[32] The variables measuring negative emotions were combined into a scale in Broidy's (2001) research.

decisions to engage in an act. If some aspect of opportunity theory were affixed to the current framework, it would account for those types of crime and deviance which are predominantly the result of a lack of capable guardians at a locale. Additionally, social learning theory seems to presume that all individuals are at the whim of change and circumstance – veritable pawns with little control over being influenced by others. No consideration is given to elements of individuality or unbiased and rational thinking among people, and each of the four tenets of the theory appears to necessitate a passive acceptance by the individual in order for the deviance to be internalized. Some other questions are left unanswered in Akers' explication. For example, are all individuals equally able to learn, or are some subgroups more susceptible than others? Since nonsocial and social influences vary in frequency and intensity, are all behaviors similarly reinforced[33]? Do structures of inequality and privilege play a role? Does proper socialization and instilling positive beliefs about individuality and agency in some people reduce the possibility of learning criminality? Is there any hope for implementing proactive strategies to counter this trend of learning deviance? These are all issues which are not addressed in the current work, but which warrant deeper inquiry.

Methodological Limitations

The techniques employed in the current research methodology do not facilitate precise generalizations to the universe of college students in the United States, as a probability sampling technique was not utilized. In addition, the demographics of participants were somewhat skewed in terms of race and socioeconomic status, even though they largely represented the overall undergraduate population of the university where the study took place. Music piracy participation may have been underreported because of the tendency of individuals to provide socially desirable answers, especially about a topic that is so hotly contested and widely discussed in many social circles (Seale, Polakowski, & Schneider, 1998). Recall bias may have also affected the data provided by participants. Individuals who were prompted to remember their music pirating behavior from years past may have been unsuccessful in accurately doing so (or doing so at all), and may have coddled their

---

[33] Akers (1985) mentions nonsocial reinforcers but does not fully develop their role.

memories by adding erroneous information or altering previously stored information in order to recollect and reveal it in a manner appropriate to what the survey questions asked. Finally, self-serving bias - where individuals demonstrate a tendency to view themselves more favorable than not - may also have been evident among respondent choices (Babcock & Loewenstein, 1997; Cross, 1977).

Notwithstanding these theoretical and methodological limitations, it is hoped that this research will cumulatively advance society's understanding of the causative elements of online intellectual property theft specifically, and - to some degree - Internet-based criminality in general. Such derived knowledge should inform decision-making related to policy and programming strategies that can be implemented to respond this form of wrongdoing in the most advantageous manner. The increasing value and role of information and the products of creative minds in our professional and personal lives mandates this empirical examination.

CHAPTER 5

Analysis

This research seeks to shed light on the elements that contribute to music piracy participation, and also assess the capacity of general strain, self-control, and social learning theory in explaining variation in the activity. To accomplish this, various statistical techniques will be employed: univariate analyses in the form of frequency distributions; bivariate analyses in terms of crosstabulations, correlations, and one-way analyses of variance (ANOVA) procedures; and multivariate analyses in the form of logistic and multinomial logistic regression models.

To test Hypothesis 1, two items were included in the questionnaire to measure proficiency and variety of Internet usage. Examining the distribution of these categories among music pirates will be possible through ANOVA, which assesses whether the population means are equal by calculating the significance of the difference between the sample means. Identifying which category of the dependent variables differs significantly from the others in its power to influence music piracy will occur through the Bonferroni Post Hoc test. To test Hypotheses 2 and 3, two types of multivariate regression analyses will be conducted. Regression allows multiple predictive factors to be examined together in the same model, to determine the influence of one component while holding the others constant. Logistic regression analyses can be performed to ascertain if general strain, self-control, and social learning theory elements significantly increase the likelihood that individuals will pirate music. Multinomial logistic regression can be similarly performed to determine whether certain theoretical components (as measured by factor scale variables) differentiate the intensity of participation among music pirates. Rationale for the use of these analytic techniques are provided with the statistical results.

DESCRIPTIVE STATISTICS

Descriptive statistics allow researchers to summarize data in an easily interpretable format, and can serve as a foundation for subsequent multivariate analyses. The following text provides some basic distributions of the important demographic characteristics of respondents in the sample, as well as crosstabulated percentages of how general participation in music piracy varies across these groups. Specifically, the variable of "total MP3s downloaded over the course of one's life" - with response categories of 0, 1-100, 101-500, 501-2000, or 2001 or more - was chosen to clarify which demographic groups participate in music piracy more than others. These univariate measures, of course, do not take into account any other variables. These figures are inclusive of a final sample size of 2,032 individuals, following listwise deletion of those cases with missing values[34].

To begin, 57.6% of the sample was female, and 7.8% of women sampled had downloaded over 2000 MP3s in their lifetime (compared to 22.8% of men sampled). Men, though, were more frequent participants in music piracy, with 22.8% having over 2000 MP3 files (as compared to 7.8% of women). Interestingly, young males have been identified as the population that disproportionately participates in *software* piracy (Rahim et al., 1999; Sims et al., 1996; Solomon & O'Brien, 1990; Wood & Glass, 1995), which mirrors these findings concerning music piracy[35].

The vast majority of the sample was White (77.9%), and the distribution of total MP3s ever downloaded across racial groups was relatively similar (see Table 9). To note, 10.1% of the sample was Black, but almost 1/4th of that demographic group (24.8%) had never downloaded an MP3. This figure indicates that Blacks may not participate in this activity to the same extent as other races -- at least at typical large

---

[34] Listwise deletion was chosen over imputation of missing data because the original sample size was 2,194, and only a small proportion (7.4%) of cases would be removed.

[35] Interestingly, the largest purchasing consumers of software are professionals usually past the college age-group, while the largest purchasing consumers of music are generally students in secondary and post-secondary education (Bhattacharjee et al., 2003). It seems that the piracy of music would negatively affect the revenue stream of that industry to a much greater degree than the influence of software piracy on the producers and developers of applications and games.

Midwestern public universities. It must be stated that if this study were conducted at a historically-Black college or university, the findings might be very different. Almost half of the sample were not employed at all (49.1%), approximately a fifth worked 20 hours a week (19.5%), and only 3.2% stated that they worked 40 hours each week. Interestingly, 22.7% of these full-time working students had downloaded over 2000 MP3s, as compared to 13.6% of those who did not work at all during the week.

The majority of the sample was 19 years of age or younger (57.6%), and 11.5% of this group had downloaded over 2000 MP3s, compared to 18.1% of those 20 years of age or older. With regard to educational level, 31.4% were freshmen, 28.9% were sophomore, 24.2% were juniors, and 15.5% were seniors. A larger proportion of seniors (19.7%) belonged to the heaviest group of MP3 participants than the other classes. Slightly over half of those sampled lived on campus in a dormitory (55.2%) and 88.9% had high-speed Internet access. Consistent with intuition, more MP3s were downloaded by this group than those who connected to the Internet via dialup modem at home and those who did not have Internet access at their place of residence.

The largest proportion of students stated that their major was housed in the College of Social Science (24.8%); the heaviest downloaders belonged to the College of Communication Arts and Sciences (21.8%) and the College of Engineering (20.7%). This might be expected because those majors require more competence and participation with computers than do some of the others, and a larger amount of proficiency may be correlated with greater MP3 downloading[36]. Nevertheless, MP3 participation is generally distributed similarly across majors, indicative of its prevalence throughout the entire student body.

---

[36] Proficiency as well as variety of Internet use are later tested in a bivariate analyses to determine their predictive role in music piracy.

Table 9. Demographic Characteristics and Participation in Pirating (N=2032)

	Sample %	Total MP3s Ever Downloaded				
		0	1-100	101-500	501-2000	2001+
Sex						
Female	56.7	16.1	14.6	30.2	31.3	7.8
Male	43.3	7.2	9.0	22.6	38.5	22.8
Race						
White	77.9	10.7	11.1	27.2	36.3	14.7
Black	10.1	24.8	15.5	24.8	22.8	12.1
Asian	5.6	10.5	19.3	33.3	27.2	9.6
Other	6.4	13.2	14.0	20.9	35.7	16.3
Employment (hrs)						
0	49.1	11.7	11.7	29.1	33.8	13.6
10	22.5	11.1	11.6	28.8	35.4	13.1
20	19.5	13.4	12.4	21.7	36.4	16.2
30	5.7	10.4	17.4	24.3	34.8	13.0
40	3.2	24.2	12.1	16.7	24.2	22.7
Age						
19 or younger	57.6	10.4	14.3	30.0	33.8	11.5
20 and older	42.5	14.7	9.3	22.7	35.2	18.1
Educational Level						
Freshman	31.4	13.3	16.1	31.2	28.5	10.8
Sophomore	28.9	7.0	10.5	28.6	41.2	12.8
Junior	24.2	13.4	9.8	23.6	36.2	17.1
Senior	15.5	18.2	10.8	20.4	30.9	19.7
Living Situation						
On-Campus Dorm	55.2	10.6	13.6	29.9	33.4	12.4
Off-Campus Apt/House	38.7	13.9	9.9	22.9	35.8	17.6
On-Campus Apt	3.7	15.8	11.8	23.7	39.5	9.2
Other	2.4	18.8	14.6	27.1	27.1	12.5
Internet Connection Home						
High-speed	88.9	10.0	11.5	27.6	36.0	15.1
Dialup	8.3	27.4	22.0	20.2	20.8	9.5
No Connection	2.8	40.4	5.3	26.3	24.6	3.5
Major in the College of:						
Social Science	24.8	15.3	12.5	25.0	34.0	13.1
Business	12.0	10.2	12.7	27.5	34.0	15.6
Natural Science	11.7	13.1	11.0	27.8	33.3	14.8
Comm. Arts/Sciences	10.6	6.5	10.6	20.4	10.7	21.8
Engineering	6.9	7.1	7.9	27.1	37.1	20.7
Human Ecology	5.7	16.5	11.3	35.7	30.4	6.1
Undecided	10.1	9.7	14.6	30.1	35.4	10.2
Other	18.2	14.3	13.5	27.8	31.8	12.7
Base Percentage of Sample:	100.0	12.3	12.2	26.9	34.4	14.3

Table 10 provides the distribution of thirteen survey items representing the primary dependent variables employed in this study. The response categories differed across these questions, and so the table demarcates five groups in a non-specific manner: zero, low, medium, high, and extreme amount of participation. Individuals were asked to recall their participation since 2000, and the data indicate that a larger amount of people were introduced to, and partook in, the behavior with each subsequent year. For instance, almost half (47.8%) had not downloaded a single MP3 file in 2000. In 2001, 34.8% did not participate at all, and in 2002, only 1/5th of those surveyed (21.9%) did not download any music. This trend is mirrored in the average number of MP3s downloaded per month over those three years as well. In 2001, 63% downloaded at least one MP3 each month; in 2002 that percentage increased to 78.1%, and by 2003 it was 80.8%.

Though data collection took place over the course of three months, it is notable that since the beginning of 2003, only 14.6% had never downloaded a music file and that 59.4% could be classified as "high" or "extreme" participants in the phenomenon. Finally, it is notable that a sizable 61.6% disclosed that they had obtained at least one complete music album in MP3 format online. This underscores the fact that MP3 file downloading is not just "a song here and a song there," but often involves calculated acquisition of the contents of entire CDs, presumably for the purposes of using those as a substitute for purchasing the album from a store.

Table 10. Distribution of Music Piracy Variables (N=2032)

	Zero	Low	Med	High	Extreme
How many MP3 files have you downloaded:	%	%	%	%	%
in the last week?	41.9	21.1	12.8	9.8	14.3
in the last month?	27.5	32.1	17.4	11.7	11.2
since the beginning of 2003?	14.6	6.8	19.2	34.4	25.0
on average per month?	19.2	48.6	18.8	8.2	5.1
on average per week one year ago?	23.4	25.2	21.3	16.2	13.9
on average per month one year ago?	21.9	31.7	22.8	14.8	8.7
on average per week exactly two years ago?	37.4	25.6	16.8	10.6	9.5
on average per month two years ago?	37.0	29.8	17.0	9.8	6.4
in 2002?	21.9	7.8	24.7	37.0	8.7
in 2001?	34.8	10.0	24.7	24.9	5.7
in 2000?	47.8	10.8	21.1	16.5	3.7
over the course of your life thus far?	12.3	12.2	26.9	34.4	14.3
How many complete albums have you downloaded?	38.4	28.6	12.5	8.6	11.9

Though not examined in any bivariate or multivariate analyses, it is informative to discuss some other findings related to MP3 participation gleaned from the survey. For instance, of those who do spend time each week looking for MP3s, 35.1% spend more than one hour engaged in that activity and 9.9% spend at least three hours. Additionally, while 36.7% download 100% and upload 0% of their participation time, 41.3 upload at least 25% of that time. Two-fifths of the sample (41.8%) have created an audio CD from MP3 files, 5.2% have made an MP3 file themselves, and 33.6% have done both. Moreover, 64.8% of respondents listen to MP3s on their computer and listen to them after burning them to CD or transferring them to a portable MP3 player. Finally, 31.4% disclosed they share their MP3 files with others, 2.8% stated that they sell them, and 4.4% stated that they do both activities.

Three questions related to ethical, moral, and legal perceptions of MP3 participation also provided some valuable insight into the minds and motives of those surveyed. A sizable 91.2% stated that receiving or providing MP3s should not be illegal. More specifically, 54% believed that MP3 participation is completely appropriate on ethical, moral, and legal grounds. Over one-fifth (21.4%) felt that it is unethical and/or immoral but still appropriate behavior, while 6.3% believed that the fact it is unethical and/or immoral renders it inappropriate. A respectable 14.5% stated that from their perspective, downloading or uploading MP3s is illegal but ethical and/or moral and therefore appropriate. Only 3.9% felt that the activity was unethical, immoral, and illegal and accordingly inappropriate. By extension, 49.4% stated that they participate because they do not believe it is illegal, while 25.4% participate even though they believe it is illegal. Among those who refrain from participating, 8% do so because they believe it is illegal, while 6.9% do so for other unspecified reasons. These figures not only highlight mass ignorance regarding the existence and applicability of copyright law to the digital domain and intellectual property found online, but also demonstrate how perceptions of what is illegal, unethical, or immoral do not necessarily constrain certain behaviors.

BIVARIATE STATISTICS

Bivariate statistics are used to measure the presence and strength of a relationship between two variables. Before discussing the findings from correlation and ANOVA tests, a summary of the construction of the independent and dependent variables is necessary. As mentioned, CFA with Promax rotation[37] was employed on the subsets of train, attitudinal and behavioral self-control, and social learning variables to ensure that each group of observable measures was specifically representative of the unobservable construct it sought to measure. The resultant continuous factor score variables were utilized as independent variables throughout the multivariate analyses. With regard to the thirteen dependent variables, a summary scale variable ranging from 13 to 65 (as each question has answer choices of 1, 2, 3, 4, or 5) was created to use in bivariate ANOVA procedures and a continuous factor score variable was used in the multivariate models.

With the final factor score variables, a bivariate correlation matrix was created to discover the existence, direction, and strength of relationships among variables (see Table 11). The strongest relationship between predictor and outcome variables was that of differential reinforcement and overall music piracy ($r = .445$, $p \leq .01$), followed by

---

[37] Promax rotation was used because resultant factors are expected to be correlated due to the theories in which the variables are grounded.

differential association (r=.332, p ≤ .01). Both the attitudinal and behavioral measures of self-control were also significantly correlated with music piracy. That is, a lower amount of self-control was linked with a higher amount of MP3 downloading. The correlations, though, were of a comparatively small magnitude.

Indicative of possible multicollinearity and a difficulty to clearly distinguish between the four tenets of social learning theory was the correlation between differential association and differential reinforcement (.682). This is not too alarming, due to the fact that Akers himself has stated that there are interrelationships among the social learning theory components and that they are not conceptually distinct (Akers, 1977; Akers et al., 1979). Specific to the MP3 phenomenon, having peer associations who participate would positively reinforce one's own participation, and the possibility of losing that peer group - which provide valuable social, emotional, and tangible rewards (MP3 files) to an individual - would serve as negative reinforcement and thereby perpetuate that person's involvement. Thus, the theoretical overlap between the two measures is obvious. Strictly concerning the theoretical variables, notable findings included a significant correlation between the attitudinal and behavioral measures of self-control (r=.070, p ≤ .01), and between strain and behavioral self-control (r=.187, p ≤ .01).

Table 11. Bivariate Correlation Matrix of Variables

	X_1	X_2	X_3	X_4	X_5	X_6	X_7	X_8	X_9	X_{10}	Y
X_1 White	--	.020	-.001	-.134*	-.059*	-.027	.148*	-.124*	.030	.097*	.049*
X_2 Male		--	.027	-.211*	.042	.041	.046*	.086*	.035	.085*	.296*
X_3 20 or older			--	.055*	-.022	.087*	-.084*	.024	.025	-.092*	.031
X_4 Strain				--	.009	.187*	-.057*	.040	.027	-.058*	-.043
X_5 Attitudinal Self-Control					--	.070*	-.084*	.003	.059*	-.076*	.050*
X_6 Behavioral Self-Control						--	.060*	.056*	.093*	.077*	.183*
X_7 Differential Association							--	-.045*	.219*	.682*	.332*
X_8 Imitation								--	.255*	-.010	.113*
X_9 Definitions									--	.226*	.144*
X_{10} Differential Reinforcement										--	.445*
Y Music Piracy											--

*$p < 0.05$ (two-tailed tests).

Analysis of Variance

Analysis of Variance (ANOVA) allows for the interpretation of mean differences in the dependent variable across the independent variables (Bachman & Paternoster, 1997). Comparisons between actual (identified) and expected variation in category averages is expressed in the F statistic, which is the ratio of the between group variation and the within group variation. If the significance of F is ≥ .05, it can be concluded that the variance in the dependent variable is the same irrespective of the independent variable. Conversely, if the significance of F is < .05, it can be concluded that the variance is different due to the influence of the predictor variable.

H_0: all DV population means are equal ($\mu_1 = \mu_2 = \mu_3$)
H_A: at least one DV population mean differs from others ($\mu_1 \neq \mu_2 \neq \mu_3$)

To reiterate, ANOVA will determine the significance of the difference between means in music piracy participation across values of the predictors. Utilizing a factor score dependent variable provides incomprehensible results when comparing mean levels. As such, the summary scale dependent measure was used, with possible values between 13 (indicating that the respondent had selected "0" for each of the thirteen piracy participation questions) and 65 (indicating that the respondent had selected the highest or largest choice for each of the thirteen piracy participation questions). Significant results were found across Sex, Race, Educational Level, type of Internet connection at home, and the College in which the respondent's major was housed (see Table 12).

Table 12. ANOVA: Demographics and Overall Music Piracy

	Mean	S.D.	F-ratio
Sex			200.252‡
Female	30.445	11.269	
Male	37.906	12.406	
Race			6.807‡
Caucasian	33.973	12.22	
Black	30.175	13.19	
Asian	33.781	11.18	
Other	35.473	12.54	
Employment (hrs)			.124
0	33.657	12.221	
10	33.515	11.292	
20	34.015	13.034	
30	33.522	12.973	
40	33.672	15.585	
Age			
19 or younger	33.456	11.918	.853
20-older	33.967	12.887	
Educational Level			2.909*
Freshman	32.679	12.453	
Sophomore	34.264	10.873	
Junior	34.581	12.707	
Senior	33.159	13.891	
Living Situation			.075
On-Campus Dorm	33.691	12.029	
Off-Campus Apt/House	34.276	12.268	
On-Campus Apt	33.599	12.696	
Other	33.479	19.941	
Internet Connection at Home			29.755‡
High-speed	34.402	12.022	
Dialup	27.399	12.811	
No Connection	29.018	14.617	
Major in the College of:			8.164‡
Social Science	32.424	12.437	
Business	35.299	13.140	
Natural Science	32.781	12.112	
Comm. Arts/Sciences	37.708	12.515	
Engineering	37.271	11.917	
Human Ecology	31.209	10.414	
Undecided	33.131	11.778	
Other	32.221	12.338	

*$p < 0.05$; †$p < 0.01$; ‡$p < 0.001$ (two-tailed tests).

Specifically, the greatest participants were male, and those who were neither White, Black, nor Asian (i.e., those who fit in the collapsed category of "Other"). The mean for Blacks was significantly different from Whites (mean difference = -3.798 p ≤ .01) and those in the "Other" category (mean difference = -5.298 p ≤ .01). Majors in the College of Communication Arts and Sciences scored the highest mean on this additive dependent variable, and that value was significantly different from those in the Colleges of Human Ecology (mean difference = 6.499 p ≤ .01), Natural Science (mean difference = 4.927 p ≤.01), Social Science (mean difference = 5.284 p ≤ .01), those whose major was Undecided (mean difference = 4.577 p ≤ .01), and those who fit in the category of "Other" (mean difference = 5.487 p ≤ .01) according to the Bonferroni Post Hoc Test, which determines which of the five predictor categories differ significantly from the others in their power to influence the dependent variable in the population. As expected, mean piracy levels were significantly higher for those with high-speed access to the Internet at their residence.

To test Hypothesis 1, ANOVA procedures for Proficiency in Internet Use and Variety of Internet Use were run against the additive measure of overall music piracy. Mean levels of participation were different depending on levels of proficiency and variety to a significant degree (see Table 13). The Bonferroni Post Hoc test indicated that those who used the Internet for 0-5 items were significantly different than those who used the Internet for 6 or more items. The mean difference of music pirating activities between those who used the Internet with the highest variety (9 or more items) compared to those who used it for 1-2 items was 11.786 (p ≤ .01). Similarly, the test revealed that those who were proficient in 0-2 items were significantly different from those who were proficient in 3 or more items. The mean difference between the highest proficiency level and 1-2 items - was 13.564 (p ≤.01). These analyses support Hypothesis 1 by empirically demonstrating that individuals with higher skill levels in using online resources, and those who take greater advantage of all that the Internet has to offer, pirate music to a larger extent than their counterparts.

Table 13. ANOVA: Proficiency and Variety of Internet Use and Overall Music Piracy

	Mean	S. D.	F-ratio
Proficiency in Internet Use			41.647‡
0 items	29.94	11.90	
1-2 items	27.94	11.82	
3-5 items	30.50	11.77	
6-8 items	34.71	11.70	
9 or more items	39.72	12.34	
Variety of Internet Use			66.282‡
0 items	26.05	12.28	
1-2 items	28.63	11.61	
3-5 items	31.54	11.34	
6-8 items	36.09	11.66	
9 or more items	42.20	12.20	

‡p < 0.001 (two-tailed tests).

Eta squared (η^2) measures how much total variation can be attributed to the variation that occurs between groups, and was obtained by dividing the Between Groups Sum of Squares by the Within Groups Sum of Squares. For Variety of Internet Use, η^2 was .082, and for Proficiency of Internet Use η^2 was .131. That is, 8.2% and 13.1% of variation in music pirating activities can be explained by variety in, and proficiency of, Internet use. As an assessment of strength, both of these variables indicate a relatively weak relationship between the explanatory and criterion variables.

MULTIVARIATE STATISTICS

Ordinary Least Squares (OLS) Regression

As a preliminary test, OLS linear regression analyses was performed, regressing the general strain, self-control, and social learning factor score predictor variables on the factor score outcome variable of overall music piracy (see Table 14). Also included were control variables of Race, Sex, and Age. With regard to the controls, a dummy variable of "White" was created since 77.9% of the sample belonged to this racial group. In an ideal model, all NonWhites would not be analyzed together. However, since such a comparatively small amount of respondents belonged to a NonWhite group, this stands out as one limitation of the current research. OLS regression assists in determining the degree to which a linear combination of certain predictors significantly explains variation in the criterion variable of music piracy.

Table 14. OLS Regression: Predictor Factor Scores on Overall Piracy Factor Score

Variables	B	Std. Error
Constant	-.291	.046
White	.042	.046
Male	.493‡	.039
20 or older	.107†	.038
Strain	.006	.020
Attitudinal Self-Control^	.068‡	.019
Behavioral Self-Control^	.125‡	.019
Differential Association	.068†	.026
Imitation	.094‡	.020
Definitions	-.006	.020
Differential Reinforcement	.380‡	.026
R^2	0.302	
Adjusted R^2	0.299	

*$p < 0.05$; †$p < 0.01$; ‡$p < 0.001$ (two-tailed tests).
^Greater magnitude in these factor scores indicates lower self-control

With regard to the demographic factors, males and those over age 20 were significantly more likely to pirate music than females and those 19 and younger, respectively, controlling for the effects of all the other variables. Strain was not significantly related to music piracy, while both the attitudinal and behavioral measures of self-control were significantly related. This is a preliminary indication that those with lower self-control pirate music to a greater degree than those with higher levels of that latent dispositional trait. Concerning the four components of social learning theory, Differential association, imitation, and differential reinforcement were found to each be significant predictors of music piracy when controlling for all other predictors, while definitions was found to be unrelated. The most influential variable, based on the size of the coefficient, was differential reinforcement[38]. This attests to the importance of perceived and actual rewards and punishments stemming from engaging in digital intellectual property theft. It also points to possible policy solutions that may be implemented in an effort to shift the cost-benefit ratio in favor of the law, so that individuals "think twice" about participation in the activity. More policy implications will be discussed in Chapter 7.

Tests for multicollinearity corroborated the notion of possible overlap in the operationalization and measurement of social learning theory tenets (Long, 1997). Tolerance and Variance Inflation Factor statistics for strain, self-control, imitation, and definitions were unproblematic, but differential association and differential reinforcement revealed a notable issue. Variance proportions for the two showed very high loadings on the same dimension. To note, a comprehensive analyses of the social learning theory measures and the difficulties inherent in conceptualizing and measuring them as distinct elements was provided in Chapter 4.

Limitations of Ordinary Least Squares (OLS) Regression

Specific regression models with ordinal-level variables have gained popularity in their use since the mid 1980s, due to biases inherent in OLS regression analyses. Analyses using outcome measures that violate the assumptions of OLS regression tend to result in biased standard errors (heteroskedasticity), abnormally distributed residuals, and probability predictions that are difficult or impossible to pragmatically reconcile (Long, 1997:39). Additionally, the functional form requirement of a linear model - that a one unit increase in x results in a constant increase in y, irrespective of the value of x - is not practical when considering probabilities as outcomes. The influence of x tends to wane as probabilities approach 0 or 1 (Long, 1997). Finally, OLS is based on a linear relationship between variables, and assumes that the dependent items are at the interval-ratio level. Also, it presupposes that the distance between the categories of the criterion variable is equal.

The dependent variables representing participation in music piracy in this analyses are all ordinal-level measures. Each one, in fact, is a

---

[38] The coefficients of the theoretical variables in the regression analyses can be compared with each other because they are factor scores and thereby standardized.

transformation of an underlying continuous variable, where neatly observable categories are specified and ordered but where the distance between them is unspecified and unknown (Winship & Mare, 1984). It cannot be assumed that the values of an ordinal variable are equidistant from each other; as such, additional parameters that represent those unknown distances (thresholds) should be included in order to more accurately assess the effect of the predictors on the criterion variable (Maddala, 1983; McKelvey & Zavoina, 1975).

Logistic Regression

The premise of this study is to test the applicability of general strain, self-control, and social learning theory on participation in digital music piracy. The thirteen questions created as dependent measures, all intended to reveal a particular frequency of pirating activity over certain time periods or durations, have five possible response choices. These include zero as the first choice, and then incrementally advance higher - depending on the question asked. For example, for the question "How many total MP3s have you downloaded over the course of your life thus far?," the response set includes "0," "1-100," "101-500," "501-2000," and "2000 or more." In general, it appears that this research should not attempt to differentiate between very specific levels of pirating activity based on certain theoretical tenets. That is, it is not useful theoretically or practically to determine that strain - for example - is not significantly related to individuals who have downloaded 1-100 MP3s over the course of their life, but is significantly related to those who have downloaded 101-500 MP3s. It is more useful, rather, to ascertain how these theoretical predictors differentiate those that do not pirate from those that do.

Accordingly, the decision was made to collapse the second, third, fourth, and fifth response choices into one category, and create a dichotomous variable for each of the thirteen dependent measures so that 0 equaled no participation, and 1 equaled participation, in digital music piracy. Thirteen separate logistic regression analyses were then run with the seven theoretical factor score variables of strain, attitudinal self-control, behavioral self-control, differential association, imitation, definitions, and differential reinforcement. Only the six most relevant and informative are discussed below.

The logit model allows for the conclusion that a unit change in x will result in a logit change in y by β, holding all other variables constant. The dependent variable employed is generally dichotomous and can take the value of 1 with a probability of success θ. The independent variable is not constrained by requirements to be linearly related, normally distributed, or to have equal variances in the groups. Indeed, a nonlinear relationship between the explanatory and criterion variables is tested using the logistic regression function, and the model is fit appropriately via maximum likelihood estimation. The logit transformation of the probability of success θ can be represented with the following equation:

$$\theta = \frac{e^{(\alpha + \beta 1 \chi 1 + \beta 1 \chi 1 + \beta i \chi i)}}{1 + e^{(\alpha + \beta 1 \chi 1 + \beta 1 \chi 1 + \beta i \chi i)}}$$

Understanding a logit change is not intuitive; therefore, odds ratios (Exp(B) values) provide a more logical way of interpreting the parameters. If the odds ratio is greater than 1, the odds of the predicted value of y=1 based on a one unit change in x are Exp(B) times larger; if less than one, the odds of the predicted value of y=1 based on a one unit change in x are Exp(B) times smaller (Long, 1997:80-81). To reiterate, the logit model specifically speaks to the underlying latent variable that stimulates the crossing of the threshold from 0 to 1 – from no participation in music piracy to participation in that act, and assesses the odds of one or the other value of the binary dependent variable (i.e., have not vs. have pirated music) occurring due to the values of the predictors.

The first model utilized the dependent variable of "How many MP3 files have you downloaded in the last month?" (see Table 15). Consistent with findings from the OLS regression model, being male increased the likelihood of having downloaded at least one MP3 in the last month by 1.986, controlling for the other variables. Attitudinal self-control was significantly related to the dependent measure, in that a lower amount increased the odds an individual downloaded at least one file in the last month by 1.159. Differential association was also a significant predictor, increasing the odds of MP3 participation by 1.273. The strongest predictor by far was differential reinforcement, and its influence increased the odds of MP3 downloading by 1.959. While all thirteen dependent variables were initially run in this analyses, the results from only the six most relevant outcome measures are provided in Tables 15 and 16 in order to avoid redundancy.

Table 15. Logistic Regression: MP3 files downloaded in last month, since 01/2003, and in average month one year ago

	MP3s in last month			MP3s since January 2003			MP3s - avg. month – 1 yr ago		
	b	S.E.	Exp(B)	b	S.E.	Exp(B)	b	S.E.	Exp(B)
Constant	1.244	.138	3.471	2.208	.183	9.095	1.012	.141	2.752
White	-.239	.137	.787	.066	.172	1.068	.132	.142	1.141
Male	.686‡	.117	1.986	.661‡	.161	1.936	.714‡	.130	2.042
20 or Older	-.516‡	.110	.597	-.326*	.149	.722	.272*	.123	1.312
Strain	.103	.058	1.108	.054	.077	1.056	-.119	.063	.888
Attitudinal Self-Control^	.147*	.057	1.159	.336‡	.078	1.400	.210†	.062	1.234
Behavioral Self-Control^	.106	.059	1.112	.186*	.081	1.205	.216†	.065	1.241
Differential Association	.242†	.076	1.273	.642‡	.101	1.900	.263†	.082	1.301
Imitation	-.023	.061	.978	-.227*	.090	.797	.033	.068	1.033
Definitions	-.051	.062	.950	-.241*	.095	.786	-.130	.070	.878
Differential Reinforcement	.673†	.074	1.959	.833‡	.091	2.301	.753‡	.079	2.124
-2 Log Likelihood	2045.471			1229.959			1781.342		
Cox & Snell R²	.156			.201			.161		
Nagelkerke R²	.232			.357			.248		

*p < 0.05; †p < 0.01; ‡p < 0.001 (two-tailed tests). ^Greater magnitude in these factor scores indicates lower self-control

Table 16. Logistic Regression: MP3s downloaded in 2002, total complete MP3 albums, and total MP3s downloaded over one's lifetime

	MP3s in 2002			Total Albums Downloaded			MP3s over lifetime		
	b	S.E.	Exp(B)	b	S.E.	Exp(B)	t	S.E.	Exp(B)
Constant	.959	.140	2.608	.332	.119	1.394	2.177	.190	8.315
White	.054	.142	1.056	-.102	.120	.903	.293	.178	1.340
Male	.864‡	.131	2.372	.567‡	.101	1.762	1.021‡	.181	2.777
20 or Older	.383†	.123	1.466	.045	.098	1.046	-.205	.160	0.315
Strain	-.047	.062	.954	.005	.051	1.005	.037	.082	1.038
Attitudinal Self-Control^	.175†	.061	1.192	.081	.049	1.084	.283‡	.082	1.334
Behavioral Self-Control^	.197†	.065	1.217	.158†	.051	1.171	.201*	.087	1.221
Differential Association	.275†	.081	1.316	.027	.067	1.028	.782‡	.109	2.201
Imitation	.011	.067	1.011	.163†	.053	1.177	-.282†	.098	0.749
Definitions	-.210†	.069	.811	.015	.053	1.015	-.314‡	.106	0.731
Differential Reinforcement	.699‡	.078	2.012	.519‡	.068	1.680	.717‡	.094	2.048
-2 Log Likelihood	1799.268			2505.288			1079.751		
Cox & Snell R²	.152			.094			.191		
Nagelkerke R²	.233			.128			.365		

*p < 0.05; †p < 0.01; ‡p < 0.001 (two-tailed tests).   ^Greater magnitude in these factor scores indicates lower self-control

The findings for the demographic variables were relatively consistent across the models. While race (as measured by the "White" dummy variable) did not affect the outcome variable, being male increased the likelihood of having pirated across all models. The effects of age were significant in all six models but the direction of the relationship alternated depending on the specific dependent variable. As such, nothing conclusive can be said about the predictive capacity of age in differentiating those who do not pirate music online from those who do.

Overall, strain was not significantly related to MP3 participation in any of the models. This contradicts Hypotheses 2, which stated that each "general" theory is appropriately named and has the capacity to explain variation in music piracy. General strain theory, according to these analyses, is not a significant predictor of the unlawful activity in question.

When controlling for the predictive effects of all the other variables, both attitudinal self-control and behavioral self-control were significant in five of the six models. These findings were also all in the expected direction, and indicated that lower self-control increases the odds of music pirating activities. When considering the model, "How many total MP3s have you downloaded over the course of your life thus far?" and a response set of either "0" or "1 or more," an increase in attitudinal self-control increased the odds of belonging to the "1 or more" group by 1.334 (see Table 16). Similarly, an increase in behavioral self-control increased the odds of having pirated at least one MP3 by 1.221. This supports Hypotheses 2, which predicted a positive significant relationship between the self-control and dependent measures. In accordance with Hypotheses 3, the elements of social learning theory were most strongly related to music piracy. Specifically, differential association was significantly and positively related to MP3 participation in five of the six models, and differential reinforcement was significant in all six.

This last model revealed findings that are perhaps most representative of music pirating activity since it concerned lifetime MP3 downloading. It had the largest Nagelkerke R^2 of any of the models (36.5% explained variance) and had the best model fit (-2 Log Likelihood = 1079.751). While general strain was not a significant predictor, both measures of self-control were significantly and positively related. Each of the four elements of social learning were significantly related, but imitation and definitions both decreased the odds that the respondent had pirated music. To note, imitation and definitions were significant in some models but the direction of their relationship was not consistent and their predictive power was comparatively small. Therefore, it is difficult to make conclusive statements about their role in music piracy participation. Differential association, though, increased the odds by 2.201, while differential reinforcement increased the odds by 2.048, that the individual had downloaded at least one MP3 over the course of his or her life.

Multinomial Logistic Regression

It is not theoretically or practically useful to determine how the theoretical factor scores explain variance at each of the five *specific* levels of MP3 participation provided as possible response choices. Similar to the example given with the logit analyses, it does not contribute to the knowledge base to know that social learning theory significantly differentiates between those who pirate 101-500 MP3s and those who pirate 1-100 MP3s. It is instructive, however, to examine the discriminating effect that the theories have on *general* levels of involvement in music piracy. Therefore, the next stage of analyses involved taking the initial thirteen dependent measures and recoding them to better understand the theoretical elements that differentiated those individuals who engaged in "Low," "Medium," and "High" amounts of MP3 downloading. This also brought about more proportionate distributions among the categories than the previous analyses in which dichotomous variables were created. To construct these three-category variables, the choices of 1 or 2 were coded as "Low," the choices of 3 and 4 as "Medium," and the choice of 5 as "High." The decision to combine 1 - which equaled zero MP3s, and 2 - which equaled the lowest number of MP3s downloaded among the possible responses for each question, was made because some individuals who have merely dabbled in the activity and experimented with the technology should arguably not be grouped with those who have downloaded a Medium or High amount of digital music[39]. This then facilitated thirteen Multinomial Logistic (MNL) Regression models; only the six most relevant and informative are presented and discussed.

---

[39] Some might posit that a differentiation must be made between "experimentation" and "occasional" use. It seems appropriate to consider those who have downloaded the lowest possible number of MP3s (apart from zero) as experimenters. Those who have downloaded any larger number should at least be considered as "occasional" participants.

MNL regression represents an extension of the logistic regression model when the nominal dependent measure has more than two levels (Hosmer & Lemeshow, 2000; Long, 1997). For this analyses, music piracy is measured at three levels – "Low," "Medium," and "High," and those in the "Low" group are the reference category for the calculation of odds ratios. MNL regression can be utilized to predict the log odds of one outcome as compared to a baseline category by producing two logits simultaneously (where there are three levels) (Hosmer & Lemeshow, 2000; Long, 1997). In this research, the two logits will represent Low as compared to Medium, and Low as compared to High.

If Low is represented as j, the equation for the ith category (i.e., Medium) is as follows:

$$\text{Log } (P_i/P_j) = B_{i0} + B_{i1}X_1 + B_{i2}X_2 + \dots + B_{ip}X_p$$

The coefficients that result must be interpreted as a change in log-odds resulting from a one-unit change in the predictor variable. This is not very intuitive, and so odds-ratios are again used. The odds of i rather than j occurring due to the influence of x can be represented as follows:

$$\Omega_{m \mid n} (x_i) = \text{Exp}(x_i[\beta_i - \beta_j])$$

The relationship of general strain, attitudinal self-control, behavioral self-control, Differential association, imitation, definitions, and differential reinforcement and the likelihood of belonging to groups representing different amounts of MP3 downloading are assessed and depicted in Tables 17 through 22. Again, while all thirteen dependent variables were initially run in this analyses, the results from only the six most relevant outcome measures are presented.

Table 17. Multinomial Logistic: How many MP3s downloaded in the last month?

	Medium			High		
Variables	b	S.E.	Exp(B)	b	S.E.	Exp(B)
Constant	-.712	.131		-2.164	.203	
White	.022	.132	1.022	-.016	.191	.984
Male	.621‡	.110	1.861	1.288‡	.166	3.624
20 or older	-.786‡	.111	.456	-.822‡	.164	.440
Strain	.116*	.056	1.123	.041	.081	1.042
Attitudinal Self-Control^	.077	.054	1.080	.137	.077	1.147
Behavioral Self-Control^	.120*	.054	1.127	.213†	.076	1.237
Differential Association	.078	.074	1.082	.166	.108	1.180
Imitation	.043	.056	1.043	.350‡	.076	1.419
Definitions	.002	.056	1.002	.052	.079	1.054
Differential Reinforcement	.502‡	.080	1.653	.627‡	.127	1.872
Chi-Square				354.988		
-2 Log Likelihood				3355.270		
Cox & Snell R²				.160		
Nagelkerke R²				.191		

*p < 0.05; †p < 0.01; ‡p < 0.001 (two-tailed tests).
^Greater magnitude in these factor scores indicates lower self-control

Note: Reference group is low lifetime music piracy (either zero participation, or the lowest possible amount of participation). Medium equals the two largest penultimate MP3 totals in the response set, while High equals the ultimate (and largest) response choice—the highest number of MP3s downloaded as available in the response set.

Music Piracy and Crime Theory

Table 18. Multinomial Logistic: How many MP3s downloaded since the beginning of 2003?

Variables	Medium			High		
	b	S.E.	Exp(B)	b	S.E.	Exp(B)
Constant	1.013	.151		-.159	.185	
White	.241	.149	1.272	.329	.181	1.390
Male	.479‡	.137	1.615	1.055‡	.159	2.871
20 or older	-.292*	.128	.747	-.538‡	.153	.584
Strain	.014	.067	1.014	.063	.079	1.065
Attitudinal Self-Control^	.247‡	.066	1.280	.291‡	.077	1.338
Behavioral Self-Control^	.113	.070	1.120	.371‡	.079	1.449
Differential Association	.470‡	.087	1.601	.438‡	.103	1.549
Imitation	-.124	.073	.883	.049	.082	1.050
Definitions	-.151*	.075	.860	-.006	.085	.994
Differential Reinforcement	.634‡	.082	1.886	1.064‡	.110	2.898
Chi-Square				564.715		
-2 Log Likelihood				3543.040		
Cox & Snell R²				.243		
Nagelkerke R²				.280		

*p < 0.05; †p < 0.01; ‡p < 0.001 (two-tailed tests).
^Greater magnitude in these factor scores indicates lower self-control

Note: Reference group is low lifetime music piracy (either zero participation, or the lowest possible amount of participation). Medium equals the two largest penultimate MP3 totals in the response set, while High equals the ultimate (and largest) response choice the highest number of MP3s downloaded as available in the response set.

Table 19. Multinomial Logistic: How many MP3s downloaded in an average month exactly one year ago?

Variables	Medium			High		
	b	S.E.	Exp(B)	b	S.E.	Exp(B)
Constant	-.668	.125		-2.815	.234	
White	.062	.124	1.064	.067	.212	1.069
Male	.397‡	.103	1.488	1.089‡	.184	2.971
20 or older	.206*	.102	1.229	.373*	.175	1.452
Strain	.062	.053	1.064	.197*	.090	1.218
Attitudinal Self-Control^	.053	.050	1.054	.178*	.085	1.195
Behavioral Self-Control^	.190‡	.052	1.210	.370‡	.083	1.448
Differential Association	.184†	.070	1.201	-.035	.116	.966
Imitation	.099	.052	1.105	.304‡	.085	1.356
Definitions	.034	.053	1.035	.176*	.089	1.193
Differential Reinforcement	.470‡	.074	1.600	.837‡	.141	2.309
Chi-Square				314.337		
-2 Log Likelihood				3398.457		
Cox & Snell R²				.143		
Nagelkerke R²				.171		

*p < 0.05; †p < 0.01; ‡p < 0.001 (two-tailed tests).
^Greater magnitude in these factor scores indicates lower self-control

Note: Reference group is low lifetime music piracy (either zero participation, or the lowest possible amount of participation). Medium equals the two largest penultimate MP3 totals in the response set, while High equals the ultimate (and largest) response choice – the highest number of MP3s downloaded as available in the response set.

Table 20. Multinomial Logistic: How many MP3s did you personally download in 2002?

Variables	Medium			High		
	b	**S.E.**	**Exp(B)**	**b**	**S.E.**	**Exp(B)**
Constant	.206	.127		-2.568	.252	
White	.316*	.128	1.372	.425	.229	1.529
Male	.672‡	.116	1.957	1.605‡	.200	4.976
20 or older	.352†	.112	1.422	.460*	.187	1.584
Strain	-.023	.057	.977	.015	.096	1.015
Attitudinal Self-Control^	.118*	.055	1.125	.185*	.092	1.204
Behavioral Self-Control^	.164†	.058	1.178	.364‡	.091	1.440
Differential Association	.256†	.074	1.291	.100	.124	1.105
Imitation	-.062	.060	.940	.177	.093	1.194
Definitions	-.104	.061	.901	-.046	.096	.955
Differential Reinforcement	.590‡	.073	1.804	.929‡	.143	2.531
Chi-Square				404.036		
-2 Log Likelihood				3136.235		
Cox & Snell R^2				.180		
Nagelkerke R^2				.219		

*$p < 0.05$; †$p < 0.01$; ‡$p < 0.001$ (two-tailed tests).
^Greater magnitude in these factor scores indicates lower self-control

Note: Reference group is low lifetime music piracy (either zero participation, or the lowest possible amount of participation). Medium equals the two largest penultimate MP3 totals in the response set, while High equals the ultimate (and largest) response choice the highest number of MP3s downloaded as available in the response set.

Table 21. Multinomial Logistic: How many total complete music albums in MP3 format have you obtained online?

Variables	Medium			High		
	B	S.E.	Exp(B)	B	S.E.	Exp(B)
Constant	-1.169	.139		-2.224	.189	
White	-.206	.138	.814	-.205	.178	.814
Male	.597‡	.118	1.816	.956‡	.154	2.601
20 or older	-.281*	.118	.755	.084	.149	1.088
Strain	.053	.060	1.054	.007	.077	1.007
Attitudinal Self-Control^	.089	.057	1.093	.146*	.073	1.157
Behavioral Self-Control^	.197†	.057	1.218	.188*	.073	1.207
Differential Association	-.074	.079	.929	-.025	.101	.976
Imitation	.222‡	.059	1.249	.328‡	.072	1.388
Definitions	.078	.061	1.081	.059	.075	1.061
Differential Reinforcement	.338‡	.082	1.401	.625‡	.118	1.868
Chi-Square				404.036		
-2 Log Likelihood				3136.235		
Cox & Snell R^2				.180		
Nagelkerke R^2				.219		

*p < 0.05; †p < 0.01; ‡p < 0.001 (two-tailed tests).
^Greater magnitude in these factor scores indicates lower self-control

Note: Reference group is low lifetime music piracy (either zero participation, or the lowest possible amount of participation). Medium equals the two largest penultimate MP3 totals in the response set, while High equals the ultimate (and largest) response choice – the highest number of MP3s downloaded as available in the response set.

Table 22. Multinomial Logistic: How many total MP3s have you downloaded over the course of your life thus far?

Variables	Medium			High		
	B	S.E.	Exp(B)	B	S.E.	Exp(B)
Constant	.496	.135		-2.073	.224	
White	.456†	.137	1.577	.511*	.205	1.668
Male	.677‡	.128	1.969	1.657‡	.180	5.246
20 or older	.148	.121	1.160	.729‡	.170	2.073
Strain	.030	.062	1.031	.050	.088	1.051
Attitudinal Self-Control^	.183†	.060	1.201	.265†	.085	1.303
Behavioral Self-Control^	.205†	.064	1.228	.391‡	.086	1.479
Differential Association	.414‡	.080	1.512	.344†	.114	1.411
Imitation	-.072	.067	.930	.162	.087	1.176
Definitions	-.036	.068	.964	-.061	.090	.940
Differential Reinforcement	.551‡	.077	1.736	1.200‡	.134	3.320
Chi-Square				549.928		
-2 Log Likelihood				3196.982		
Cox & Snell R^2				.237		
Nagelkerke R^2				.282		

*p < 0.05; †p < 0.01; ‡p < 0.001 (two-tailed tests).
^Greater magnitude in these factor scores indicates lower self-control

Note: Reference group is low lifetime music piracy (either zero participation, or the lowest possible amount of participation). Medium equals the two largest penultimate MP3 totals in the response set, while High equals the ultimate (and largest) response choice the highest number of MP3s downloaded as available in the response set.

To begin, the Chi-Square statistic was significant across each model and indicated that the group of independent variables is significantly linked to the respective dependent variables in the analyses. Concerning the theoretical measures, general strain was significantly and positively related in only two of the six models. The dependent variables in these models were: "How many MP3 files have you downloaded in the last month?" and "How many MP3s did you download in an average month exactly one year ago?" Nonetheless, the strength of general strain in predicting music piracy was comparatively unimpressive, and so overall not much can be said about the capacity of that theory to explain MP3 participation.

When considering the number of MP3 files downloaded by the respondent in an average month exactly one year ago, low attitudinal self-control increased the odds of an individual's participation in "High" as compared to "Low" amounts of music piracy, while low behavioral self-control increased the odds of MP3 participation in both "Medium" as compared to "Low," and "High" as compared to "Low" amounts. Imitation significantly differentiated those who downloaded "Low" amounts of MP3s from those who downloaded "High" amounts, increasing the odds of belonging to the "High" group by 1.356. Differential reinforcement was the strongest predictor, and had the greatest effect when evaluating its influence on the "High" group; that theoretical tenet increased the odds of belonging to the "Medium" group by 1.600 and increased the odds of belonging to the "High" group by 2.309. This trend was consistently found throughout all of the multinomial logistic analyses.

The last model - "How many total MP3s have you downloaded over the course of your life thus far?" - indicated the best fit based on the Chi-Square statistic (see Table 30). Being male increased one's likelihood of belonging to the "Medium" and "High" group, as compared to the "Low" group, while being age 20 or older increased one's likelihood of belonging to the "High" group as compared to the "Low" group. Attitudinal and behavioral self-control were both significantly and positively related. That is, lower self-control (measured either through attitudinal or behavioral variables) increased the odds that an individual participated in "Medium" or "High" amounts of MP3 downloading. To note, behavioral self-control had a stronger influence than did attitudinal self-control. With regard to the social learning theory variables, differential association was a significant predictor and increased the odds of belonging to the "Medium" group by 1.512 and the odds of belonging to the "High" group by 1.411. Differential reinforcement was also significant and increased the odds of belonging to the "Medium" group by 1.736 and the "High" group by 3.320.

Imitation was significantly and positively related in three of the six models. Though further exploration of this variable is required, the role of behavior, attitudes, techniques, and beliefs to observe and emulate on the Internet may differentiate music pirates among their quantity of music piracy participation, but not between non-pirates and pirates.

Definitions was significant in two of the six models, but the direction of its influence was not constant and the coefficients were quite small. Accordingly, not much can be said about its influence - and this finding resonates across all of the statistical models in this research.

CHAPTER 6

Explaining the Relevance of the Crime Theories

The preceding analyses has clarified the relationship between the three general criminological theories and digital music piracy. Two hypotheses were supported; one was rejected. A host of questions stemming from the findings merit discussion in an attempt to crystallize the statistical relationships into concrete knowledge. To begin, what are some possible reasons as to why general strain theory was not a significant predictor of music piracy? Individuals who experience strain from certain negative life experiences are probably not more likely to venture online to download intellectual property from Internet sources. Though asserted as a "general" theory and purportedly universal in its explanatory power to all forms of wrongdoing, this was not the case when examining frequency of online music pirating behavior as the outcome variable in this study. This could be for a variety of reasons. General strain theory may not be extensible to cyberspace and to research that commingles real-life and the online realm. It also may be that negative affect ensuing from strain is reconciled through behaviors or actions in real-life, rather than reserved for manifestation when a person is in front of a computer connected to the Internet.

In addition, these traditional measures of strain involving the experience of real-life stressors and misfortunes may be inappropriate for analyzing this particular phenomenon. Strain perhaps needs to be specifically *measured* as resulting from the inability to obtain or purchase the desired commodity of music, rather than as resulting from problems in one's day-to-day living experience. This coheres with initial conceptualizations of Robert Merton's (1938) strain. Merton argued that persons are limited in their access to socially approved goals and the means to achieve those goals. Music is valued by a great number of

Americans, and meets a variety of psychological, emotional, and social needs. Possessing certain songs or recordings is a broad desire among many, and the acquisition of music is a culturally-promulgated goal for at least some subgroups in America (e.g., teenagers). The legitimate method to obtain music is by purchasing it on audio CD from a retail establishment, which requires financial resources. Accordingly, restricted access to music may lead to feelings of strain, which can be compounded by the strain resulting from a lack of funds requisite to resolve the initial strain.

Five modes of adaptation were proffered by Merton (1938) in order to counter the resultant dissonance: conformity, innovation, ritualism, retreatism, and rebellion. Innovation is carried out by individuals who accept culturally- and socially-promulgated goals, but have been thwarted in their attempts to achieve them in a legitimate fashion, and so are inclined to develop another (unethical or unlawful) method to do so (Merton, 1938). The criminological literature base tends to utilize generic measures of strain that are not specific to the dependent variable, and the current research followed that trend. However, perhaps greater consideration of the *uniqueness of the crime* is necessary when conceptualizing and operationalizing predictors. As such, four questions included in the survey but not initially designated as strain measures may be useful in more precisely (but not perfectly) measuring strain in general as a predictive influence. These included: "I would be more likely to download/upload MP3s if I could not afford the purchase price of the music on CD?"; "I would be more likely to download/upload MP3s if I needed the music and wouldn't be able to obtain it any other way?"; "I would be more likely to upload/download MP3s because I can't afford to waste money on a music CD that might only have 1 or 2 good songs?"; "I would be more likely to upload/download MP3s because without the ability to evaluate the music, I will not be able to determine if I really want to purchase it on CD?." These focus on strain induced by financial limitations – likely the most prominent type among university students, even if many come from middle-class families.

To test the utility of these more specific measures, a factor score variable was created from these items, and had a high reliability alpha value (.766) and factor loadings over .7. This variable was run through the same logistic and multinomial regression models, and while stronger support was found for general strain theory as a positively related predictor of music piracy, variability and mixed results were still found to some extent across the models. As such, a relationship between general strain and MP3 participation is identifiable but not consistent among the various measures of the phenomenon. general strain, then, must be operationalized in a more informed manner, based on the inconclusive results of the current analyses.

Finally, copyright infringement through MP3s may be considered by some as a white-collar crime, simply due to its technologically-advanced and comparatively sophisticated nature. Under that assumption, it is useful to compare music piracy with another white-collar crime - embezzlement - since the latter involves traditional strain to some degree. Donald Cressey (1953) argued that embezzlement occurred when an individual had an unsharable financial problem and could use his or her position of trust to "get back in the black," could justify the behavior as acceptable and necessary, and was presented with the right opportunity. Music piracy does not seem to result from the "unsharable financial problem" of not being able to afford a music CD, even though rationalizations are used and an attractive opportunity is presented. Indeed, obtaining digital music to satisfy a personal desire cannot be equated to the misappropriation of funds to address a financial need for survival. Strain, then, may only play a determinative role in wrongdoing that is related to a significant and life-impacting necessity.

The second question arising from the results is as follows: Why was low attitudinal and behavioral self-control significantly and positively related to digital music piracy? Intuitively, one would think that an individual's inability to regulate and constrain his or her behavior in the real world would translate into an inability to refrain from participation in questionable online activities when presented with an attractive opportunity. This was depicted in the analyses, which generally showed that lower self-control - both measured behaviorally and attitudinally - increased participation in the phenomenon. Interestingly, mean scores created from both types of self-control measures indicated that the distribution of responses were negatively skewed. This is inconsistent with general estimations of self-control among university students; one might believe that because of their enrollment and participation in higher learning, they possess more self-control than their counterparts who are not enrolled in a university. Based on the measures employed in this study, however, the attitudes and behaviors of students seem to decidedly indicate a lack of self-control – which then seems to manifest itself in music piracy to some degree. Why, then, does this lack of self-control result in pirating music online, rather than shoplifting it from a retail store? This question warrants some discussion.

Gottfredson and Hirschi (1990) remark that criminal acts require little skill or planning. It seems, though, that MP3 participation involves methodical actions which - while quickly routinized - still necessitate a certain amount of skill and planning. Conversely, shoplifting a music CD from a retail establishment involves only the spontaneous seizing of an attractive opportunity. Prior to these findings, one might conclude that the former would be favored by those with more self-control, and the latter by those with less self-control. The sample involved in this study, however, has revealed a disproportionate amount of low self-control (based on the response choices in the survey items). Furthermore, it is likely that most – if not all - individuals are attracted by the possibility of acquiring music at no cost. Music is a valued commodity for the emotional, psychological, and relational benefits it provides among the college-aged population, and this demographic group typically has little discretionary income to purchase CDs at their whim.

If one assumes that individuals are equally motivated to obtain free music, perhaps one of the primary variables that distinguish those of the college age-group (17-24) who would engage in larceny from a store from those who would partake in music piracy online is their *level* of low self-control. While this particular sample of university students indicated a disproportionate amount of low self-control, it is possible that they still have more self-control in general than those who are not in school but are still of the same age. As such, those enrolled in higher education – though lacking in self-control because of their age – are more inclined to learn the methodical actions to download music from the Internet for free than to shoplift it because they do have more self-control than their non-college-going peers. Furthermore, it is very possible that students simply do not equate downloading with "stealing," as the former is everyday behavior while the latter is not. Even if they do view downloading and shoplifting in a similar light, it is also possible that the former is considered a "smarter" and more admirable crime, and therefore attracts much more participation. Both of these notions merits deeper inquiry in future studies.

The third question is relevant to the strongest theoretical predictor: why does differential reinforcement increase the likelihood and amount of music piracy among respondents? Evidently, the consequences that result from the behavior are very potent influences in its perpetuation and perhaps even its escalation. It is highly likely that the beneficial outcome of receiving valued goods at no cost (MP3 files) increases participation in downloading. Similarly, the relative lack of punitive repercussions in the form of detection, apprehension, and penalty promotes the behavior as well. Intrinsic and extrinsic rewards, and the comparative lack of punishment, commingle to create the predominant contributive element in music piracy. Sanctions do not seem to effectuate much in the way of deterrence; this will be discussed further in Chapter 7. Policy intended to reduce the frequency and prevalence of this phenomenon must somehow decrease the rewards that accompany participation.

The fourth question concerns the reasons behind the role of differential association as the second strongest predictor. As previously stated, MP3 participation is a wildly social event online, and techniques, motives, rationalizations, and beliefs in support of the activity are taught through peer associations. Indeed, the prevailing atmosphere on the Internet is incontrovertibly pro-MP3, and thousands of venues exist where computer-mediated communication between individuals can encourage and foster the behavior. As increasing amounts of new participants internalize the attitudes and actions that contribute to music piracy, they then fulfill an instructive role to others who might be fresh to the "scene." This consequently and continually enlarges the circle of individuals who partake in the phenomenon. Differential association was significant in five of the six binary logistic models, and in four of the six multinomial logistic models. That is, the tenet largely differentiates between nonpirates and pirates, and also – to some extent - the *amount* of music piracy committed by pirates. This is consonant with the role that differential association is believed to play in introducing individuals to wrongdoing, and the fact that it is the first occurring component of social learning theory (Akers, 1979). To summarize, peer associations acquaint people to the behavior and reinforce its appropriateness. Once a person becomes acquainted with MP3s, the intensity of associations appears to affect the *level* of immersion in music piracy.

The fifth question is related to the contributory role of imitation in differentiating music pirates in their *amount* of MP3 participation (e.g., Low from Medium, Low from High) in three of the six models, but not differentiating persons who pirate from those who do not. A possible explanation is as follows. Once individuals are introduced to the activity, their frequency of participation would presumably increase upon observing and learning other methods of obtaining MP3 files, and other sources and venues on the Internet from where they might be downloaded. Thus, people do not begin to pirate music by imitating someone else's pirating activities; commencement appears to stem from differential association. Rather, a person's initial involvement is deepened after emulating the actions of those who they encounter in cyberspace. While this corroborates the general chronological ordering of the social learning theory elements, it is contrary to the findings in Akers et al. (1979), who presumed that imitation has its greatest effect in the initial phases of participation rather than in maintaining the activity.

The sixth and final question is: why were definitions largely irrelevant in explaining any variation in music pirating activity? To remind the reader, definitions are evaluative criteria designating behaviors as good or bad and thus qualifying them as acceptable or appropriate (Akers et al., 1979). They are similar to Sykes and Matza's (1957) techniques of neutralization, but are shared by a group and are a byproduct of social interaction. It can be speculated that definitions are not necessary to define MP3 participation as "right" and "justifiable" simply because of its ubiquity. The presence of hundreds of thousands of individuals online might serve to preempt any questions as to the acceptability of the activity. That is, if so many people do it, how could it be wrong? No definitions, then, must be actively embraced in order to resolve or overcome any qualms or misgivings about participation. One might participate simply because MP3 files are available, easily obtainable, and provide great benefits with little to no cost.

CHAPTER 7

Implications of the Research

The preceding analyses have attempted to contribute to the theoretical knowledge base by testing the purported universal applicability of three general criminological theories. Specifically, Gottfredson and Hirschi's (1990) self-control theory and certain tenets of Akers' (1985) social learning theory were determined to be related to participation in digital music piracy. Technical and social policy considerations merit discussion for the purposes of suggesting responses that can be implemented by private- and public-sector institutions. It is hoped these will curtail the pervasiveness of copyright infringement and lead to increased protection of, and respect toward, the value of intellectual property. Implications specific to the two relevant theories are first discussed.

POLICY IMPLICATIONS OF SELF-CONTROL THEORY

According to Gottfredson and Hirschi, self-control is a personality characteristic largely developed and refined during early childhood. They also argue that it is age-invariant - or tends to stay constant over the course of a person's life. Unfortunately, this does not assist much in the way of suggesting policy solutions that societal institutions can enact to increase self-control among its members, apart from appropriate and adequate parenting of children and perhaps broader socialization at an early age.

As mentioned earlier, Gottfredson and Hirschi state that individuals with low self-control will be more inclined towards crime to most efficiently accomplish a goal or resolve a conflict. Accordingly, deterrence may be a way to curtail goal achievement or conflict resolution through unlawful means. Even though low self-control - an internal constraining mechanism - is explicated as an invariant personality trait,

135

perhaps the external constraining mechanism of deterrence can reduce the likelihood of seizing antinormative or unlawful opportunities.

An example can be provided to illustrate the concept of deterrence. Many college students know of the illegality associated with driving under the influence of alcohol (DUI). They can intuitively understand why it is a criminal offense, and they are accustomed to stories - perhaps on television or in print - of intoxicated individuals causing their own death, or the death of family, friends, or strangers. As such, a tangible loss or harm is visible to potential and actual drunk drivers. Second, almost everyone is aware of the harsh punishment (fines, attorney and court costs, incarceration, loss of driving privileges, etc.) that follow a DUI arrest and conviction, and the fact that the chance for arrest and conviction is nontrivial. Most people are accordingly deterred from drinking and then driving.

This example points to issues related to certainty and severity of punishment (Beccaria, 1968; Paternoster, 1987; Paternoster & Piquero, 1995). However, the threat of detection, apprehension, and punishment has largely been nonexistent when considering the MP3 phenomenon, although well-intentioned efforts have been made. As mentioned earlier, from September 2003 to June 2005 the RIAA has filed 11,700 lawsuits against individuals around the United States for illegally distributing music online (Associated Press, 2005; CNN.com, 2004; Slashdot.org, 2005). When the RIAA filed its first round of 261 civil lawsuits[40] in the second half of 2003 and 532 in January 2004, piracy participation on peer-to-peer file exchange networks dropped off substantially. Nonetheless, participation began to creep up relatively soon thereafter as the likelihood of a music pirate's detection and apprehension was identified as very small among the millions of persons who took part in the phenomenon. While the utility of the RIAA's strategy has yet to be clearly determined, perhaps more private-sector companies in the copyright industries must litigate with certainty and severity against violators to provide external constraints on the behavior.

Perhaps private-sector litigation must be coupled with increased vigilance by law enforcement and other regulating entities. Intellectual property theft is an act subject to civil and criminal penalties, and is expressly prohibited by the law. This negative definition by itself,

---

[40] Civil, rather than criminal, lawsuits were filed because it was difficult to rally the attention of law enforcement.

however, does not appear to deter people from downloading unauthorized MP3s. Software piracy has been tackled by federal law enforcement agencies (Wikipedia, 2004), and music piracy should perhaps similarly merit at least some allocation of resources by the national government.

Finally, there is no tangible and visible harm associated with participating in downloading copyrighted music from the Internet. This might be addressed through increased use of music artists and bands speaking out against piracy because of losses incurred to them and the industry. Recently, both motion picture actors and musicians have spoken out in advertisements against movie and music piracy. A consequent reduction in digital intellectual property theft has not been explicitly identified, but perhaps has put a name and face on a heretofore unknown victim of the behavior. Cumulatively, these policies may prove fruitful by positively shaping behavioral choices when an attractive opportunity for wrongdoing presents itself.

POLICY IMPLICATIONS OF SOCIAL LEARNING THEORY

It appears that peer associations are quite influential in an individual's acceptance of, and participation in, digital music piracy. These associations presumably provide behavioral models to emulate, and also champion a belief system that supports the activity while minimizing or ignoring perspectives that are dissonant. It is not practical or functional to attempt to control interactions between individuals with the intent of preventing the manifestation of negative influences that stem from peer association or imitation. What appears to be more utilitarian and effective is a concentrated effort to address the contributive role of differential reinforcement, which then may serve to attenuate the influence of differential association.

The salience of differential reinforcement can be addressed in two general ways. Not only must technology be enlisted to conform and direct behavior to adhere to lawful standards, but general social and individual sentiment towards the appropriateness of piracy must be modified through cognitive restructuring[41] endeavors. More specifically, the following initiatives may prove valuable toward this end: the industry's adoption of

---

[41] Cognitive restructuring occurs when a person identifies antisocial, irrational, incorrect, or otherwise negative beliefs and replaces them with prosocial, rational, correct, or otherwise positive statements.

a new business model that takes advantage of digital dissemination of music; the employment of copy protection schemes to restrict the uncontrolled distribution of songs; the proactive countering of cognitive factors that impel or induce participation in piracy, and the creation of a normative culture where legal mandates and moral sentiment do not contradict or clash, and where individuals feel individually and socially compelled to abide by those legal standards. These are discussed in detail in the following text with the intent of depicting their capacity to decrease the rewards and increase the possibility of punishment associated with MP3 participation.   Indeed, the most useful approach might be to incorporate elements from all of these policy suggestions to most aptly produce the desired change in a person's thoughts and actions.

EMBRACING A NEW BUSINESS MODEL

Since the flourishing of the MP3 phenomenon, the producers of music have struggled to develop ways to continue generating revenue while combating piracy. For example, the top five major record companies and a number of smaller labels have offered a selection of music downloads – some free and some at a price - for digital audio enthusiasts. Also, partnerships are being established in increasing fashion between the top labels and Internet companies to capitalize on the benefits (marketing, promotion, distribution, innovation) associated with the digital music invasion of cyberspace, real space, and popular culture (Borland & Hu, 2001; RIAA, 2000d). This has lent itself to the continued viability of the respective companies, and has served to meet the listening needs (and win the allegiance) of a respectable number of people. As such, embracing the potential of digital music and assimilating it into a business model may actually prove to be a wise and lucrative strategy.

In 1999, the first year in which MP3s gained a large following, the record industry experienced an 8% growth in revenue (from $13.7 billion to $14.6 billion) (Ploskina, 2000). Supporters of the technology contend that these figures would have been higher had the industry embraced the new paradigm at its onset, rather than seeking to quell the "digital music revolution" through litigation. Perhaps it is not too late, as at least two licensed P2P services - Peer Impact, and Snocap - are set to be introduced to consumers in the second half of 2005 (Associated Press, 2005). The former allows individuals to find and purchase songs from an initial catalogue of 500,000 as provided through partnerships with major record labels. The latter is engineered to track the distribution of songs online, and inform record labels when an individual attempts to disseminate an unlicensed track. Both of these *finally* reveal a willingness on the part of the recording industry to utilize P2P technology as a vehicle of distribution to generate revenue. Notwithstanding, if a new model for promotion, reproduction, and distribution for online music had been created and implemented immediately following the explosion of the MP3 phenomenon, the industry may have reaped much greater rewards.

Considering how much appeal digital music has for individuals, there are additional ways that recording labels could provide a valued product and capitalize on existing demand in a manner that meets the needs of both producers and consumers. For instance, they should offer promotional singles for free download and discounts on buying an album after downloading a free song. They should make their entire music database available in digital format to the online consumer, including those artists and tracks from decades ago which never benefited from CD capabilities. The release of new music albums using the Internet as the sole vehicle for dissemination may be a profitable strategy as well. New revenue models could be implemented for music, including digital distribution, subscription access, personalized radio, and pay-per-listen webcasts. Marketing strategies should be better tailored to those who will most likely purchase a particular artist's work because of the panoptic nature of the World Wide Web (Breen, 2000). For example, emails could be sent to individuals who sign up at an artist's web site in order to apprise them of that artist's media or public appearances (including concerts), or news about a current or forthcoming album. Accordingly, promotional campaigns driving visitors to particular web sites for artists' music, merchandise, concert tickets, and special contests can aid in amassing a giant database of users most interested in the music and most likely to purchase the products available.

To illustrate, musician Tom Petty made available full-length MP3 tracks from a soon-to-be-released album on his web site in 1999, requiring only that a visitor provide a valid email address so that news and information related to Tom Petty could be delivered to that person's inbox every so often (Kibbee, 1999). This provided the musician and record company with a sizeable database of Tom Petty fans, who could then be targeted for concert ticket and merchandise sales, and who would presumably be the most likely candidate to purchase such items. David Bowie, another popular rock artist, was also a trailblazer in using the Internet to solidify his relationship with fans, expand his popularity on a global scale, and to market his creative talent. Bowie offered free downloads of songs from upcoming albums and even live concerts to the visitors of his web site (Robertson, 2000). Additionally, he gave fans the opportunity to write lyrics to one of his songs to be selected for inclusion on his new album. Robertson (2000) compares Internet music pioneers such as Bowie to "drug dealers" who give fans free "stuff" such as digital music in the hopes of winning their allegiance and their future business in the form of album purchases, concert tickets, and merchandise[42]. An increasing number of musicians and bands are providing free tracks for download on their web sites to promote their records. Perhaps this needs to be the role that *all* musicians should adopt with increasing frequency in order to capitalize on the ubiquity of the Web and its users' hunger for information and multimedia.

Furthermore, there appears to be much potential for artists to have more personal freedom to create music without submitting to the demands and constraints imposed by record companies, thereby maintaining more control and creative license in their work. Concurrently, there is an ever-present need to bridge the gap between themselves and their fans through an online presence. As such, web sites offering space and advertising for independent artists proliferated - some of which include garageband.com, purevolume.com, and vitaminic.com. This trend should continue as musicians increasingly embrace the value of utilizing the Internet to promote and publicize their music. Another way that the music industry might embrace MP3s would be through the widespread adoption of ID3v2, a labeling system allowing for extra information such as lyrics, song ratings, copyright information, encrypted files, hyperlinks, CD cover art, and the artist's web page, to be embedded into individual music tracks (Nilsson, 2000). Upon playback of a track, this meta information would be capable of providing the listener with the option to obtain more information about the artist or song. It can also be tied to retailers who sell the music or band merchandise, concert tickets, and a variety of other goods and services that fans might appreciate.

A more harmonious relationship with the consumer population should result as the industry demonstrates they are *willing to work with the public* to satisfy their music needs by utilizing digital music technology, rather

---

[42] Indeed, some MP3 supporters argue that the old music business model should be replaced by a new framework that concentrates on selling merchandise (clothes, posters, stickers) and concert tickets associated with the artist, and making music more of a service than a commodity (Philips, 2000).

than opposing any change to the status quo. Wholehearted adoption of the technology may also reduce costs to both business and the environment as manufacturing, packaging, and physical distribution costs are largely eliminated. Finally, creativity and innovation may be further encouraged because a global market is now readily available. As the entire process is simplified, positive outcomes should result for musicians and consumers in the short term, and for the music industry in the long run.

COPY PROTECTION SCHEMES

The duplication of music prior to the MP3 phenomenon was prohibitively difficult for the average consumer, and a retrospective look at the evolution of media on which music is sold attests to this fact. When the predominant medium was the vinyl record, the general public simply could not afford equipment to reproduce them. The cassette tape introduced the possibility of duplication at low cost, but quality noticeably degraded with each successive generation, and was time-consuming due to the need to play from the source and record to the destination cassette in real-time. A similar trend was evidenced in the evolution of video players. Prior to the introduction of the video cassette recorder, reproduction of movies was next to impossible; following its mainstream adoption, duplication did take place with greater frequency but also suffered from the problem of quality loss[43]. In both these cases, many individuals came to the conclusion that obtaining the best listening experience was worth purchasing the official recording, and a general consensus arose that pirated recordings were of inferior quality.

Digital audio tapes (DATs), following their introduction in 1987, became popular in the professional recording industry due to their relatively affordable price and storage features. However, they were never fully embraced by the consumer population because of the prohibitive cost of DAT players and the fact that a tax was added with each DAT sold in order to compensate the record labels for losses stemming from piracy facilitated by the product (Amter, 2001). Further, digital copies of

---

[43] To note, the very legality of video cassette recorders was challenged in front of the U. S. Supreme Court, where it was determined that they had "substantial noninfringing use" and afforded time-shifting so that individuals could view a previously-aired program at a later time ("Sony Corp. v. Universal Studios," 1984).

recordings could only be made from an original source, as a bit or flag was set on each duplicate digital recording signifying that it was, in fact, a clone. Termed Serial Copying Management System (SCMS), this prevented the creation of another generation of copies from that clone. Sony MiniDiscs were another technological advance that failed to catch on among consumers in the United States, despite their popularity overseas. They allowed for portable digital recording onto a small disc, incorporated SCMS and provided functionality previously unknown (Woudenberg, 2003). Both DATs and MiniDiscs did not engender mass music piracy simply because of the difficulties associated with easy duplication and their comparative lack of mainstream adoption.

Audio compact discs (CDs) were brought to market in 1982, became popular in the late 1980s, and have since been the medium of choice in terms of recorded music (Amter, 2001). Movies and videos on digital video discs (DVDs) were introduced in 1996 and have acquired considerable market share from video cassette tapes since the beginning of the 21st century. Their ubiquity has provided relatively insecure *digital* sources of music and movie data that were similarly difficult to duplicate in their initial years of existence. With the continued exponential growth in technological capabilities, however, increasingly easy-to-use methods to extract media content and preserve the fidelity of the audio and/or video are emerging. The size of data files is also not as relevant as in the past, due to the growing pervasiveness of fast connections and large hard drives[44]. When considering the previous mediums in light of the current advances, it is interesting to note that the digital music and movie phenomenon is the first time that the general populace has possessed the ability to copy and propagate high-quality creative works - and thereby dictate their own experience of audiovisual media.

As such, two competing interest groups need to reach common ground in terms of their demands and perceived rights in order for the controversy that surrounds digital music to be resolved. Consumers - who have become accustomed to obtaining an incredibly large amount of high-quality music from a variety of time periods and genres at little to no cost - want this trend to continue. Furthermore, they desire no limitations that inconvenience their ability to transfer songs to portable players or burn them to recordable CDs. Producers - who had been accustomed to

---

[44] As of June 2005, brand name hard drives with capacities around 250 megabytes were available for $175 or less.

significant control over the distribution, marketing, and cost of music prior to the MP3 phenomenon - desire adequate compensation and revenue generation for their talent and investments, and to continually to maintain a fanbase that will perpetually be a source of income.

It is incontestable that many artists, primarily those independent and unsigned, are quite willing to advance the distribution of digital copies of their music on the Internet, simply because of their love for music and their desire to promote their musical efforts. At the same time, there are hundreds of artists (primarily those accustomed to obtaining royalties whenever their music is sold or used) who vehemently discourage the illegal copying of their music online. They argue that while those artists who openly allow and support online dissemination of their work should have the freedom to continue in that vein, those who disagree with the practice should be able to protect their creations from unlawful duplication, and a mechanism should be in place to afford this defense. With this in mind, individuals have demonstrated that they increasingly prefer the convenience of obtaining high-quality music online rather than through a retail establishment due to continued growth in broadband availability and computer technology to the general public. In order to align with the interests and objectives of the producers and to meet the consumer demand for downloadable tracks online, some constraining factor must compel individuals to purchase music through authorized Internet-based distributors, as opposed to freely downloading music from P2P file-exchange networks.

Digital rights management (DRM) is one solution being advanced by several IT and media companies such as Microsoft, Apple, Sony, and Xerox Corporation. It seeks to restrict the uncontrolled distribution of digital files by embedding protective code inside the music file. This allows the media to be used through DRM-enabled software or hardware, or for a limited time, or solely for one computer system, rendering itself unusable if transferred elsewhere. DRM-encoded files are not only protected in transfer to the end user, but also are protected from use beyond what is authorized. This is termed "persistent protection" - as the content is secured continually due to inherent control mechanisms (Stamp, 2002, 2003).

DRM allows for the creation of a digital music infrastructure that allows the music labels to have more control over the consumer's listening experience. Through unfettered music piracy, consumers have been bringing the intellectual property of others into the public domain without appropriate permission. As such, DRM may be useful in restoring the balance between the interest of the public and the rights of creators and owners. In the ideal state for the recording industry, then, music will no longer be shared with impunity but will be delivered to those who pay for the right to listen to it, and will only be playable by approved, DRM-compliant devices (MP3.com, 1999; Weekly, 2000). In terms of fiscal incentives, DRM has also been billed as the recording industry's saving grace due to its potential to thwart piracy and to increase their ability to dictate how music will be obtained and utilized – presumably in a way that generates revenue in as profitable a way as traditional sales from brick-and-mortar retail stores. By way of illustration, DRM was requisite before Apple went public with its iTunes digital music store in May 2003 (Long, 2003; Zeiler, 2003)[45]. Apple knew that if the music files they offered were insecure and easily duplicated between individuals online, their financial profit would greatly decrease. Furthermore, their business relationships with record labels who made available catalogues of legitimate digital songs would be critically damaged.

Typically, the security of valuable digital content has relied on the "honor" system where delivery to an authorized customer takes place using cryptographic methods but can be accessed and then saved in an insecure method on the recipient's hard drive – which of course allows for the illegal re-distribution of that unprotected content to other individuals. Piracy will continue on a large scale, then, unless the content – e-books, movies, music – is indissolubly integrated with a protection scheme that controls its use. One might argue that the implementation of technical measures to protect content is both effortful and futile because all software-based limitations will inevitably be broken. This notion has merit, but does not invalidate the use of rigorous DRM methodologies to secure content. The overarching goal is to make the reverse-engineering and cracking of security controls a more difficult alternative than simply purchasing the content. Also, the security control must "fail well" (Schneier, 2000, 2003). This means that when it is compromised, the loss

---

[45] iTunes has been a terrific success, selling two million songs to Macintosh users in its first sixteen days of existence (Zeiler, 2003). As of June 2005, over 430 million songs have been purchased worldwide (Reuters, 2005). It is supported by many recording artists and the music industry because it encodes music in the more secure Advanced Audio Coding (AAC) file compression format, restricts usage to three computers authorized by a single individual, and because its inherent "sharing" functionality is restricted to five users on a local area network.

and damage is isolated and localized so that greater loss and damage is minimized.

A brief description of a typical DRM technology tied to the distribution of digital music can illuminate this technical policy solution. Rather than providing insecure, easily reproducible MP3 files to interested individuals online, the music is packaged in an encrypted form – rendering it unplayable unless a key is lawfully obtained (i.e., purchased) from the owner or authorized distributor of the content. Public-key encryption can facilitate the secure exchange of keys via the Internet between parties[46]. Apart from the key, a license must also be obtained which specifies the rights an individual has with the digital content at hand. Perhaps the person can only play the song a particular number of times, or for a certain number of days (Cravotta, 2000; de Fontenay, 1999; Weekly, 2000). Perhaps the person has unlimited ability to listen to the music when, where, and how he or she desires. This would be defined in the license and would be related to a price that intuitively increases according to the freedoms afforded. Indeed, the license generally contains the key that decrypts the secured music file for playback, and is often hosted on separate Internet-based servers which coordinate delivery to a DRM-enabled software application (such as Microsoft Windows Media Player) on the end user's system[47].

When the encrypted music file is downloaded, it cannot be enjoyed unless the corresponding key is obtained via purchase of the appropriate license. In the "license predelivery" method, the software that is performing the request and download of the media file is also granted delivery of the license and key concurrently in a seamless and transparent manner. Alternatively, "license postdelivery" involves the acquisition of the license and key in a separate and additional process from the initial music file download, and often requires the provision of payment and personal information (e.g., age group, musical preferences, purchasing habits) to the producer. As is evident, the former is the most convenient

---

[46] For technical details related to this process, please see (Diffie, 1988; Diffie & Hellman, 1976).

[47] It should be noted that the allegiance of the purchasing population must be maintained and their interests and preferences considered prior to the implementation of any DRM scheme that might not resonate positively with them. These solutions vary in the level or degree of restrictions imposed upon end users, and may need to be reevaluated in light of the desires of consumers to enjoy music in a hassle-free and uncomplicated manner.

and unobtrusive, but does not provide a wide range of options for delivery and information gathering.

Another distinction concerning the secure delivery of digital content is also relevant. In a "tethered" scheme, the DRM-based media player contacts a particular web server and requests a decryption key to the music file *every time* an individual attempts its playback – consequently requiring a dedicated connection to the Internet[48]. The decryption key is destroyed after playback ensues, which provides robust security at the expense of inconveniencing the user to always be connected. More commonly employed is the "untethered" scheme, where the DRM-based media player requests the appropriate key *once* and keeps it with the media file on the local machine, rather than obtaining it each time the file is played.

Incorporating both predelivery and postdelivery methods in the distribution of all secure music online appears to be a promising technological solution. The initial license provided during predelivery can be limited in its scope, thereby providing a evaluation period of sorts to an individual. Once that evaluation period expires, the DRM-based media player can connect to a server that dispenses a license allowing for unlimited and unrestricted playback upon provision of two pieces of data: information necessary for a purchase transaction, and information related to demographics and listening preferences for future marketing purposes. If the end user has enjoyed the music file during the initial period, he or she can legitimately buy it and continue to derive its benefits. Conversely, if the end user did not, he or she can choose to decline the invitation for purchase and move on. Consumer desires of quick, easy acquisition of a valued commodity with unrestricted usage can thus be balanced with the creator and producer demands of control over, and adequate remuneration for, their digital intellectual property.

A major obstacle to the universal adoption of DRM is the fact that many companies are devising protective technologies that are not interoperable with one another. Unprotected, commonplace MP3 files are playable on a variety of operating systems with a variety of software

---

[48] A similar practice is identifiable in the software industry, as developers are writing their applications and games so that their execution triggers a small amount of data to be sent to the company or business which released the product ("phoning home," so to speak) in order to verify the legitimacy of the serial number used to unlock the full capabilities of the program.

media players, while DRM-encoded files often require proprietary software for playback. Efforts are underway to develop a standardized language of interaction[49] so that license, key, and usage data in secure music files can be extracted and utilized across applications and operating systems without action or even awareness on the part of the end user. However, it may be that open standards with exhaustive documentation may allow for the creation of software and music players that ignore the metadata that restricts functionality, thereby allowing for circumvention of the DRM technology. If it becomes easy to implement DRM in a standardized way across platforms, it may be similarly easy to devise a method to enjoy the media content without adherence to the restrictions in place. The reality of this point has yet to be determined.

Some interim solutions have been brought to market due to the delay in a standardized DRM adoption. Recording labels have released new albums from their top artists and bands on copy-protected CDs, which take advantage of the differences in how audio CD players and computer CDROM drives read data from discs. The way in which the data is written to the CD allows for its playback in the former but not in the latter. In theory, this strategy had potential for success, but in reality has infuriated and frustrated consumers by causing operating systems and software to lock up and crash (Mariano, 2002; Oakes, 2000). Additionally, issues relating to the degradation of consumer rights also surfaced, as many individuals contend they should be able to listen to the music they purchase in any capacity without restrictions. It remains to be seen what impact DRM will have on the digital music phenomenon. As of 2005, DRM-encoded iTunes, Rhapsody, and Napster-to-Go files have all garnered some popularity among consumers, but no single DRM implementation has captured the lead as a viable overarching solution to the problem of music piracy.

Incidentally, Weekly (2000) voices a concern that proponents of secure digital music must address before copy-protected formats have any potential to become standardized. A software application, when reading an encrypted or otherwise-secure audio track, must decrypt it and direct it to the computer's sound card in an unprotected raw format for it to be

---

[49] The XML-based languages currently under development for secured digital content include ODRL (http://www.odrl.net) and XrML (http://www.xrml.org), and the reader is encouraged to visit their respective web sites for more information.

played. If a secure sound recording can be outputted to a sound card, it must at some point be rendered insecure before playback can ensue. At that point, it is vulnerable for usurping and copying into a digital file format by software on a computer system. As a consequence, individuals so inclined can easily develop a piece of software that can intercept and duplicate the contents of that file as it is passed off from the operating system to the sound card. Then, they can save the data in a format once again suitable for unrestricted duplication and dissemination without any limitations or perceivable negative repercussions, thereby invalidating all of the security and copy protection measures that were implemented. Some programs that perform these functions are available commercially at a very reasonable cost[50]. Also, newer sound cards such as those made by Creative Labs allow consumers to digitally record any audio played through the sound card with no loss in quality. Finally, other individuals can still exploit the "analog hole" by utilizing a device to record music from the audio speakers themselves – which admittedly reduces the fidelity of the recording but still provides an acceptable duplicate of the music at no cost (Wikipedia, 2003).

The DRM facilities heretofore mentioned are primarily software-based, and circumvention of protective controls - through techniques such as those mentioned above - remains a distinct possibility. To augment the difficulty inherent in breaking the controls, joint software and hardware initiatives are underway, such as Microsoft's forthcoming "Next-Generation Secure Computing Base for Windows" operating system core, which works in conjunction with Intel's Trusted Computing Platform Alliance[51]. In basic terms, digital content is linked with the unique hardware in each individual's system, effectively binding it to one location and one person (Carroll, Juarez, Polk, & Leininger, 2002). By extension, breaking the security of one digital file on one system will not open it up for exploitation and misappropriation by others. The security, then, fails "well" (Schneier, 2000, 2003).

Microsoft has emphasized that insecure and unprotected content acquired prior to the introduction of their secure computing base will still be playable on their new DRM-enabled systems (Carroll et al., 2002).

---

[50] Total Recorder (www.totalrecorder.com) and Super MP3 Recorder Pro (www.audio-mp3-recorder.com) are two examples.
[51] Microsoft's Next-Generating Secure Computing Base was previously given the code name Palladium.

Nonetheless, once the majority of new music and movie releases are DRM-encoded and distributed solely online, individuals will be forced to participate in the secure schema through legitimate purchase in order to obtain and enjoy the commodity. While the ramifications for users of other operating systems such as Linux and BSD have yet to be determined and demand consideration, this seems the most promising technical approach to effect the protection of copyrighted content, and to stem the tide of unfettered intellectual property theft. Nonetheless, past experience underscores the very real potential for compromise in technological solutions, and therefore a complimentary initiative that addresses cognitive, behavioral, psychological, and sociological stimuli is warranted. Steve Jobs, CEO of Apple Computer, has echoed the same sentiment: "Piracy is a behavioral issue, not a technological one" (Taylor, 2002).

COGNITIVE RESTRUCTURING INITIATIVES

The proactive countering of cognitive, behavioral, psychological, and sociological influences of music piracy is as important as the implementation of reactive technological measures. For instance, when the boundaries of lawful behavior are clearly defined, it will seemingly be more challenging for potential offenders to justify their deviant actions. Deviance, then, may be reduced in severity and frequency with the use of laws, legal sanctions, or threats of sanction (Tittle, 1980). As applied to the setting of higher education, if acceptable and unacceptable computing behavior is plainly spelled out by university administration through the use of ethical codes substantively similar to laws and legal sanctions, the incidence of piracy among students may be attenuated. Engendering a respect for intellectual creations and property among students is an essential function of higher learning, particularly when it involves a networked environment where duplication and dissemination of works without the author or owner's permission can proliferate easily and with great celerity.

Tittle (1980) has stated that levels of wrongdoing may be decreased if laws are crafted and made known defining the behavior as illegal and prescribing penalties for its violation. Online intellectual property theft - inclusive not only of music but also of other forms of digital content - must somehow be designated as completely unacceptable in order for individuals to abstain from participation. The Campus Computing Project found in 2003 that 80 percent of public, and 78 percent of private, universities have policies in place explicitly prohibiting individuals from downloading copyrighted content (Word, 2003). A sample statement from the author's alma mater emphasizes that the university does not condone intellectual property theft:

> "Examples of unacceptable use of your network account include sharing copyrighted files through file sharing or peer-to-peer software such as Kazaa, Morpheus, Gnutella, or other similar program. If you do not adhere to this policy your network access and e-mail account may be suspended." (Michigan State University, 2003)

The presumed goal of such a declaration is to increase awareness of the illegal nature of the activity irrespective of its prevalence. For instance, at this author's alma mater, a feature article on the unacceptability of downloading unauthorized MP3s was printed in the school newspaper on the first day incoming freshmen in Fall 2003 were able to check into their residence halls. The article stated that the university receives approximately 35 complaints each day from music and movie industry representatives who have scanned the network utilizing software which identifies the host IP of the computer facilitating the data transfer of copyrighted material (Frank, 2003).

Furthermore, all students who registered their computer to use the broadband network resources on campus were required to indicate that they would comply with the following statement:

> "I acknowledge if I share copyrighted material from my network connection using a program like Kazaa, Morpheus, Gnutella or other file sharing program or method I will be subjected to disciplinary action which will minimally include the loss of my network connection. I also risk losing more than my campus Internet connection. Owners of copyrighted material may sue me, or press a criminal complaint against me which could face [sic] heavy fines—or even imprisonment." (Rondeau, 2003)

Such statements are often utilized in conjunction with campus-wide Acceptable Use Policies (AUPs) that delineate general appropriate and inappropriate use of computer systems and software. For example, they prohibit the unlawful access, infiltration, disruption, and damage of systems or networks belonging to others. Further, they typically specify adjudicatory measures such as disconnection of individual Internet connections in preference to the examination of the contents of user data due to strict adherence to principles supportive of academic freedom and privacy (e.g., Middle Tennessee State University, 2001). This practice promotes an environment conducive to the advancement of knowledge through its unrestricted expression and dissemination, while still designating penalties for transgressors.

Civil and criminal prosecution are specified as possible sanctions, but most matters - at least at the university studied - are resolved internally after contacting the infringing individual and requiring their discontinuation of the unacceptable activity. First-time violators are sent an email by network authorities on campus to immediately cease their activity; second- and third-time infringers are subject to loss of their Internet connection, academic suspension or even expulsion. To note, though, this piecemeal, case-by-case approach of addressing computer-related infractions does not help to inform the entire student population of the wrongfulness of the action. As such, a more panoptic initiative that can precipitate widespread change in the thought processes of individuals towards the activity may be more useful. As an example, incoming freshmen in Fall 2003 at the University of California in Berkeley who desired to use their dorm-room high-speed Internet connection were required to attend a 30-minute orientation session that focused heavily on the illegality and punitive repercussions of file-sharing (Brand, 2003)[52].

Finally, the RIAA has developed a campaign to work in conjunction with colleges and universities to increase awareness of copyright issues on the Internet and to foster a respect and appreciation for the intellectual property and creative output of others[53]. University administrators can order educational materials from the association and can institute programming to encourage ethical and lawful conduct on the Internet, and it is hoped that such a partnership will curb the rate of copyright violations among college student populations nationwide[54]. In addition, the

---

[52] A technical measure was also introduced to complement the cognitive initiative - a limit of five gigabytes of data can be transferred both upstream and downstream by students each week (Brand, 2003). To note, though, this would still allow approximately 1,250 downloads of four megabyte MP3s to be obtained and will perhaps only rarely become an issue among students.

[53] See http://www.soundbyting.com

[54] In order to determine the efficacy of codes, ethical training, warning signs, disclaimers, and entreatments to students from university personnel in reducing the frequency of music piracy through increased awareness and sensitivity, longitudinal studies must be performed following such policy implementation.

Recording Industry Association of America, the Motion Picture Association of America, the National Music Publishers' Association, and the Songwriters Guild of America have jointly crafted and disseminated letters to colleges and universities to increase their awareness of the phenomenon, request that steps be taken to monitor bandwidth and block access to P2P networks, recommend software tools that will aid in bandwidth management, and impose punitive action as necessary[55].

Irrespective of who plays the role, it is clear that some social institution or authority must teach individuals that stealing a product from a retail store and stealing a product over the Internet are both examples of theft - illegal activity necessitating prohibition and penalty.

External to the university environment, law enforcement has not developed any substantive campaign to inform individuals about copyright infringement and intellectual property theft, and may never view these acts as significant enough to warrant such policy. The recording industry and certain high-profile musicians and celebrities have spoken out against the unauthorized transfer of digital music files, but are perhaps too distant and remote for individuals to actually relate to and agree with. Curbing music piracy through personal admonishments and informative initiatives may be fruitful, but more individuals must perceive the problem as serious and contribute to such efforts.

Unfortunately, the distinction between right and wrong among copyright-infringing behaviors appears amorphous, unclear, and susceptible to varying interpretations. As such, society must step up and address this issue through the specific and conspicuous delineation of appropriate and inappropriate computing behavior. With regard to future research, it would be instructive to compare statistics of music piracy before individuals were made familiar (or reminded) of its intrinsic unlawfulness, to see if any general deterrence resulted from the conscience-raising effort. It might be determined that the inability to cultivate cognitive restructuring among those particularly prone to engage in online deviance has in some respects fostered and perpetuated the problem of music piracy.

---

[55] Appendix C provides a sample letter for the reader.

SHAPING MORALITY TO COHERE WITH LEGALITY

Tyler (1996) provides an interesting commentary on the ineffectiveness of deterrence measures in facilitating compliance with law among individuals, and instead points to the relevance of two related concepts: morality and legitimacy. He argues that intellectual property law is, in itself, impotent to dissuade copyright infringement because it is economically and pragmatically impossible to implement mechanisms to raise probabilities of detection, apprehension, and punishment past a threshold where they will induce conformity.

Regulation on the Internet has been attempted since 2003 through the filing of civil lawsuits by the RIAA who offered copyrighted music for unauthorized downloading from their computer systems (Bowman, 2003; CNN.com, 2004; Dean, 2003). The Department of Justice has hinted toward criminal prosecution and incarceration of music pirates for the purposes of "preserving the viability of America's content industries," but this has yet to occur outside of the realm of commercial software (McCullagh, 2002). Unquestionably, priorities are set by the general public, and law enforcement must cater to the demands of social and political pressures. Further, the police simply do not have the resources (as of yet) to expend on combating this form of theft, and societal members generally rail against privacy-compromising intrusions into their lives. Even if such resources were allocated and such "big-brother" practices allowed - thereby increasing the likelihood of penalties for transgressors - the impact of the initiatives would wane and eventually cease to exist as individuals come to a realization that the perceived risks are either less significant than previously imagined, or that there are other methods to circumvent the model of justice in place. When coupled with the widespread opportunities for copyright infringement, threats of punitive action designed to stimulate compliance will remain unproductive.

The objective, according to Tyler (1996), should be to gain voluntary cooperation among the citizenry through a reshaping of their conceptions of morality and legitimacy. The former concerns a person's beliefs towards wrong and right behavior, while the latter concerns a felt obligation to abide by the law. Tyler (1996) asserts that individuals largely engage in behavior not because of the degree or chances of risks and rewards, but because it aligns with their sense of morality. By way of illustration, the role of morality in determining actions - to a *greater* degree than the threat of sanctions - has been identified in a host of research studies (e.g., Christensen & Eining, 1991; Eining & Christensen, 1991; Grasmick & Bursik, 1990; Grasmick & Green, 1980; Grasmick et al., 1993; Nagin & Paternoster, 1993; Paternoster, 1989; Paternoster & Simpson, 1996).

By extension, dissonance in moral beliefs is apparently not experienced by individuals who contemplate and then participate in copyright infringement. Law is most effective when it coheres with the moral consensus of its subjects, and a climate must be created where individuals not only experience moral qualms when considering or partaking in intellectual property theft, but one in which overall law conformance is expected and culturally obligated. This notion is not new; centuries ago, Jeremy Bentham ([1781] 1970) stated that the restraining power legal sanctions have stems in large part from their connection to social sanctions. In the online realm, there are not yet any viable social sanctioning mechanisms in place. This consequently places the onus for the promotion and preservation of Internet propriety not only on the courts to develop legal sanctions, the private-sector to develop technological safeguards, and law enforcement to execute the law, but also on society to engender an appreciation and respect for digital property and copyright.

Second, individuals must view the laws, its process of creation, and the authority figures in charge of its promulgation and administration as legitimate, and thereby feel compelled to respect and obey them. Both morality and legitimacy contain a notion of justice and fairness, as citizens will voluntarily subscribe and support only that which they believe was devised and implemented in a manner they deem evenhanded and proper. Future research should identify what individuals conceive as fair when it comes to downloading, copying, and distributing intellectual property, and policy makers should attempt to embrace and then modify those public perceptions to collimate with the written law.

In sum, Tyler (1996) maintains that deterrence and preventive measures (e.g., through technology) only hold short-term worth, while affecting societal conceptions of morality and legitimacy have long-term implications, and is decidedly the policy road to travel to engender lasting positive change in this area. The deterrence approach in this subject area appears with Acceptable Use Policies and similar warnings that vilify music piracy, while the preventive approach is observable in DRM schemes. Both of these have been discussed, and the astute reader will be able to identify inherent vulnerabilities and weaknesses in their actual implementation. Tyler's (1996) suggestion to create a society inclined towards morality appears somewhat idealistic, and no practical steps are articulated towards this end. In accordance, perhaps the combination of deterrent and preventive measures – though admittedly short-term – can serve as stepping-stones in the direction of widespread positive change in shaping behavior through informal social control.

CONCLUSION

The present study has sought to test the applicability of three "general" criminological theories to online intellectual property theft in the form of digital music piracy. It has determined that self-control and social learning theory are extensible to crimes that are nontraditional in content and in context, while general strain theory is not. Furthermore, it has fostered an awareness of the factors that result in adoption of the behavior and assimilation into the social group that supports and perpetuates it. Policy solutions intended to curb the prevalence of copyright violations have also been suggested and discussed.

To a large extent, the majority of criminological research results in similar findings - a great proportion of variance in the dependent variable is due to elements that are not accounted for in the research, despite the fact that most studies seek to test the expected influence of theoretically- and conceptually-relevant independent variables. Notwithstanding the constant variability in the human condition and the consequent unpredictable nature of any action – criminal or otherwise, are social science researchers to be content with small R^2 values and little clarity as to the strongest contributive elements of a phenomenon? Is there more to it than our weak-to-moderate findings, with which we seem so content? If so, the "big picture" may not be as elusive as the statistics show (or, for that matter, do not show). It appears obtainable with a three-pronged approach: 1) by altering traditional conceptualizations of the makeup of criminal behavior; 2) by rallying elements from other disciplines outside the social sciences to improve our predictive models; and 3) by integrating into a functional whole the most salient elements of multiple theoretical frameworks. Now that we have greater clarity as to the relevance of general strain, self-control, and social learning, future research should continue to answer Sutherland's (1947; 1973) call and expand our paradigmatic scope even further by following these three paths.

The digital music phenomenon has achieved unprecedented media coverage, public accolade and adoption, and legislative attention since its introduction into the popular culture. The technology and associated infrastructure which has developed to support its growth and pervasiveness has augured great promise for the future of intellectual property distribution. However, the wild proliferation of copyright infringement in the face of traditional business models and extant copyright law has demonstrated a weakness which may negatively affect the innovation, development, and value of intellectual property and creative works as the Internet plays a larger role in our information-based society. Intelligent analysis of the expropriation of music online will shape determinations of how valuable digital works of *all* kinds can and should be disseminated over the Internet. As society becomes further ensconced in the Information Age, this is critical. It is hoped that the current research has taken a sizable step forward in this regard.

Bibliography

A & M Records Inc. et al. v. Napster Inc. (2001). *No. 00-16403.*
Retrieved February 12, 2001, from http://www.riaa.com/
pdf/napsterdecision.pdf

Adams, M. S. (1996). Labeling and differential association: Toward a
general social learning theory of crime and deviance. *American
Journal of Criminal Justice, 20*(2), 147-164.

Agnew, R. (1985). A revised strain theory of delinquency. *Social
Forces, 64,* 151-167.

Agnew, R. (1989). A longitudinal test of the revised strain theory.
Journal of Quantitative Criminology, 5, 373-387.

Agnew, R. (1992). Foundation for a General Strain Theory of Crime
and Delinquency. *Criminology, 30*(1), 47-87.

Agnew, R. (1997). Stability and change over the life course: A strain
theory explanation. In T. P. Thornberry (Ed.), *Developmental
Theories of Crime and Delinquency* (pp. 101-132). New
Brunswick, NJ: Transaction.

Agnew, R. (1998). The approval of suicide: A social-psychological
model. *Suicide and Life-Threatening Behavior, 28*(2), 205-225.

Agnew, R. (1999). A general strain theory of community differences in
crime rates. *Journal of Research in Crime and Delinquency, 36*(2),
123-155.

Agnew, R., & Brezina, T. (1997). Relational problems with peers,
gender, and delinquency. *Youth & Society, 29*(1), 84-111.

Agnew, R., Brezina, T., Wright, J. P., & Cullen, F. T. (2002). Strain,
personality traits, and delinquency: Extending general strain
theory. *Criminology, 40*(1), 43-71.

Agnew, R., Cullen, F. T., & Burton, V. S. J., et al. (1996). A new test of classic strain theory. *Justice Quarterly, 13*(4), 681-704.

Agnew, R., & Peters, A. A. R. (1986). The techniques of neutralization: An analysis of predisposing and situational factors. *Criminal Justice and Behavior, 13*(1), 81-97.

Agnew, R., & White, H. R. (1992). An Empirical Test of General Strain Theory. *Criminology, 30*(4), 475.

Akers, R. L. (1977). *Deviant behavior: A social learning approach.* Belmont, CA: Wadsworth.

Akers, R. L. (1985). *Deviant behavior: A social learning approach* (3 ed.). Belmont, CA: Wadsworth.

Akers, R. L. (1991). Self-control as a general theory of crime. *Journal-of-Quantitative-Criminology, 7*((2)), 201-211.

Akers, R. L. (1992). Linking sociology and its specialties. *Social Forces, 71*, 1-16.

Akers, R. L. (1994). *Criminological Theories.* Los Angeles: Roxbury.

Akers, R. L. (1996). Is differential association/social learning cultural deviance theory? *Criminology, 34*(2), 229-256.

Akers, R. L. (1998). *Social learning and social structure: A general theory of crime and deviance.* Boston: Northeastern University Press.

Akers, R. L., & Cochran, J. K. (1985). Adolescent marijuana use: A test of three theories of deviant behavior. *Deviant Behavior, 6*(4), 323-346.

Akers, R. L., Krohn, M. D., Lanza-Kaduce, L., & Radosevich, M. (1979). Social learning and deviant behavior: A specific test of a general theory. *American Sociological Review, 44*, 636-655.

Akers, R. L., & Lee, G. (1996). A longitudinal test of social learning theory: Adolescent smoking. *Journal of Drug Issues, 26*(2), 317-343.

Angus Reid Worldwide. (2000a). *Despite the use of MP3 technology being widespread among Internet-enabled Canadians, cd-buying behaviour remains strong.* Retrieved September 24, 2001, from http://www.angusreid.com/media/content/displaypr.cfm?id_to_vie w=985

Angus Reid Worldwide. (2000b). *MP3 technology bridging Internet generation gap.* Retrieved October 1, 2001, from http://www.angusreid.com/media/content/displaypr.cfm?id_to_view= 1042

Apter, T. (2001). *The Myth of Maturity*. London: W. W. Norton & Company.

Arneklev, B. J., Grasmick, H. G., Tittle, C. R., & Bursik, R. J. (1993). Low Self-control and Imprudent Behavior. *Journal of Quantitative Criminology, 9*, 225-247.

Aseltine, R. H., Gore, S., & Gordon, J. (2000). Life stress, anger and anxiety, and delinquency: An empirical test of general strain theory. *Journal of Health and Social Behavior, 41*(3), 256-275.

Associated Press. (2005). *Rethinking the File-Swap Morass*. Retrieved June 24, 2005, from http://www.wired.com/news/digiwood/ 0,1412,68000,00.html?tw=wn_tophead_2

Babcock, L., & Loewenstein, G. (1997). Explaining bargaining impasse: The role of self-serving biases. *Journal of Economic Perspectives, 11*, 109-126.

Bachman, R., & Paternoster, R. (1997). *Statistical methods for criminology and criminal justice*. New York: McGraw-Hill.

Bandura, A. (1969). *Principles of behavior modification*. New York: Holt, Rinehart, Winston.

Bandura, A. (1973). *Aggression: A social learning analysis*. Englewood Cliffs, NJ: Prentice-Hall.

Bandura, A. (1977). *Social learning theory*. Englewood Cliffs, NJ: Prentice-Hall.

Bandura, A., & Walters, R. (1963). *Social learning and personality development*. New York: Holt, Rinehart, Winston.

Banerjee, D., Cronan, T. P., & Jones, T. W. (1998). Modeling IT ethics: A study in situational ethics. *MIS Quarterly, 22*(1), 31-60.

Beccaria, C. (1968). *On Crimes and Punishments* (H. Paolucci, Trans.). Indianapolis: Bobbs-Merrill.

Benson, M. L. (1985). Denying the guilty mind: Accounting for involvement in a white-collar crime. *Criminology, 23*(4), 583-608.

Benson, M. L., & Moore, E. (1992a). Are White-Collar and Common Offenders the Same - an Empirical and Theoretical Critique of a Recently Proposed General-Theory of Crime. *Journal of Research in Crime and Delinquency, 29*(3), 251-272.

Benson, M. L., & Moore, E. (1992b). Are White-collar and Common Offenders the Same? An Empirical and Theoretical Critique of a Recently Proposed General Theory of Crime. *Journal of Research in Crime and Delinquency, 29*, 251-272.

Bentham, J. (Ed.). ([1781] 1970). *An Introduction to the Principles of Morals and Legislation*. London: The Athlone Press.

Berst, J. (1997). *Has your web site been stolen?* Retrieved April 28,
    1997, from http://www.zdnet.com/anchordesk/story/story_864.html
Bettig, R. V. (1996). *Copyrighting culture.* Boulder, CO: Westview.
Bhattacharjee, S., Gopal, R. D., & Sanders, G. L. (2003). Digital music
    and online sharing: software piracy 2.0? *Communications of the
    ACM (CACM), 46*(7), 107-111.
Black, J. (2003). *Big Music's Broken Record.* Retrieved February 13,
    2003, from http://www.businessweek.com/technology/content/
    feb2003/tc20030213_9095_tc078.htm
Borland, J., & Hu, J. (2001). *Napster signs on to sell major labels'
    music.* Retrieved January 2, 2004, from http://news.com.com/2100-
    1023-267840.html?legacy=cnet
Bowman, L. M. (2000). *Musicians praise, bash Napster.* Retrieved
    October 21, 2000, from http://www.zdnet.com/zdnn/stories/news/
    0,4586,2643361,00.html
Bowman, L. M. (2003). *RIAA to sue thousands of file swappers.*
    Retrieved June 25, 2003, from http://zdnet.com.com/2100-1105_2-
    1020876.html
Brand, W. (2003). *Students warned on downloads.* Retrieved
    September 1, 2003, from http://www.oaklandtribune.com/Stories/
    0,1413,82~1726~1575835,00.html
Breen, C. (2000). *Steal this song.* Retrieved November 8, 2001, from
    http://www.cnn.com/2000/TECH/computing/07/07/digital.music.sp
    ecial.idg/index.html
Brezina, T. (1998). Adolescent maltreatment and delinquency: The
    question of intervening processes. *Journal of Research in Crime
    and Delinquency, 35*(1), 71-99.
Brezina, T., Piquero, A. R., & Mazerolle, P. (2001). Student anger and
    aggressive behavior in school: An initial test of Agnew's macro-
    level strain theory. *Journal of Research in Crime and Delinquency,
    38*(4), 362-386.
Broidy, L. M. (2001). A test of general strain theory. *Criminology,
    39*(1), 9.
Broidy, L. M., & Agnew, R. (1997). Gender and crime: A general strain
    theory perspective. *Journal of Research in Crime and Delinquency,
    34*(3), 275-306.
Brownfield, D., & Sorenson, A. (1993). Self-control and Juvenile
    Delinquency: Theoretical issues and an Empirical Assessment of
    Selected Elements of a General Theory of Crime. *Deviant
    Behavior, 14*, 243-264.

Brownfield, D., & Thompson, K. (1991). Attachment to peers and delinquent behavior. *Canadian Journal of Criminology, 33*, 45-60.

Buckley, M. R., Wiese, D. S., & Harvey, M. G. (1998). An investigation into the dimensions of unethical behavior. *Journal of Business Education, 73*(5), 284-290.

Burgess, R., & Akers, R. (1966). A differential association-reinforcement theory of criminal behavior. *Social Problems, 14*, 128-147.

Burton, V. S., Cullen, F. T., Evans, T. D., Alarid, L. F., & Dunaway, R. G. (1998). Gender, self-control, and crime. *Journal of Research in Crime and Delinquency, 35*(2), 123-147.

Calpo, G. (2000). *MP3 bitrate comparison.* Retrieved June 20, 2000, from http://www.pinoyware.com/fliptech/bitrate.shtml

Carroll, A., Juarez, M., Polk, J., & Leininger, T. (2002). *Microsoft "Palladium": A Business Overview.* Retrieved October 1, 2003, from http://www.microsoft.com/presspass/features/2002/jul02/0724Palladiumwp.asp

Catalano, R. F., Kosterman, R., & Hawkins, J. D., et al. (1996). Modeling the etiology of adolescent substance abuse: A test for the social development model. *Journal of Drug Issues, 26*(2), 429-455.

Chantler, N. (1996). *Profile of a Computer Hacker.* Florida: Infowar.

Christensen, A. L., & Eining, M. M. (1991). Factors influencing software piracy: Implications for accountants. *Journal of Information Systems*, 67-80.

Cloward, R. A., & Ohlin, L. E. (1963). *Delinquency and opportunity: a theory of delinquent gangs* (4th ed.). New York: The Free Press.

CNN.com. (2000a). *MP3.com beats street: Online music service reports loss of 9 cents a share, revenue rises sharply.* Retrieved August 3, 2001, from http://cnnfn.cnn.com/2000/10/19/technology/earns_mp3/index.htm

CNN.com. (2000b). *MP3.com ordered to pay up to $250 million in music copyright case.* Retrieved October 3, 2001, from http://www.cnn.com/2000/LAW/09/06/mp3.lawsuit.01/index.html

CNN.com. (2000c). *Napster heads to court.* Retrieved October 5, 2001, from http://www.cnnfn.cnn.com/2000/07/03/companies/napster/

CNN.com. (2004). *More song swappers sued.* Retrieved January 24, 2004, from http://money.cnn.com/2004/01/21/technology/riaa_suits/index.htm

Cochran, J. K., Wood, P. B., Sellers, C. S., & Chamlin, M. B. (1998). Academic Dishonesty and Low Self-control: An Empirical Test of a General Theory of Crime. *Deviant Behavior, 19,* 227-255.

Cochran, J. K., Wood, P. B., Sellers, C. S., Wilkerson, W., & Chamlin, M. B. (1996). *Academic dishonesty and low-self-control: An empirical test of a general theory of crime.* Paper presented at the American Society of Criminology, Chicago, IL.

Cohen, A. K. (1955). *Delinquent boys: The culture of the gang.* Glencoe, IL: The Free Press.

Cohen, L. E., & Felson, M. (1979). Social change and crime rate trends: A routine activities approach. *American Sociological Review, 44,* 588-607.

Coleman, J. W. (1989). *The criminal elite: the sociology of White-collar crime.* New York: St. Martin's Press.

Congress, t. (1997). *Bill summary and status: No Electronic Theft (NET) Act.* Retrieved October 15, 2001 from http:// www.thomas.loc.gov/cgi-bin/bdquery/ z?d105:HR02265:@@@L

Consumer Electronics News. (2003). *Compressed Audio Player Market Will Continue to Surge Ahead as Consumers Snap Up Diverse Array of Devices, Says IDC.* Retrieved June 12, 2003, from http://www.prnewswire.com/cgi-bin/stories.pl?ACCT= SVBIZINK8.story&STORY=/www/story/06-12-2003/ 0001964220&EDATE=THU+Jun+12+2003,+09:09+AM

Copyright Office of the United States. (1998). *Summary of Digital Millennium Copyright Act of 1998.* Retrieved September 24, 2001, from http://www.loc.gov/copyright/legislation/dmca.pdf

Copyright Office of the United States. (2000a). *Copyright Basics, Circular 1.* Retrieved October 4, 2001, from http://www.loc.gov/ copyright/circs/circ1.html

Copyright Office of the United States. (2000b). *Copyright law of the United States of America and related laws contained in Table 17 of the United States Code.* Retrieved October 1, 2000, from http://www.loc.gov/copyright/title17/circ92.pdf

Cravotta, N. (2000). *The Internet-audio (r)evolution.* Retrieved February 3, 2000, from http://www.findarticles.com/cf_0/m0EDN/ 3_45/59969530/print.jhtml

Crawford, K. (2005). *Hollywood wins Internet piracy battle.* Retrieved June 27, 2005, from http://money.cnn.com/2005/06/27/ technology/grokster/

Crawford, W. (2000). New sounds for a new millennium? *Online, 24*(2), 82-84.

Cressey, D. R. (1953). *Other people's money.* New York: The Free Press.

Cross, P. (1977). Not can but will college teaching be improved. *New Directions in Higher Education, 17*(1).

CyberAtlas. (2001). *Piracy extends beyond software to digital content,* 2001, November 9, from http://cyberatlas.internet.com/big_picture/ applications/article/0,1323,1301_920681,00.html

Davis, M. (2003). *Penn State seeks out student piracy.* Retrieved May 1, 2003, from http://www.redandblack.com/vnews/display.v/ ART/2003/05/01/3eb12b203a281

de Fontenay, E. (1999). *The music industry enters the digital age.* Retrieved September 24, 2001, from http://www.musicdish.com/ survey/downloads/MP3report.pdf

Dean, K. (2003). *RIAA hits students where it hurts.* Retrieved April 5, 2003, from http://www.wired.com/news/digiwood/ 0,1412,58351,00.html

Denning, D. (1998). *Information Warfare and Security.* Reading: Addison-Wesley.

Dessent, B. (2005a). *BitTorrent FAQ and Guide: Background Information.* Retrieved May 2, 2005, from http://btfaq.com/serve/ cache/3.html

Dessent, B. (2005b). *BitTorrent FAQ and Guide: How does BitTorrent compare to other forms of file transfer?* Retrieved May 2, 2005, from http://btfaq.com/serve/cache/4.html

Diffie, W. (1988). The first ten years of public-key cryptography. *Proceedings of the IEEE, 76,* 560-577.

Diffie, W., & Hellman, M. E. (1976). New directions in cryptography. *IEEE Transactions on Information Theory, 22,* 644-654.

DMA. (2000). *Web Music.* Retrieved September 28, 2001, 2001, from http://www.digmedia.org/whatsnew/web_music.html

Dordick, H. S. (1986). *Intellectual property: Protecting rights and privileges in an electronic age.* New York: Clark Boardman.

Duke Law School. (2005). *MGM Studios v. Grokster.* Retrieved May 1, 2005, from http://www.law.duke.edu/publiclaw/ supremecourtonline/certgrants/2004/mgmvgro.html

Dyrness, C. (2002). *Setting sites on nabbing pirates: Stolen web design a growing problem,* 2002, September 18, from http:// newsobserver.com/business/story/1741179p-1753793c.html

Eining, M. M., & Christensen, A. L. (1991). A psycho-social model of software piracy: The development of a test model. In R. Dejoie, G. Fowler & D. Paradice (Eds.), *Ethical Issues in Information Systems* (pp. 134-140). Boston: Boyd & Fraser.

Electronic Frontier Foundation. (2005). *MGM v. Grokster.* Retrieved May 1, 2005, from http://www.eff.org/IP/P2P/MGM_v_Grokster/

Etzioni, A. E., O. (1999). Face-to-face and computer-mediated communities, a comparative analysis. *The Information Society, 15,* 241-248.

Evangelista, B. (2003). *Film industry crusades for piracy laws,* 2003, May 12, from http://www.rockymountainnews.com/drmn/technology/article/0,1299,DRMN_49_1954561,00.html

Evans, T. D., Cullen, F. T., Burton, V. S., Dunaway, R. G., & Benson, M. L. (1997). The social consequences of self-control: Testing the general theory of crime. *Criminology, 35*(3), 475-504.

Flaherty, L., Pearce, K., & Rubin, R. (1998). Internet and face-to-face communication: Not functional alternatives. *Communication Quarterly, 46*(3), 250-268.

Frank, S. (2003). *Downloads could result in discipline.* Retrieved August 15, 2003, from http://www.statenews.com/print.phtml?pk=18447

Garner, B. A. (Ed.). (1999). *Black's Law Dictionary* (7th ed.): West Group Publishing.

Gentile, G. (2003). *Film industry trying to stop pirates.* Retrieved April 18, 2003, from http://www.dailytexanonline.com/vnews/display.v/ART/2003/04/18/3e9fb66f698c9

Gibbs, J. J., & Giever, D. (1995). Self-Control And Its Manifestations Among University Students: An Empirical Test Of Gottfredson And Hirschi's General Theory. *Justice Quarterly: JQ, 12*(2), 231.

Gibbs, J. J., Giever, D., & Martin, J. S. (1998). Parental management and self-control: An empirical test of Gottfredson and Hirschi's general theory. *The Journal of Research in Crime and Delinquency, 35*(1), 40.

Gilbert, S. W., & Lyman, P. (1989). Intellectual property in the information age: Issues beyond the copyright law. *Change, 21,* 23-28.

Google. (2004). *Year-End Google Zeitgeist: Search patterns, trends, and surprises.* Retrieved May 20, 2003, from http://www.google.com/press/zeitgeist2004.html

Gopal, R. D., & Sanders, G. L. (1997). Preventive and deterrent controls for software piracy. *Journal of Management Information Systems, 13*(4), 29.

Gopal, R. D., & Sanders, G. L. (1998). International software piracy: Analysis of key issues and impacts. *Information Systems Research, 9*(4), 380-397.

Gopal, R. D., Sanders, G. L., Bhattacharjee, S., Agrawal, M., & Wagner, S. (2004). A behavioral model of digital music piracy. *Journal of Organizational Computing and Electronic Commerce, 14*(2), 89-105.

Gottfredson, M., & Hirschi, T. (1990). *A general theory of crime.* Stanford, CA: Stanford University Press.

Grasmick, H. G., & Bursik, R. J. (1990). Conscience, significant others, and rational choice: Extending the deterrence model. *Law and Society Review, 24*, 837–861.

Grasmick, H. G., & Green, D. E. (1980). Legal punishment, social disapproval and internalisation as inhibitors of illegal behavior. *The Journal of Criminal Law and Criminology, 71*(3), 325-335.

Grasmick, H. G., Tittle, C. R., Bursik, R. J., & Arneklev, B. J. (1993). Testing the core empirical implications of Gottfredson and Hirschi's general theory of crime. *The Journal of Research in Crime and Delinquency, 30*(1), 5.

Hafner, K., & Markoff, J. (1991). Cyberpunk: outlaws and hackers on the computer frontier.

Hall, J. (1935). *Theft, Law and Society.* Boston: Little Brown & Co.

Haney, C. (2000). *Microsoft fears e-book piracy.* Retrieved August 29, 2001, from http://www.pcworld.com/news/article/0,aid,18262,00.asp

Harari, O. (1999). You say you want a revolution? *Management Review, 88*(10), 30-33.

Harmon, A. (2001). *Software double bind,* Retrieved August 13, 2001, from http://www.nytimes.com/2001/08/13/technology/ebusiness/13NECO.html

Harris, L. J. (1969). *Nurturing new ideas.* Washington, DC: Bureau of National Affairs.

Harris, M. (2003). *Now playing: movie piracy crackdown. Film industry fights back against illegal recording,* 2003, May 2, from http://www.canada.com/edmonton/edmontonjournal/story.asp?id=F90C17FC-7E1A-4954-9CAB-8114B633B58A

Hawkins, J. D., Herrenkohl, T., Farrington, D. P., Brewer, D., Catalano, R. F., & Harachi, T. W. (1998). A review of predictors of youth violence. In R. Loeber & D. P. Farrington (Eds.), *In serious & violent juvenile offenders: Risk factors and successful interventions*. Thousand Oaks, CA: SAGE Publications.

Healy, J. (2003). *4 pay steep price for free music*. Retrieved May 2, 2003, from http://www.latimes.com/la-fi-settle2may02,0,6007000.story

Heid, J. (1997). *So long, CDs*. Retrieved October 3, 2001, from http://www.macworld.zdnet.com/1999/07/features/MP3.html

Heimer, K. (1997). Socioeconomic status, subcultural definitions, and violent delinquency. *Social Forces, 75*, 799-834.

Higgins, G. E. (2005). Can low self-control help with the understanding of the software piracy problem? *Deviant Behavior, 26*(1), 1-24.

Higgins, G. E., & Makin, D. A. (2004). Does social learning theory condition the effects of low self-control on college students' software piracy? *Journal of Economic Crime Management, 2*(2).

Hinduja, S. (2001). Correlates of Internet software piracy. *Journal of Contemporary Criminal Justice, 17*((4)), 369-382.

Hinduja, S. (2003). Trends and patterns among software pirates. *Ethics and Information Technology, 5*(1), 49-61.

Hirschi, T. (1969). *Causes of delinquency*. Berkeley: University of California Press.

Hirschi, T., & Gottfredson, M. (1993). Commentary: testing the general theory of crime. *Journal-of-Research-in-Crime-and-Delinquency, 30*((1)), 47-54.

Hoffman, J. P., & Miller, A. S. (1998). A latent variable analysis of general strain theory. *Journal of Quantitative Criminology, 14*(1), 83-110.

Hoffmann, J. P., & Su, S. S. (1997). The conditional effects of stress on delinquency and drug use: A strain theory assessment of sex differences. *Journal of Research in Crime and Delinquency, 34*(1), 46-78.

Hosmer, D. W., & Lemeshow, S. (2000). *Applied logistic regression*. New York: John Wiley and Sons.

IFPI. (2002). *IFPI Music Piracy Report*. Retrieved September 15, 2003, from http://www.ifpi.org/site-content/library/piracy2002.pdf

Im, J. H., & Van Epps, P. D. (1991). Software piracy and software security in business schools: An ethical perspective. *Data Base, 22*(3), 15-21.

International Standards Organization. (2003). *Introduction.* Retrieved October 20, 2003, from http://www.iso.ch/iso/en/aboutiso/introduction/index.html

Jacobs, F., & Allbritton, C. (2001). *E-book publishers face piracy panic.* Retrieved January 1, 2001, from http://www.cnn.com/2001/TECH/computing/01/01/e.book.piracy.panic.idg/

Jay, E. D. (2000). *Survey of napster users.* Retrieved October 4, 2001, from http://www.riaa.com/PDF/jay.pdf

Johnston, M. (2000). *E-book industry warned of piracy threat.* Retrieved September 25, 2000, from http://www.idg.net/idgns/2000/09/25/EBookIndustryWarnedOfPiracyThreat.shtml

Jones, C. (2000). *RIAA sues MP3.com.* Retrieved October 2, 2001, from http://www.wired.com/news/politics/0,1283,33634,00.html

Junger, M., & Tremblay, R. E. (1999). Self-control, accidents, and crime. *Criminal Justice and Behavior, 26*(4), 485-501.

Kaplan, H. B., Johnson, R. J., & Bailey, C. A. (1987). Deviant peers and deviant behavior: Further elaboration of a model. *Social Psychology Quarterly, 50*(3), 277-284.

Karagiannis, K. (1999, July). Digital audio and MP3. *Electronics Now, 70,* 22-24.

Keane, C. M., Paul S; Teevan, James J. (1993). Drinking and driving, self-control, and gender: Testing a general theory of crime. *The Journal of Research in Crime and Delinquency, 30*(1), 30.

Kibbee, R. (1999). *The choice conundrum. MP3: Digital Music for the Millennium?* Retrieved September 25, 2001, from http://www.musicdish.com/survey/downloads/MP3report.pdf

Kievit, K. (1991). Information systems majors/non-majors and computer ethics. *Journal of Computer Information, 32*(1), 43-49.

King, B. (2000a). *Napster: Music's friend or foe?* Retrieved September 29, 2001, from http://www.wired.com/news/print/0,1294,36961,00.html

King, B. (2000b). *New school of thought on piracy.* Retrieved September 29, 2001, from http://www.wired.com/news/print/0,1294,36875,00.html

King, B. (2001). *MP3 Types Call Telcos for Help.* Retrieved January 5, 2004, from http://www.wired.com/news/business/0,1367,45208,00.html

Knight Systems. (2000). *The top ten.* Retrieved July 7, 2000, from http://www.searchterms.com

Krochmal, M. (1998). *Music industry unprepared for MP3.* Retrieved October 1, 2001, from http://www.techweb.com/story/ TWB19980716S0010

Krohn, M. L., Skiller, W. F., Massey, J. L., & Akers, R. (1985). Social learning theory and adolescent cigarette smoking: A longitudinal study. *Social Problems, 32*(5), 455-473.

Lanier, M., & Henry, S. (1998). *Essential Criminology.* New York: Free Press.

Latonero, M. (2000). *Survey of MP3 usage: Report on a university consumption community.* Retrieved October 5, 2001, from http://www.entertainment.usc.edu/publications/mp3.pdf

Learmonth, M. (2000). *Finally, some numbers on Napster.* Retrieved October 2, 2001, from http://www.thestandard.com/article/ display/0,1151,15502,00.html

Lersch, K. M. (1999). Social learning theory and academic honesty. *International Journal of Comparative and Applied Criminal Justice, 23*(1), 103-114.

Lessig, L. (1997). Intellectual property and code. *St. Johns Journal of Legal Commentary, 11*(635).

Lessig, L. (1999a). *Code and Other Laws of Cyberspace.* New York: Basic Books.

Lessig, L. (1999b). Commons and Code. *Fordham Intellectual Property, Media and Entertainment Law Journal, 9*(459).

Lipton, B. (1998). *New music pirates face lawsuits.* Retrieved September 18, 2001, from http://www.news.com/News/Item/ 0,4,22060,00.html

Long, J. S. (1997). *Regression Models for Categorical and Limited Dependent Variables.* Thousand Oaks, CA: Sage.

Long, P. D. (2003). *iTunes and the technology beyond MP3.* Retrieved July 1, 2003, from http://www.syllabus.com/article.asp?id=7895

Longshore, D., & Turner, S. (1998). Self-control and criminal opportunity: Cross sectional test of the general theory of crime. *Criminal Justice and Behavior, 25*(1), 81.

Longshore, D., Turner, S., & Stein, J. A. (1996). Self-control in a Criminal Sample: An Examination of Construct Validity. *Criminology, 34*, 209-228.

Luckenbill, D. F., & Miller, S. L. (1998). Defending intellectual property: State efforts to protect creative works. *Justice Quarterly, 15*(1), 93-120.

Maddala, G. (1983). *Limited dependent and qualitative variables in econometrics.* New York: Cambridge University Press.

Mariano, G. (2002). *Apple: Play music at your own risk.* Retrieved August 25, 2003, from http://news.com.com/2100-1023-912695.html

Marsh, H. W., & Hau, K. T. (1999). Confirmatory factor analysis: Strategies for small sample sizes. In R. H. Hoyle (Ed.), *Statistical strategies for small sample research.* Thousand Oaks, CA: Sage.

Matsueda, R. L. (1982). Testing control theory and differential association: A causal modeling approach. *American Sociological Review, 47,* 489-504.

Matsueda, R. L., & Anderson, K. (1998). The dynamics of delinquent peers and delinquent behavior. *Criminology, 36*(269-308).

Mazerolle, P. (1998). Gender, general strain, and delinquency: an empirical examination. *Justice Quarterly, 15*(1), 65-91.

Mazerolle, P., Brame, R., Paternoster, R., Piquero, A., & Dean, C. (2000). Onset age, persistence, and offending versatility: comparisons across gender. *Criminology, 38*(4), 1143-1172.

Mazerolle, P., & Maahs, J. (2000). General strain and delinquency: An alternative examination of conditioning influences. *Justice Quarterly, 17*(4), 753-778.

Mazerolle, P., & Piquero, A. (1998). Linking exposure to strain with anger: An investigation of deviant adaptations. *Journal of Criminal Justice, 26*(3), 195-211.

McCullagh, D. (2002). *DOJ to swappers: Law's not on your side.* Retrieved September 12, 2003, from http://news.com.com/2100-1023-954591.html?tag=fd_top

McKelvey, R., & Zavoina, W. (1975). A statistical model for the analysis of ordinal level dependent variables. *Journal of Mathematical Sociology, 4,* 103-120.

Mendels, P. (1999). *University cracks down on MP3 trade.* Retrieved September 20, 2001, from http://www.ou.edu/archives/it-fyi/0723.html

Menta, R. (2000). *The merits in the mp3.com lawsuit.* Retrieved October 5, 2001, from http://www.mp3newswire.net/stories/2000/MP3courtpoint.html

Merton, R. K. (1938). Social structure and anomie. *American Sociological Review, 3,* 672-682.

Merton, R. K. (1968). *Social Theory and Social Structure.* New York: Free Press.

Messner, S. F., & Rosenfeld, R. (1994). *Crime and the American Dream*. Belmont, CA: Wadsworth.

Michigan State University. (2003). *Acceptable use of your account*. Retrieved November 15, 2003, from https://mail.msu.edu/upgrade/pilotupgrade2.html

Middle Tennessee State University. (2001). *Computer and Network Acceptable Use Policy*. Retrieved March 15, 2001, from http://www.mtsu.edu/misc/policy.html

Midgley, C. (2000). *History of MP3? MP3 for the Mac - best of MP3 for Apple Macs*. Retrieved September 29, 2001 from http://www.mp3mac.co.uk/Pages/History_of_MP3.html

Miller, J. K., & Gergen, K. J. (1998). Life on the line: The therapeutic potentials of computer-mediated conversation. *Journal of Marital and Family Therapy, 24*(2), 189-202.

Mindenhall, C. (2000). *Music pho the masses*. Retrieved January 21-27, 2000 from http://www.laweekly.com/ink/00/09/cyber-mindenhall.php

Moore, R., & McMullan, E. C. (2004). Perceptions of Peer-to-Peer File Sharing Among University Students. *Journal of Criminal Justice and Popular Culture, 11*(1).

MP3 Newswire. (2000). *RIAA defeats MP3.com in court*. Retrieved September 28, 2001, from http://www.mp3newswire.net/stories/2000/MP3courtruling.html

MP3.com. (1998). *RIAA wins restraining order against MP3 recording device*. Retrieved October 9, 2001, from http://www.mp3.com/news/112.html

MP3.com. (1999). *Glut yourself on more SDMI dirt - Editorial*. Retrieved October 2, 2001, from http://www.mp3.com/news/311.html

Nagin, D. S., & Paternoster, R. (1993). Enduring individual differences and rational choice theories of crime. *Law & Society Review, 27*(467-96).

Napster.com. (2005). *What is Napster?* Retrieved May 4, 2005, from http://www.napster.com/what_is_napster.html

Nijmeh, G. (2001). *Behind the files: History of MP3*. Retrieved July 20, 2002, from http://www.mp3-cdburner.com/History-Of-MP3s.shtml

Nilsson, M. (2000). *ID3v2 made easy*. Retrieved October 20, 2001, from http://www.id3.org/easy.html

Oakes, C. (2000). *Copy-protected CDs taken back.* Retrieved August 20, 2003, from http://www.wired.com/news/technology/ 0,1282,33921,00.html

Office of Technology Assessment. (1986). *Intellectual property rights in an age of electronics and information.* Washington, DC: U.S. Government Printing Office.

Orcutt, J. D. (1987). Differential association and marijuana use: A closer look at Sutherland (with a little help from Becker). *Criminology, 25*(2), 341-358.

Pasick, A. (2004). *File-sharing network thrives beneath the radar.* Retrieved November 4, 2004, from http://in.tech.yahoo.com/ 041103/137/2ho4i.html

Paternoster, R. (1987). The deterrent effect of the perceived certainty and severity of punishment: A review of the evidence and issues. *Justice Quarterly, 4*(2), 173-218.

Paternoster, R. (1989). Decisions to participate in and desist from four types of common delinquency: Deterrence and the rational choice perspective. *Law and Society Review, 23*, 7-40.

Paternoster, R., & Brame, R. (1998). The structural similarity of processes generating criminal and analogous behaviors. *Criminology, 36*, 633-669.

Paternoster, R., & Brame, R. (2000). On the association among self-control, crime, and analogous behaviors. *Criminology, 38*(3), 971-982.

Paternoster, R., & Mazerolle, P. (1994). General Strain Theory and Delinquency - a Replication and Extension. *Journal of Research in Crime and Delinquency, 31*(3), 235-263.

Paternoster, R., & Piquero, A. (1995). Reconceptualizing deterrence: An empirical test of personal and vicarious experiences. *Journal of Research in Crime and Delinquency, 32*(3), 251-286.

Paternoster, R., & Simpson, S. (1996). Sanction Threats and Appeals to Morality: Testing a Rational Choice Model of Corporate Crime. *Law & Society Review, 30*, 549-583.

Patrizio, A. (1999). *DOJ cracks down on MP3 pirate.* Retrieved September 27, 2001, from http://www.wired.com/news/politics/ 0,1283,21391,00.html

Patterson, J. (1998). *The history of computers during my lifetime - the 1980's,* Retrieved June 3, 2002, from http://www.pattosoft.com.au/ jason/Articles/HistoryOfComputers/1980s.html

Petersen, S. (2000). *Music's new killer app: Napster*. Retrieved March 21, 2001, from http://comment.zdnet.co.uk/story/0,,t479-s2113471,00.html

Petreley, N. (2000). *How record companies could embrace Napster and maintain profits*. Retrieved September 27, 2001, from http://www.idg.net/go.cgi?id=250024

Pew Internet & American Life Project. (2000). *13 million Americans 'freeload' music on the Internet; 1 billion free music files now sit on Napster users' computers*. Retrieved October 5, 2000, from http://www.pewinternet.org/reports/pdfs/MusicReportFull.pdf

Philipkoski, K. (1999a). *The student jukebox sting*. Retrieved October 1, 2001, from http://www.wired.com/news/culture/0,1284,32444,00.html

Philipkoski, K. (1999b). *University snoops for MP3s*. Retrieved October 2, 2001, from http://www.wired.com/news/MP3/0,1285,32478,00.html

Philips, C. (2000). *Recording chief critiques criticisms of her industry*. Retrieved October 1, 2001, from http://www.lawtimes.com/business/20000427/t000039445.html

Piquero, A. R., & Rosay, A. B. (1998). The Reliability and Validity of Grasmick, et al.'s Self-control Scale: A Comment on Longshore, et al. *Criminology, 36*, 157-173.

Piquero, A. R., & Tibbetts, S. (1996). Specifying the Direct and Indirect Effects of Low Self-control and Situational Factors in Offenders' Decision Making: Toward a More Complete Model of Rational Offending. *Justice Quarterly, 3*, 481-510.

Piquero, N. L., & Sealock, M. D. (2000). Generalizing general strain theory: An examination of an offending population. *Justice Quarterly, 17*(3), 449-484.

Plant, M. A. & Plant, M. L. (1992). *Risktakers: Alcohol, drugs, sex and youth*. London: Tavistock/Routledge.

Ploskina, B. (2000). *Record industry shoots itself with MP3 bullet*. Retrieved October 1, 2001, from http://www.zdnet.com/intweek/stories/news/0,4164,2551103,00.html

Pratt, T. C., & Cullen, F. T. (2000). The empirical status of Gottfredson and Hirschi's general theory of crime: A meta-analysis. *Criminology, 38*(3), 931-964.

Quantum Corporation. (2000). *The Growing Need for Gigabytes*. Retrieved October 3, 2001, from http://www.quantum.com/src/tt/sh_needs.htm

Rahim, M. M., Seyal, A. H., & Rahman, N. A. (1999). Software piracy among computing students: A Bruneian scenario. *Computers and Education, 32,* 301-321.

Reciprocal Inc. (2000a). *Measuring the influence of music file sharing.* Retrieved October 12, 2001, from http://www.reciprocal.com/pdf/ Reciprocal_VNU_report.pdf

Reciprocal Inc. (2000b). *Reciprocal/VNU entertainment study reveals online file sharing as likely cause of decline in college market album sales.* Retrieved October 12, 2001, from http:// www.reciprocal.com/prm_rel05242000.asp

Reiman, J. H. (1995). *The rich get richer and the poor get prison.* (4th ed.). New York: Wiley.

Reuters. (2005). *Apple updates iTunes music system, adds podcast.* Retrieved June 28, 2005, from http://www.reuters.com/audi/ newsArticle.jhtml?type=technologyNews&storyID=8918047

RIAA. (2000a). *Anti-Piracy: Effects.* Retrieved July 20, 2001, from http://www.riaa.com/Protect-Campaign-3.cfm

RIAA. (2000b). *Complaint for copyright infringement against mp3.com.* Retrieved October 10, 2001, from http:// www.riaa.com/PDF/MP3_Complaint.pdf

RIAA. (2000c). *Digital music laws.* Retrieved September 24, 2001, from http://www.riaa.com/Copyright-Laws-4.cfm

RIAA. (2000d). *FAQ on Napster and Digital Music.* Retrieved September 20, 2001, from http://www.riaa.com/Napster.cfm

RIAA. (2000e). *Federal Laws.* Retrieved October 15, 2001, from http://www.riaa.com/Copyright-Laws-2.cfm

RIAA. (2000f). *Napster lawsuit Q&A.* Retrieved August 25, 2002, from http://www.riaa.com/Napster.cfm

RIAA. (2000g). *The NET Act.* Retrieved January 25, 2001, from http://www.riaa.com/Protect-Online-2.cfm

RIAA. (2000h). *Soundbyting: Top ten myths.* Retrieved October 3, 2001, from http://www.soundbyting.com/html/top_10_myths/ myths_index.html

RIAA. (2000i). *Who we are.* Retrieved August 4, 2001, from http://www.riaa.com/About-Who.cfm

RIAA. (2003). *Tracking music trends in America.* Retrieved October 3, 2003, from http://www.riaa.com/MD-Tracking.cfm

Robertson, M. (2000). *MP3.com Response to RIAA Lawsuit Letter.* Retrieved October 3, 2001, from http://www.MP3.com/ response.html

Rodriguez, N. (2005). *RIAA files 405 new lawsuits*. Retrieved May 2, 2005, from http://www.dailytrojan.com/media/paper679/news/2005/04/14/News/Riaa-Files.405.New.Lawsuits-924373.shtml

Rogers, M. K. (2001). *A social learning theory and moral disengagement analysis of criminal computer behavior: An exploratory study*. Unpublished doctoral dissertation, University of Manitoba, Winnipeg.

Rondeau, E. (2003). *Universities seek methods to curb illegal file sharing*. Retrieved September 5, 2003, from http://www.statenews.com/article.phtml?pk=18857

Rosen, H. (2000). *RIAA Lawsuit Letter to MP3.com*. Retrieved September 28, 2001, from http://www.MP3.com/response2.html

Rosoff, S. M., Pontell, H. M., & Tillman, R. (2002). *Profit without honor: white-collar crime and the looting of America*. Upper Saddle River, NJ: Prentice Hall.

Roth, D. (1999). Desperately seeking MP3: A writer's quest. *Fortune, 140*(6), 264.

Royal Canadian Mounted Police. (2000). *Computer crime, can it affect you?* Retrieved November 10, 1999, from http://www3.sk.sympatico.ca/rcmpccs/cpu-crim.html

Schneier, B. (2000). *Secrets and Lies: Digital Security in a Networked World*. New York: John Wiley & Sons.

Schneier, B. (2003). *Beyond Fear: Thinking Sensibly about Security in an Uncertain World*. New York: Copernicus Books.

Schoen, S. (2002). *BPDG one-page critique*. Retrieved June 4, 2002, from http://bpdg.blogs.eff.org/archives/000121.html

Seale, D. A., Polakowski, M., & Schneider, S. (1998). It's not really theft! Personal and workplace ethics that enable software piracy. *Communication Abstracts, 21*(4).

Sellers, C. S. (1999). Self-control and intimate violence: An examination of the scope and specification of the general theory of crime. *Criminology, 37*(2), 375-404.

Sharman Networks. (2005). *Kazaa Media Desktop*. Retrieved June 19, 2005, from http://www.kazaa.com/us/index.htm

Sherizen, S. (1997). Criminological concepts and research findings relevant for improving computer crime. In R. C. Hollinger (Ed.), *Crime, Deviance and the Computer* (pp. 298-305). Aldershot: Dartmouth.

Sims, R. R., Cheng, H. K., & Teegen, H. (1996). Toward a profile of student software piraters. *Journal of Business Ethics, 15*(8), 839.

Singleton, R. A. J., & Straits, B. C. (1999). *Approaches to Social Research* (3rd ed.). New York: Oxford University Press.

Skinner, B. F. (1953). *Science and human behavior.* New York: MacMillan.

Skinner, B. F. (1957). *Verbal learning.* New York: Appleton-Century-Crofts.

Skinner, B. F. (1971). *Beyond Freedom and Dignity.* New York: Knopf.

Skinner, B. F., & Fream, A. M. (1997). A social learning theory analysis of computer crime among college students. *Journal of Research in Crime and Delinquency, 34,* 495-518.

Slashdot.org. (2005). *RIAA File-Sharing Lawsuits Top 10,000 People Sued.* Retrieved April 30, 2005, from http://yro.slashdot.org/yro/05/04/30/1913227.shtml?tid=123&tid=141&tid=103&tid=95&tid=17

Smith, G. V., & Parr, R. L. (1989). *Valuation of intellectual property and intangible assets.* New York: Wiley.

Solomon, S., & O'Brien, J. A. (1990). The effect of demographic factors on attitudes toward software piracy. *Journal of Computer Information Systems,* 40-46.

Sony Corp. v. Universal Studios. (1984). 464 U.S. 417; 220 U.S.P.Q. 665.

Spring, T. (2000). *Swap MP3s, go to jail?* Retrieved October 12, 2001, from http://www.cnn.com/2000/TECH/computing/04/14/MP3.crackdown.idg/index.html

Stamp, M. (2002). Risks of digital rights management. *Communications of the ACM, 45*(9), 120.

Stamp, M. (2003). Digital rights management: The technology behind the hype. *Journal of Electronic Commerce Research, 4*(3), 102-112.

Steffensmeier, D. (1989). On the Causes of White-Collar Crime - an Assessment of Hirschi and Gottfredson Claims. *Criminology, 27*(2), 345-358.

Stenger, R. (2000). *Campuses seek compromise over popular bandwidth hog.* Retrieved September 28, 2001, from http://www.cnn.com/2000/TECH/computing/03/01/napster.ban/

Stenneken, J. (1999). *MP3 Research Survey.* Retrieved September 28, 2001, from http://www.joasten.webprovider.com/

Rolling Stone. (2000). MP3 Survey. *Rolling Stone.*

Sutherland, E. (1947). *Principles of criminology* (3rd ed.). Philadelphia: J.B. Lippincott.

Sutherland, E. (1949a). *White collar crime*. New York: Holt, Rinehart, and Winston.

Sutherland, E. (1973). *On analyzing crime*. Chicago: The University of Chicago Press.

Sutherland, E. (Ed.). (1949b). *The white collar criminal*. New York: Philosophical Library.

Swiatecki, C. (2000a). *I want my MP3*. Retrieved September 20, 2001, from http://www.statenews.com/editions/041400/ms_MP31.html

Swiatecki, C. (2000b). *Stiff fines, jail can't deter Napster users*. Retrieved September 20, 2001, from http://www.statenews.com/editions/041400/ms_MP32.html

Sykes, G. M., & Matza, D. (1957). Techniques of neutralization: A theory of delinquency. *American Sociological Review, 22*, 664-670.

Tarde, G. (Ed.). ([1890] 1903). *Gabriel Tarde's laws of imitation*. New York: Henry Holt.

Taylor, C. (2002, May 12). Burn, Baby, Burn. *TIME*.

Thong, J. L., & Yap, C. S. (1998). Testing an ethical decision-making theory: The case of softlifting. *Journal of Management Information Systems, 15*(1), 213-237.

Thurrott, P. (2003). *Hacker Exploits Chink in iTunes DRM Armor*. Retrieved January 10, 2004, from http://www.windowsitpro.com/Article/ArticleID/40972/40972.html

Tittle, C. R. (1980). *Sanctions and social deviance: The question of deterrence*. New York: Praeger Publishers.

Tremblay, R. E., Boulerice, B., Arseneault, L., & Niscale, M. J. (1995). Does low self-control during childhood explain the association between delinquency and accidents in early adolescence? *Criminal Behaviour and Mental Health, 5*, 439-451.

Tyler, T. R. (1996). Compliance with intellectual property laws: A psychological perspective. *International Law and Politics, 29*, 219-235.

Vold, G. B., Bernard, T. J., & Snipes, J. B. (1998). *Theoretical criminology* (Fourth ed.). New York: Oxford University Press.

Wagner, S. C. (1998). *Software Piracy and Ethical Decision Making*. Buffalo: State University of New York at Buffalo.

Walsh, A. (2000). Behavior genetics and anomie/strain theory. *Criminology, 38*, 1075-1107.

Walther, J. B. (1992). Interpersonal effects in computer-mediated interaction: A relational perspective. *Communication Research, 19*, 50-88.

Walther, J. B., Anderson, J. F., & Park, D. W. (1994). Interpersonal effects in computer-mediated interaction: A meta-analysis of social and antisocial communication. *Communication Research, 21*(4), 460-487.

Warr, M. (2002). *Companions in crime: The social aspects of criminal conduct.* Cambridge: Cambridge University Press.

Warr, M., & Stafford, M. (1991). Influence of delinquent peers: What they think or what they do? *Criminology, 29*, 851-866.

Webnoize. (2000). *Napster university: From file swapping to the future of entertainment.* Retrieved September 21, 2001, from http://research.webnoize.com

Weekly, D. (1998). *MP3 Summit Report.* Retrieved October 3, 2001, 2001, from http://www.MP3.com/news/064.html

Weekly, D. (2000). *The MP3 Explosion.* Retrieved October 8, 2001, from http://david.weekly.org/MP3book/ch1.php3#7

Weisbard, E. (2000). *At Pho, a thousand e-mails a month track the great digital debate: Keeping up with the Napsters.* Retrieved May 10-16, 2000, from http://www.villagevoice.com/issues/0019/weisbard.php

Wikipedia. (2003). *Analog Hole.* Retrieved August 29, 2003, from http://www.wikipedia.org/wiki/Analog_Hole

Wikipedia. (2004). *Operation Buccaneer.* Retrieved June 10, 2004 from http://en.wikipedia.org/wiki/Operation_Buccaneer

Wikipedia. (2005). *BitTorrent.* Retrieved May 2, 2005, from http://en.wikipedia.org/wiki/Bittorrent

Winfree, T. L., Jr., Backstrom, T. V., & Mays, G. L. (1994). Social learning theory, self-reported delinquency, and youth gangs: a new twist on the general theory of crime and delinquency. *Youth & Society, 26*(2), 147-177.

Winship, C., & Mare, R. D. (1984). Regression models with ordinal variables. *American Sociological Review, 49*(4), 512-525.

Wong, E. Y. H. (1995). How do we teach computer ethics? A short study done in Hong Kong. *Computers and Education, 25*(4), 179-191.

Wong, G., Kong, A., & Ngai, S. (1990). A study of unauthorized software copying among post-secondary students in Hong Kong. *The Australian Computer Journal, 22*(4), 114-122.

Wood, P. B., Cochran, J. K., Pfefferbaum, B., & Arneklev, B. J. (1995). Sensation-seeking and delinquent substance use: An extension of learning theory. *Journal of Drug Issues, 25*(1), 173-193.

Wood, P. B., Pfefferbaum, B., & Arneklev, B. J. (1993). Social psychological correlates of delinquency. *Journal of Crime and Justice, 16*, 111-130.

Wood, W., & Glass, R. S. (1995). Sex as a determinant of software piracy. *Journal of Computer Information Systems, 36*(2), 37-40.

Word, R. (2003). *University's software kicks off downloaders.* Retrieved November 22, 2003, from http://www.chron.com/ cs/CDA/ssistory.mpl/tech/news/2242112

Woudenberg, E. (2003). *Minidisc FAQ.* Retrieved October 30, 2003, from http://www.minidisc.org/minidisc_faq.html#SCMS

Wright, B. R. E., Caspi, A., Moffitt, T. E., & Silva, P. A. (2001). The effects of social ties on crime vary by criminal propensity: A life-course model of interdependence. *Criminology, 39*(2), 321-351.

Zeiler, D. (2003). *Hackers bite Apple in its iTunes.* Retrieved May 22, 2003, from http://www.sunspot.net/technology/custom/ pluggedin/bal-mac052203,0,6600950.column?coll=bal-business-indepth

Survey Instrument

Questionnaire on Participation in and Attitudes Towards MP3s

Thank you for taking the time to fill out the following questionnaire. Its purpose is to obtain an understanding of college students' perceptions of, familiarity with, and attitudes toward, their use of digital music (MP3s) from the Internet.

Your input is valuable to us and will aid in:

1. assessing the extent to which the Internet has become an integral part of students' lives.
2. examining your ideas of acceptable and unacceptable conduct on the Internet.

Please select an answer for each of the following questions based on your personal circumstances/knowledge. Also, don't spend too long on any one statement; just input your initial reaction on the scantron form provided.

This survey should take approximately 20 minutes to complete. Risks to subjects in this study are minimal, and only concern emotional or psychological harm when requested to contemplate and reveal participation in certain deviant behaviors. With regard to any and all information provided by you as a respondent, your privacy will be protected to the maximum extent allowable by law.

This survey is completely voluntary and anonymous. You are free to skip any question. Do not write your name or any other identifying information on the questionnaire or scantron.

I would sincerely appreciate your honest answers in order to obtain a reliable measure.

My methodology is as follows: I am going into an assortment of classrooms from varying disciplines with the permission of the professor in charge, and administering this questionnaire. I will verbally inform the students of the confidentiality and anonymity of the survey, as well as the fact that participation is voluntary. This information is also provided at the top of each questionnaire. Additionally, when I introduce myself to the classes I visit, I will explain the purposes of the research, the expected time it should take for them to fill out the survey provided, and that there is no cost associated with participating except for the time spent in composing a response. I will also make potential respondents cognizant that only group totals will be consolidated and released at the culmination of the project. This is primarily to protect the rights of the respondents and to garner a reliable cross-section for measuring the relevant constructs.

If you have questions about the study, please feel free to contact Dr. Mahesh Nalla by phone: (517) 355-2228, fax: (517) 432-1787; email: nalla@msu.edu, or regular mail: 560 Baker Hall, East Lansing, MI 48824. In case you have questions or concerns about your rights as a research participant, please feel free to contact Ashir Kumar, MD, Michigan State University's Chair of University Committee on Research Involving Human Subjects by phone: (517) 355-2180, fax: (517) 432-4503, email: ucrihs@msu.edu, or regular mail: 202 Olds Hall, East Lansing, MI 48824.

You indicate your voluntary agreement to participate by beginning this questionnaire.

FEEL FREE TO TEAR OFF AND TAKE THIS COVER SHEET HOME IN CASE YOU HAVE ANY QUESTIONS IN THE FUTURE.

Negative events often occur in our lives. For the following questions, please answer A for TRUE and B for FALSE

OVER THE LAST SIX MONTHS, I HAVE:	TRUE	FALSE
1. Received a bad grade in a class	A	B
2. Broken up with an intimate partner	A	B
3. Experienced weight gain or loss	A	B
4. Been fired or laid off from a job	A	B
5. Had money problems (i.e., had difficulty paying tuition, rent, bills)	A	B
6. Been a victim of a crime	A	B

Take a moment to reflect on your personality, and for each of the following questions, please respond as follows: A = STRONGLY DISAGREE, B = DISAGREE, C = NEUTRAL, D = AGREE, E = STRONGLY AGREE

	SD	D	N	A	SA
7. I often do what brings me pleasure here and now.	A	B	C	D	E
8. When things get complicated, I tend to quit or withdraw.	A	B	C	D	E
9. I find no excitement in doing things I might get in trouble for.	A	B	C	D	E
10. I try to look out for others first, even if it means making things difficult for myself	A	B	C	D	E
11. I *don't* lose my temper very easily.	A	B	C	D	E
12. I feel better when I am on the move rather than sitting and thinking.	A	B	C	D	E

Below are some questions related to certain behaviors in which some students have participated. For each of the following questions, please respond as follows: A = TRUE, B = FALSE

OVER THE LAST YEAR, I HAVE:	TRUE	FALSE
13. I have skipped more than 10 class periods in the past year.	A	B
14. I have lied to a professor/instructor either via email, telephone, or in person at least once in the past year.	A	B
15. I have plagiarized on a school assignment at least once in the past year.	A	B
16. I have drank alcohol before I turned 21.	A	B
17. I have driven a vehicle while under the influence of alcohol at least once in the past year.	A	B

Take a moment to reflect some more on yourself, and for each of the following questions, please respond as follows: A = STRONGLY DISAGREE, B = DISAGREE, C = NEUTRAL, D = AGREE, E = STRONGLY AGREE

	SD	D	N	A	SA
18. I am optimistic about my future.	A	B	C	D	E
19. I have difficulty maintaining long-term relationships.	A	B	C	D	E
20. I actively expect the best from people and situations.	A	B	C	D	E
21. My emotional life is unstable.	A	B	C	D	E
22. I am able to express the feelings I have, whether happy, sad, angry, frustrated, or confused.	A	B	C	D	E
23. I am not comfortable with myself when around others.	A	B	C	D	E
24. I have difficulty achieving long term goals.	A	B	C	D	E
25. I am happy.	A	B	C	D	E

26. How many student organizations (like the Debate Team, Campus Crusade, Outing Club, etc.) did you <u>regularly</u> participate in over the past year?

A. 0
B. 1
C. 2
D. 3
E. 4 or more

27. How many sports did you <u>regularly</u> participate in (including running/working out) over the past year?

A. 0
B. 1
C. 2
D. 3
E. 4 or more

28. On average each month, how many times do you participate in religious activities such as attending a church, temple, or scripture study session?

A. 0
B. 1
C. 2-3
D. 4-5
E. 6 or more

29. I have a _____ amount of friends in the area.

A. Very low
B. Low
C. moderate
D. High
E. Very high

30. I would rate my self-esteem as:
A.   Very low
B.   Low
C.   moderate
D.   High
E.   Very high

31. On a scale of 1-5 (with 1 = "cold, distant, and completely dysfunctional" and 5 = "healthy and warm"), how would you rate the quality of your relationship with your parent(s) or guardian(s)?
A.   1
B.   2
C.   3
D.   4
E.   5

32. On a scale of 1-5 (with 5 = very strongly), how strongly have your *parents* shaped your personal perspective on life?
A.   1
B.   2
C.   3
D.   4
E.   5

33. On a scale of 1-5 (with 5 = very strongly), how strongly have your *friends* shaped your personal perspective on life?
A.   1
B.   2
C.   3
D.   4
E.   5

Consider your participation with MP3s, and for each of the following questions, please respond as follows: A = STRONGLY DISAGREE, B = DISAGREE, C = I DO NOT PARTICIPATE WITH MP3s, D = AGREE, E = STRONGLY AGREE

	SD	D	~~MP3~~	A	SA
34. It is a great benefit to sample new music through MP3s.	A	B	C	D	E
35. It is a great benefit to be able to transfer assorted MP3s onto an audio/data CD or a portable MP3 player so that I can have music on-the-go.	A	B	C	D	E
36. I feel practically no threat of sanction or punishment for use of MP3s.	A	B	C	D	E
37. It makes me feel good to download a song that I have wanted.	A	B	C	D	E
38. I have learned the techniques of using MP3s from television or print media.	A	B	C	D	E
39. I have learned the techniques of using MP3s from online sources (web pages, chat rooms, etc).	A	B	C	D	E
40. I was introduced by another person online to MP3s.	A	B	C	D	E
41. MP3 use is excusable and justifiable.	A	B	C	D	E
42. One of the reasons I download MP3s is because I will not purchase the music.	A	B	C	D	E
43. One of the reasons I download MP3s is because I feel the recording industry has been overcharging the general public for music tapes and CDs.	A	B	C	D	E
44. One of the reasons I download MP3s is because many musicians and the recording industry make millions of dollars anyway, and downloading MP3s of their songs does not really cut into their income.	A	B	C	D	E
45. My friends support my MP3 usage.	A	B	C	D	E
46. I associate with others in real life (offline) who are supportive of MP3 usage.	A	B	C	D	E
47. I have introduced others in real life (offline) to MP3s.	A	B	C	D	E
48. I was introduced by another person in real life to MP3s.	A	B	C	D	E
49. I am embarrassed that I use MP3s.	A	B	C	D	E
50. I am proud that I use MP3s.	A	B	C	D	E

Consider your participation with MP3s, and for each of the following questions, please respond as follows: A = STRONGLY DISAGREE, B = DISAGREE, C = I DO NOT PARTICIPATE WITH MP3s, D = AGREE, E = STRONGLY AGREE

	SD	D	~~MP3~~	A	SA
51. I associate with others online who exchange MP3s with me.	A	B	C	D	E
52. I do not care what others think of me.	A	B	C	D	E
53. I enjoy participating in a new, controversial technology.	A	B	C	D	E
54. I feel good about myself if I am able to help or benefit someone with an MP3.	A	B	C	D	E
55. I have learned the techniques of using MP3s from my family	A	B	C	D	E
56. I have learned the techniques of using MP3s from my friends	A	B	C	D	E
57. In general, I tend to do what the majority does.	A	B	C	D	E
58. It is a great benefit to me to be able to access music freely.	A	B	C	D	E
59. MP3s do not really hurt musicians or the record industry.	A	B	C	D	E
60. Musicians and the record industry should embrace MP3 technology and use it to their advantage.	A	B	C	D	E
61. One of the reasons I download MP3s is because I <u>cannot</u> purchase the music.	A	B	C	D	E
62. One of the reasons I download MP3s is because I think music should be free.	A	B	C	D	E
63. One of the reasons I download MP3s is because people I know do it.	A	B	C	D	E
64. One of the reasons I download MP3s is so I can sample new music without having to buy the CD.	A	B	C	D	E
65. People I know offline (in the real world) like me, appreciate me, or benefit from me because I use MP3s.	A	B	C	D	E
66. People I know offline (in the real world) frown on my use of MP3s.	A	B	C	D	E
67. People I know online frown on my use of MP3s.	A	B	C	D	E
68. People I know online like me, appreciate me, or benefit from me because I use MP3s.	A	B	C	D	E

Consider your participation with MP3s, and for each of the following questions, please respond as follows: A = STRONGLY DISAGREE, B = DISAGREE, C = I DO NOT PARTICIPATE WITH MP3s, D = AGREE, E = STRONGLY AGREE

	SD	D	~~MP3~~	A	SA
69. Transferring MP3s in general should be allowed as long as individuals use the music for personal purposes, and are not making money off of them.	A	B	C	D	E
70. Use of MP3s is a "cool" thing.	A	B	C	D	E

Regardless of whether you participate with MP3s, please consider the situations and circumstances which would make you more likely to do so. For each of the following questions, please respond as follows: A = STRONGLY DISAGREE, B = DISAGREE, C = NEUTRAL, D = AGREE, E = STRONGLY AGREE

I WOULD BE MORE LIKELY TO DOWNLOAD/UPLOAD MP3s.....	SD	D	N	A	SA
71. if I could not afford the purchase price of the music on CD?	A	B	C	D	E
72. since numerous sources offering MP3s for free download are readily available online?	A	B	C	D	E
73. since there are no clear-cut rules, laws, regulations, or even guidelines when it comes to MP3 file exchanges?	A	B	C	D	E
74. if all my friends and classmates were doing it?	A	B	C	D	E
75. if it were known that the recording industry "could afford it" and would never miss the tiny amount of proceeds lost from just a few MP3s here or there?	A	B	C	D	E
76. if it were known that law enforcement agencies, universities, and authorities in general couldn't care less about MP3 file exchanges, lack adequate abilities to detect or combat the activity, and have bigger things to worry about?	A	B	C	D	E
77. if it were held that the music industry, to some extent, <u>deserves</u> to have their music distributed freely online considering the fact that they rip off consumers?	A	B	C	D	E

Regardless of whether you participate with MP3s, please consider the situations and circumstances which would make you more likely to do so. For each of the following questions, please respond as follows: A = STRONGLY DISAGREE, B = DISAGREE, C = NEUTRAL, D = AGREE, E = STRONGLY AGREE

I WOULD BE MORE LIKELY TO DOWNLOAD/UPLOAD MP3s.....	SD	D	N	A	SA
78. if it were held that no one is really getting hurt from the downloading and uploading of MP3s online?	A	B	C	D	E
79. because any rules or laws that seek to prevent individuals from exchanging MP3s are misguided and ill-conceived?	A	B	C	D	E
80. because hardly anyone has been caught or punished or has been subject to even the slightest repercussions for downloading and/or uploading MP3s online?	A	B	C	D	E
81. if I needed the music wouldn't be able to obtain it any other way?	A	B	C	D	E
82. if a family member, friend, or significant other needed the music?	A	B	C	D	E
83. if the music will be used to complete a project for school or work, or to achieve other school-related and career-related goals?	A	B	C	D	E
84. since it is okay if I do something questionable every now and then - it is better than a frequently dishonest person engaging in questionable deeds over and over again?	A	B	C	D	E
85. because I deserve something for free sometimes?	A	B	C	D	E
86. if it were prevalent all over the Internet, and if a lot of people were doing it?	A	B	C	D	E
87. if it were held that no one else seems to care whether or not they get caught?	A	B	C	D	E
88. if it were held that others are benefiting from it, and so why shouldn't I?	A	B	C	D	E
89. because I can't afford to waste money on a music CD that might only have 1 or 2 good songs?	A	B	C	D	E

Regardless of whether you participate with MP3s, please consider the situations and circumstances which would make you more likely to do so. For each of the following questions, please respond as follows: A = STRONGLY DISAGREE, B = DISAGREE, C = NEUTRAL, D = AGREE, E = STRONGLY AGREE

I WOULD BE MORE LIKELY TO DOWNLOAD/UPLOAD MP3s.....	SD	D	N	A	SA
91. because the anonymous nature of the Internet affords privacy and somewhat of a shield from detection; and so, why not take advantage?	A	B	C	D	E
92. because no one really cares about what I do online - it is just too removed from the "real world"?	A	B	C	D	E

Consider your CURRENT participation with MP3s, and for each of the following questions, please select from the answer choices provided.

93. How many MP3 files have you personally downloaded *in the last week*?
A.   0
B.   1-5
C.   6-10
D.   11-20
E.   More than 20

94. How many MP3 files have you personally downloaded *in the last month*?
A.   0
B.   1-25
C.   26-50
D.   51-100
E.   More than 100

95. How many MP3 files have you personally downloaded *since the beginning of 2003*?

A.   0
B.   1-10
C.   11-50
D.   51-250
E.   More than 250

96. How many MP3s do you, *on average*, download *per month*?

A.   0
B.   1-25
C.   26-50
D.   51-100
E.   More than 100

Consider your participation with MP3s exactly ONE YEAR AGO from today, and for each of the following questions, please select from the answer choices provided.

97. Approximately how many MP3 files did you personally download *in an average week exactly one year ago*?

A.   0
B.   1-5
C.   6-10
D.   11-20
E.   More than 20

98. Approximately how many MP3 files did you personally download *in an average month exactly one year ago*?

A.   0
B.   1-25
C.   26-50
D.   51-100
E.   More than 100

Consider your participation with MP3s exactly TWO YEARS AGO from today, and for each of the following questions, please select from the answer choices provided.

99. Approximately how many MP3 files did you personally download *in an average week exactly two years ago?*
A.   0
B.   1-5
C.   6-10
D.   11-20
E.   More than 20

100. Approximately how many MP3 files did you personally download *in an average month exactly two years ago?*
A.   0
B.   1-25
C.   26-50
D.   51-100
E.   More than 100

Consider your participation with MP3s in years past, and for each of the following questions, please select from the answer choices provided.

101. How many MP3 files did you personally download in 2002?
A.   0
B.   1-10
C.   11-100
D.   101-1000
E.   More than 1000

102. How many MP3 files did you personally download in 2001?
A.   0
B.   1-10
C.   11-100
D.   101-1000
E.   More than 1000

103. How many MP3 files did you personally download in 2000?
A.   0
B.   1-10
C.   11-100
D.   101-1000
E.   More than 1000

104. How many *total* complete music albums in MP3 format have you obtained online?
A.   0
B.   1-5
C.   6-10
D.   11-20
E.   More than 20

105. How many *total* MP3s have you downloaded over the course of your life thus far?
A.   0
B.   1-100
C.   101-500
D.   501-2000
E.   2001 or more

106. Of the total MP3s you have, what percent are <u>NOT</u> personally created from CDs you own, or are <u>NOT</u> of songs that you definitely own on CD?
A.   0% (they are all from CDs I own or are of songs that I own on CD)
B.   1%-30% (a small amount are not from CDs I own or of songs that I own on CD)
C.   31%-60% (a moderate amount are not from CDs I own or of songs that I own on CD)
D.   61%-90% (a large amount are not from CDs I own or of songs that I own on CD)
E.   Over 90% (almost all are not from CDs I own or of songs that I own on CD)

107. How many hours each week do you spend looking for or obtaining MP3s?
A.   I don't look for or obtain MP3s (zero hours)
B.   Less than 1
C.   1-2 hours
D.   3-4 hours
E.   5-6 hours

108. The breakdown of my time spent online downloading MP3s (to your computer) and uploading (from your computer) is approximately:
A.   I do not participate with MP3s
B.   0% of the time downloading, and 100% uploading
C.   25% of the time downloading, and 75% uploading
D.   75% of the time downloading, and 25% uploading
E.   100% of the time downloading, and 0% uploading

109. I have:
A.   Created an audio CD from MP3 files
B.   Made an MP3 file myself (from an audio CD or from another sound source)
C.   Both of the above
D.   None of the above

110. With my MP3 files, I do the following:
A.   Listen to them on my computer
B.   Listen to them after burning them to CD or transferring them to a portable MP3 player
C.   Both of the above
D.   None of the above (but I do have MP3 files)
E.   I don't have any MP3 files

111. With my MP3 files, I do the following:
A.   Share them with others
B.   Sell them
C.   Both of the above
D.   None of the above (but I do have MP3 files)
E.   I don't have any MP3 files

112. Do you believe that receiving or providing MP3s should be illegal?
A.   Yes
B.   No

113. From *your* perspective, downloading or uploading MP3s is:
A.   Completely appropriate (ethically, morally, legally)
B.   Unethical/Immoral but still appropriate
C.   Unethical/Immoral and thereby inappropriate
D.   Illegal but Ethical/Moral and thereby appropriate
E.   Unethical/Immoral/Illegal and thereby inappropriate

114. Do you refrain from obtaining MP3s because you believe it is illegal?
A.   Yes, I refrain because I believe it is illegal
B.   No, I participate even though I believe it is illegal
C.   Yes, I refrain but not because I believe it is illegal, but for other reasons such as the fact it hurts artists/bands, recording labels, and the music industry, or the fact that it does not sit well with me
D.   No, I participate because I do not believe it is illegal
E.   I do not obtain MP3s because I am not familiar with them or have no need/desire to do so.

For each of the following questions, please select from the answer choices provided.

115. Race:
A.   Caucasian/White
B.   African American/Black
C.   Asian/Pacific Islander
D.   Hispanic/Latino
E.   Other

116. Sex:
A.   Female
B.   Male

117. Age:
A.   17 or younger
B.   18-19
C.   20-21
D.   22-23
E.   24 or older

118. Year of Studies:
A.   Freshman
B.   Sophomore
C.   Junior
D.   Senior
E.   Graduate Student

119. What is your parents' annual household income?
A. $0 to $19,999
B. $20,000 to $29,999
C. $30,000 to $39,999
D. $40,000 to $49,999
E. $50,000 or more

120. My employment (job) status:
A.   I do not have a job
B.   I work approximately 10 hours a week
C.   I work approximately 20 hours a week
D.   I work approximately 30 hours a week
E.   I work approximately 40 hours a week

121. I live in an:
A.   On-Campus Residence Hall (dorm room)
B.   On-Campus Apartment
C.   Off-Campus Apartment or House
D.   Other

122. Where I reside during the school year (dorm room, apartment, house, etc.), I am generally connected to the Internet via:
A.   high speeds, on the Ethernet network or with a Cable or DSL connection
B.   slower speeds, where I dial in through my telephone line using my computer modem
C.   I cannot connect to the Internet at my place of residence during the school year

123. In the following list, please count up the number of activities for which you regularly use the Internet, and answer accordingly.

___Email, Chat/IRC
___Research for school work
___File Transfer
___Using the Newsgroups
___Product and Travel Information
___Online Stock Trading
___Online Shopping
___Online Auctions
___Online Games
___Online Banking
___To collect information related to news, sports, or the weather
___To collect information related to personal interests and hobbies
___Web Design

A.   0 items
B.   1-2 items
C.   3-5 items
D.   6-8 items
E.   9 or more items

124. In the following list, please count up the number of activities that you have ever done online, and answer accordingly.

___changed my browser's "startup" or "home" page
___made a purchase online for more than $100
___participated in an online game
___participated in an online auction
___changed my "cookie" preferences
___participated in an online chat or discussion (not including email, ICQ, or AOL Instant Messenger, or similar instant messaging programs)
___listened to a radio broadcast or music clip online
___made a telephone call online
___created a web page
___set up my incoming and outgoing mail server preferences

A. 0 items
B. 1-2 items
C. 3-5 items
D. 6-8 items
E. 9 or more items

In the "SECTION" section of your Scantron, in the section where you would usually record your identifying information (DO NOT do so on this survey as it is anonymous), please bubble in one of the following three-digit numbers to indicate the college in which your major is housed.

001. College of Agriculture and Natural Resources
002. College of Arts and Letters
003. College of * Business/Graduate School of Management
004. College of Communication Arts and Sciences
005. College of Education
006. College of Engineering
007. College of Human Ecology
008. College of Human Medicine
009. * College
010. College of Natural Science
011. College of Nursing
012. College of Osteopathic Medicine
013. College of Social Science
014. College of Veterinary Medicine
015. I have not decided on a major as of yet
016. I do not know where my major is housed
017. None of the above

* Identifying information was removed to keep confidential the location of the university at which the research was conducted.

Disentangling Social Learning Theory

Table A: Factor Analyses of all Social Learning Theory Variables

	1	2	3	4
Differential Association (α=.774)				
My friends support my MP3 usage	.823	-.086	.040	-.003
I associate with others in real life (offline) who are supportive of MP3 usage	.750	-.136	-.005	.089
I was introduced by another person in real life to MP3s.	.585	-.183	-.076	.588
I have learned the techniques of using MP3s from my friends	.563	-.050	.065	.596
Differential Reinforcement (α=.862)				
It is a great benefit to sample new music through MP3s.	.814	-.147	.125	-.269
It is a great benefit to be able to transfer assorted MP3s onto an audio/data CD or a portable MP3 player so that I can have music on-the-go	.794	-.115	.142	-.288
It makes me feel good to download a song that I have wanted	.735	-.019	.137	-.141
It is a great benefit to me to be able to access music freely	.762	.107	.047	.134
Imitation (α=.595)				
I have learned the techniques of using MP3s from television or print media	-.085	.648	.494	.141
I have learned the techniques of using MP3s from online sources (web pages, chat rooms, etc)	.102	.597	.590	-.014
I associate with others online who exchange MP3s with me	.053	.465	.292	.043
Definitions (α=.658)				
One of the reasons I download MP3s is because I *will not* purchase the music	.183	.517	-.425	.137
One of the reasons I download MP3s is because I feel the recording industry has been overcharging the general public for music tapes and CDs	.407	.467	-.360	-.237
One of the reasons I download MP3s is because many musicians and the recording industry make millions of dollars anyway, and downloading MP3s of their songs does not really cut into their income	.326	.579	-.375	-.069
One of the reasons I download MP3s is because I think music should be free	.199	.558	-.301	.065

All fifteen social learning theory variables α=.773

Table B: Differential Association and Differential Reinforcement Factor Analysis

	Component 1
DA - My friends support my MP3 usage	.828
DA - I associate with others in real life (offline) who are supportive of MP3 usage	.760
DA - I was introduced by another person in real life to MP3s.	.605
DA - I have learned the techniques of using MP3s from my friends	.574
DR - It is a great benefit to sample new music through MP3s.	.830
DR - It is a great benefit to be able to transfer assorted MP3s onto an audio/data CD or a portable MP3 player so that I can have music on-the-go	.808
DR - It makes me feel good to download a song that I have wanted	.740
DR - It is a great benefit to me to be able to access music freely	.771

α=.878

Table C: Imitation and Definitions Factor Analysis

	Component 1	Component 2
I have learned the techniques of using MP3s from television or print media	.172	.825
I have learned the techniques of using MP3s from online sources (web pages, chat rooms, etc)	.185	.830
I associate with others online who exchange MP3s with me	.209	.554
One of the reasons I download MP3s is because I think music should be free	.638	.254
One of the reasons I download MP3s is because I *will not* purchase the music	.656	.153
One of the reasons I download MP3s is because I feel the recording industry has been overcharging the general public for music tapes and CDs	.736	.111
One of the reasons I download MP3s is because many musicians and the recording industry make millions of dollars anyway, and downloading MP3s of their songs does not really cut into their income	.775	.203

α=.659

APPENDIX C

Sample Letter from the RIAA

Used by permission from the Recording Industry Association of America.

[UNIVERSITY]   October 3, 2002
[TITLE FIRST LAST NAME]
[ADDRESS]
[CITY], [ST] [ZIP]

Dear [University/College President]:

We are writing to you as representatives of America's creative community on an urgent matter regarding copyright infringement by some university students.

We are concerned that an increasing and significant number of students are using university networks to engage in online piracy of copyrighted creative works. The educational purpose for which these networks were built is demeaned by such illegal behavior and is inconsistent with the ethical principles underlying the university community. We believe there must be a substantial effort, both disciplined and continuous, to bring this piracy under control. Because this issue pertains to various interests within a university community, we ask that you forward copies of this letter to your General Counsel/Chief Legal Officer, as well as your Director of Information Technology/Information Systems, your Chief Financial Officer, and your Dean of Student Affairs.

In the past few years, Peer to Peer (P2P) network use has dramatically grown. P2P technology is not only exciting — it may fundamentally change the way digital works are legitimately distributed. However, student trafficking in music, movies, software, video games and other copyrighted material without authorization on P2P networks not only raises issues of copyright infringement, it is an invitation to invasions of student privacy, viruses and numerous potential security threats to the university's network. A number of forward-looking educational institutions have led the way and have adopted informational and corrective policies aimed at preventing such infringing activity. We applaud these initiatives and would like to support this movement by working with colleges and universities to help establish Codes of Conduct and other procedures to stop theft of creative content.

Copyright Infringement is Theft

The students and other users of your school's network who upload and download infringing copyrighted works without permission of the owners are violating Federal copyright law. "Theft" is a harsh word, but that it is, pure and simple. As Deputy Assistant Attorney General John Malcolm recently stated, "Stealing is stealing is stealing, whether it's done with sleight of hand by sticking something in a pocket or it's done with the click of a mouse." It is no different from walking into the campus bookstore and in a clandestine manner walking out with a textbook without paying for it.

201

Sheldon E. Steinbach, General Counsel of the American Council on Education, said of such illegal file "sharing" activities:

"Why is this issue important to higher education institutions? First, educational institutions are in the business of forming students' minds. A fundamental part of this formation is teaching about ethics, personal responsibility, and respect for the rule of law. Colleges and universities should not be in the business of condoning or promoting unlawful activities."

Additional education about the law with regard to uploading and downloading movies, music, software, games, etc., is essential. Students must know that if they pirate copyrighted works they are subject to legal liability. A number of colleges and universities have already taken positive steps by putting in place codes of online conduct. They include such schools as the University of North Carolina, Drake University, and the University of Michigan.

Increasing Bandwidth Use Associated with P2P

Not only is piracy of copyrighted works illegal, it can take up a significant percentage of a university's costly bandwidth. A recent article in the *Chronicle of Higher Education* reported that one university discovered P2P uploading accounted for 75% of its entire bandwidth. In that case, 75% of that university's bandwidth was being used primarily by individuals outside of the university. When students run P2P applications and offer files for upload, much of the bandwidth drain is likely to be users outside of the university downloading files from students. One student offering a dozen infringing files on P2P may be serving those files up to hundreds, if not thousands, of users around the world. The non-university users downloading these illegal files take bandwidth away from students and members of the university community intending to use the network for educational purposes.

Many universities use bandwidth management tools to reduce bandwidth demands from illegal and improper use of the university networks. These tools can be used to take such steps as monitoring for inappropriate use, metering the bandwidth available to each student, setting caps on upload speeds, and blocking access to infringing P2P services. The Sergeant at Arms of the United States Senate has recently announced it would block the Senate's network users from accessing P2P networks. Other government, corporate, and educational institutions have put in place measures to prevent illegal use of P2P services. There are a number of companies that offer these bandwidth management tools, and we have attached a list of some of those companies for your information. Of course, P2P technology is exciting and holds great promise as a means of legitimately distributing works — it is the misuse of this technology by entities such as KaZaa, Grokster and Morpheus that causes problems for digital networks.

Security and Privacy Risks from P2P

P2P also poses serious network security and student privacy risks. For example, it has been widely reported that KaZaa, one of the most popular P2P applications, has software imbedded that allows a third party company to take over a portion of the user's computer and bandwidth. P2P software is also susceptible to worms and viruses.

specifically designed to exploit P2P applications. Many P2P users are not fully aware that their most personal documents may be available for millions of users to download.

*   *   *   *   *   *   *   *   *   *   *   *

This is a serious challenge that calls for immediate, concrete action. As a president of an educational institution and a leader in the university community, we ask for your leadership in addressing student piracy on your network. Specifically, we urge you to adopt and implement policies that:

- Inform students of their moral and legal responsibilities to respect the rights of copyright owners
- Specify what practices are, and are not, acceptable on your school's network
- Monitor compliance
- Impose effective remedies against violators

We have attached a list of Internet links to selected university Codes of Conduct to demonstrate some of the positive steps already being taken in the university community to address the issues implicated by misuse of university networks. The Internet poses challenges to all institutions with digital networks, and we believe that these colleges and universities have done a commendable job in responding to these emerging challenges.

We appreciate your taking careful account of these serious matters and hope that you will take the time to share with us your comments and observations. We stand ready to be of assistance in any way you might find helpful and look forward to working with you on this project of mutual interest.

Hilary Rosen
Chairman and CEO,
Recording Industry Association of America

Jack Valenti
President and CEO,
Motion Picture Association of America

Edward P. Murphy
President and CEO,
National Music Publishers' Association

Rick Carnes
President,
The Songwriters Guild of America

ATTACHMENT

Selected University Acceptable Use Policies

Drake University
http://www.drake.edu/it/cio/AcceptableUse.html
http://www.drake.edu/it/cio/Copyright.html

The University of North Carolina at Chapel Hill
http://www.unc.edu/policy/copyinfringe.html
http://www.unc.edu/policy/copyright_primer.html

University of Michigan
http://www.umich.edu/~policies/responsible-use.html
http://www.umich.edu/~policies/digital-media.html

Companies That Offer Bandwidth Management

Allot Communications
http://www.allot.com/

NetReality
http://www.net-reality.com/

Packeteer, Inc.
http://www.packeteer.com/

Palisade Systems, Inc.
http://www.palisadesys.com

You may contact signatories of this letter at:

RIAA	MPAA	NMPA	SGA
1330 Connecticut Ave, NW	1600 Eye Street, NW	475 Park Avenue South	1500 Harbor Blvd
Suite 300	Washington, DC 20006	29th Floor	Weehawken, NJ 07086
Washington, DC 20036	www.mpaa.org	New York, NY 10016	www.songwriters.org
www.riaa.org		www.nmpa.org	

Index